Dream States

Smart Cities, Technology, and the
Pursuit of Urban Utopias

John Lorinc

Coach House Books, Toronto

first edition

 Canada Council Conseil des Arts
for the Arts du Canada
 ONTARIO ARTS COUNCIL
CONSEIL DES ARTS DE L'ONTARIO
an Ontario government agency
un organisme du gouvernement de l'Ontario
 Canadä

Published with the generous assistance of the Canada Council for the Arts and
the Ontario Arts Council. Coach House Books also acknowledges the support of
the Government of Canada through the Canada Book Fund and the Government
of Ontario through the Ontario Book Publishing Tax Credit.

LIBRARY AND ARCHIVES CANADA CATALOGUING IN PUBLICATION

Title: Dream states : smart cities, technology, and the pursuit of urban utopias /
John Lorinc.
Names: Lorinc, John, author.
Identifiers: Canadiana (print) 20210353279 | Canadiana (ebook) 20210354836 | ISBN
9781552454282 (softcover) | ISBN 9781770566811 (PDF) | ISBN 9781770566804 (EPUB)
Subjects: LCSH: City planning—Technological innovations. | LCSH: Smart cities. |
LCSH: Urban policy. | LCSH: Urbanization.
Classification: LCC HT166 .L67 2022 | DDC 307.1/216—dc23

In memory of John A. Honderich, 1946–2022

Table of Contents

Introduction

'Always the question of how to get through the city.'
– China Miéville, *The City & the City* (2009)

The series of renderings had a dreamy, vaguely sci-fi feel. The images were populated, as architectural drawings always are, with people strolling, sitting, or chatting. Children, seniors, couples, some on bikes, a few in wheelchairs. The open spaces looked busy yet uncrowded.

But the ambience strongly suggested something very different than the garden-variety visual language that architectural firms produce in order to sell condos, office buildings, or public spaces. The structures, though high-rises, appeared to be constructed from wooden beams enclosing inviting, light-filled interiors. Some had generous protruding balconies tapering gracefully downward, creating a kind of intimacy over the café-strewn pedestrian plazas below. Other renderings depicted fantastical curved bridges or luxuriant winter scenes, with string lights, falling snow, and people skating on a canal off in the distance.

The effect was transfixing and even surreal – a completely conjured cityscape that would never exist, created by two of the world's top architectural firms, Snøhetta and Heatherwick Studio, in the service of what had become a profoundly contentious development scheme.

These drawings surfaced in February 2019, not quite two years after Sidewalk Labs, Google's smart city spinoff, arrived in Toronto with a promise to take a derelict piece of Toronto's post-industrial waterfront and build a new neighbourhood 'from the internet up.' The company, founded by former New York City deputy mayor Dan

Doctoroff, pledged to develop the so-called Quayside precinct with cutting-edge green design, a generous provision of affordable housing, tall-timber buildings, and new ideas for programming public spaces. Designed primarily for pedestrians, the area would rest atop networks of underground tunnels for pneumatic waste collection as well as autonomous delivery vehicles that would shunt courier packages between loading docks and their ultimate destinations in Quayside's high-rise residential apartments.

However, the project's main advantages had to do with the features you couldn't visualize: all manner of wireless connectivity, thousands of wireless digital sensors situated in both private and public spaces, broadband networks, and a seemingly limitless array of online applications intended to turn Quayside into what Sidewalk claimed would be the world's smartest neighbourhood. If the project on the initial smaller site succeeded, the company planned to expand its smart city concept to the redevelopment of a much larger brownfield area nearby.

As the company's name suggested, Sidewalk wanted Quayside to become a living urban experiment, its digital features – from programmable public spaces to high-tech environmental smarts in the area's buildings – scaled and then exported to other cities around the world.

Along with a contingent of other reporters covering cities and tech, I'd been writing regularly about this futuristic scheme, trying to figure out what, exactly, this company – a well-capitalized marriage of Silicon Valley techies and New York real estate insiders – was selling.

We never did find out. Scarcely a year after the release of those exotic renderings, Sidewalk abruptly announced that it was cancelling its Toronto plans, ostensibly due to the onset of the global COVID-19 pandemic, but also, it seemed clear, because of the relentless criticism that had dogged Sidewalk and its smart city master plan since virtually the moment it launched in October 2017. For many critics, Sidewalk's corporate ties to Google simply could not be explained away.

❖

These futuristic imaginings and the company's vision of an extensively wired community surfaced about a decade or so into the birth of the global smart city movement – a confection of savvy marketing, software applications, and a dizzying range of electronic devices all meant to somehow optimize cities, thereby solving or at least ameliorating problems from congestion to emissions to street violence. As the name implies, smart cities are somehow more evolved than traditional cities, although the precise definition is fuzzy and extensively debated among academics. The term itself first surfaced in the late 2000s and is tied closely to other urbanism trends, including the growing prevalence within cities of information and communications technologies, as well as discussion about concepts like 'creative cities,' 'intelligent cities,' and economic clusters.

Sidewalk Labs' ostensible vision of the smart city can also be understood as a point of intersection between two long-running themes in the evolution of metropolitan regions: the projection of utopian futures as a means of solving the social ills of the present, and the promises of engineered urban technologies that can be scaled, customized, and then pressed into service as a way of fostering commerce, innovation, and even social or political reform. As University of London geographer David Pinder observes, '[U]topia is frequently seen as an imaginative projection of a new place or state' (Pinder 2005, 15).

From the earliest periods of urban development, monarchs, philosophers, and eventually planners and architects have sought to design and build cities that aspire to some kind of idealistic vision. As Pinder, a scholar of the utopian urban tradition, explains, these have ranged from spiritual beliefs that informed the physical layout of ancient cities to the conjuring of political utopias as a means of addressing deep questions ranging from the nature of justice to the problems of poverty or social decay.

Urban-focused technology has equally deep roots, as engineers, governments, inventors, and eventually profit-minded entrepreneurs devised solutions to the kinds of problems that have always arisen whenever humans decide to create settlements: how to move around, how to ensure access to clean water, how to dispose of waste, how to create durable structures suited for the density of urban spaces, and how to communicate efficiently.

While the history and evolution of urban space has been wrought from commerce, war, social upheaval, and the complicated diffusion of ideas, the story of city-building, in many ways, is also about the collision between utopian dreams and engineered solutions. Both have sought to improve or perfect the urban condition. There have been many examples, particularly since the dawn of the industrial era, when these two impulses converged or aligned, yet others where they came into direct conflict. Time is also a factor, as the utopian solutions to one era's failings become the political or technological conundrums of the next. Or vice versa.

The rise and fall of Sidewalk's Toronto venture has spawned dozens of academic studies, grassroots political movements, and policy reforms, as well as an international reconsideration of the promise of smart city technology in the light of deep concerns about privacy, data security, and the unchecked financialization of urban space. But the company's very deliberate elision of utopianism and technology presents an opportunity to focus on the ways in which cities have provided a stage upon which these competing visions of social life play out.

Especially in a period when the vast majority of human beings live in urban regions, cities offer incredible opportunities, but also crushing pressures and seemingly intractable inequities. The city, in some ways, is a geography of problems and solutions, chasing one another through time and space. These most complex of human institutions spark the imaginations of those who aspire to build a better world, either using dreams or inventions.

Sidewalk, like the hundreds of tech companies that have gravitated toward the multi-billion-dollar smart city industry since the early 2010s, sought to do both. The reasons behind its failure offer some important lessons about the future of the post-pandemic city.

❖

This book grew out of several years of reporting I did on the smart city movement, which turned into an extended series in the *Toronto Star* that was supported very generously through a fellowship provided by the Atkinson Foundation.

In my first journalistic encounter with the concept of smart cities, I wrote a feature for the *Globe and Mail*, in 2015, on the emergence of these technologies. One example struck a chord. I interviewed Mike Flowers, a tough-talking New York lawyer who had served in Iraq with military intelligence and somehow wound up working for then-mayor Michael Bloomberg. Bloomberg made his billions selling and analyzing financial data, and he was determined to bring that same ethic into the lumbering, archaic world of municipal government.

Flowers, who liked to refer to Bloomberg as 'the old man,' worked as part of a small flying squad of data scientists in the mayor's office. He would go to various New York City departments and beg them to hand over sprawling databases of granular building-level information about fire code violations, upgrades, liens, tax arrears, and so on. Using what he described as a 'data bridge,' Flowers and his team poured all those data sets into one giant spreadsheet that had a separate entry for every municipal address in New York. Then they started looking for patterns, 'querying' the spreadsheet to look for common traits of buildings where there had been fires. They eventually found the proverbial needle in the haystack and reckoned they could begin sending notices to landlords whose buildings showed similar patterns of neglect, reasoning that these structures were more likely to fall victim to fire. It was, fundamentally, a data-driven prevention strategy, geared in this case to mitigate fire risk.

But Flowers, no wide-eyed technophile, knew enough to gut check this process. He would go on ride-alongs with seasoned New York bylaw inspectors. They'd swing by a building that the data patterns had flagged as a potential fire trap, and sometimes the inspectors, following a quick look-around, would spot a counterfactual – a detail that suggested the building didn't pose the risk that the data predicted. Those conclusions, Flowers told me, were based on experience, observation, and common sense – all traits, he noted, that couldn't be automated.

The mayor's efforts to bring data science to municipal decision-making didn't stop at city hall. In one of his signature moves, he invited technical research institutions from around the world to bid on the opportunity to build a world-class technology and engineering campus on city-owned land in order to fill a gap in New York's university offerings.

Bloomberg had made huge donations to academic public health institutions, but he saw this initiative as a way to seed start-ups, attract venture capital, and build an east coast tech hub to rival Boston. Among the winning projects was something called the Center for Urban Science and Progress, a degree-granting research joint venture between NYU, Carnegie Mellon University, and several other academic partners, including the University of Toronto and a host of blue-chip tech giants. It describes its field – 'urban informatics' – as the 'interdisciplinary application of science, technology, engineering, and mathematics in the service of urban communities across the globe.'

Intrigued, I wrote several more stories about the use of data analytics to confront urban issues from air pollution to policing. One project, developed in Saskatoon, aimed to use predictive analytics to identify Indigenous youth who were at risk of running away. From a great distance, the initiative, a joint venture by the University of Saskatchewan and the Saskatoon police department, might have seemed well-intentioned. But once you peeled the onion, it became clear this somewhat creepy project – the data required included personal information from social service agencies – had more to do with treating the symptoms than addressing root causes.

And then Sidewalk Labs rode into town. In many ways, the company's gambit was the journalistic gift that kept on giving. It had all the ingredients – money, politics, real estate speculation, sci-fi technology, and combatants with global reputations and deep pockets. What's more, it seemed that Sidewalk, which conspicuously eschewed the phrase 'smart cities,' appeared intent on disrupting the multi-billion-dollar smart city industry, then dominated by tech giants like Cisco, IBM, and Siemens. After all, *disruption*, in those halcyon pre-pandemic years, was an investor-friendly euphemism for the tech sector's compulsion to overwhelm, wreck, and monopolize whatever stood in its way. Google and Sidewalk, in other words, seemed motivated by a desire to disrupt cities – an objective historically used to describe the work of marauders, invading armies, and natural disasters.

The first section of the book is about the long history of the relationship between cities and city-building technology, everything from some of the most fundamental forms of architecture to the digital connectivity of our era. In the history of urbanism, the engineering technologies that enabled city-building have often been depicted as playing a supporting role to more dramatic architectural and social developments, and were frequently regarded as the non-political work of technical experts. Yet, as the U.S. historian Mark Rose pointed out in a 1988 paper entitled 'Machine Politics: The Historiography of Technology and Public Policy,' city-altering technologies must always be understood to exist within a broader political context. 'The history of urban government [represents] a story of technological achievement and sophisticated financing, a story of greater breadth and complexity than has yet been recorded' (Rose).

The bulk of the book's second section offers a deep dive into this giant family of predominantly digital innovations that have emerged from tech giants and start-ups alike, as well as the far-reaching policy, political, and even philosophical questions these systems pose. *Dream States* is also tied to my interest in city-building, public space, urban history, and the myriad technologies that emerged over centuries, giving rise to the emergence of the modern metropolis. Indeed, I'd argue that the two litmus tests for any twenty-first-century smart city technology is whether it both stands the test of time and advances the cause of city-building.

In discussing technology, I have relied in part on the broad definition developed by the German-Canadian physicist and peace activist Ursula Franklin. Her view of technology, articulated in the 1989 Massey Lectures, went far beyond the realm of gadgets and inventions.

Technology, she asserted, encompassed systems, methods, and processes, some of which were holistic, like the work of artisans, and others that were essentially prescriptive and thus employed by governments, companies, and other institutions as instruments of 'compliance and conformity.' Others, like the Spanish sociologist Manuel Castells, add that technology can be defined as the 'use of scientific knowledge to specify ways of doing things in a reproducible manner' (Castells 1996, 30).

The chapters that follow will also examine the complicated space where urban technology intersects with what one might describe, very broadly, as the theories of the city. Some are utopian fictions and social critiques, while others take a sociological, observational, or even quantitative approach to explaining the nature of urban life. A few have sought to combine both into programmatic approaches to city-building and social reform.

The city is one of humanity's oldest inventions, and constantly expanding settlements have served as the backdrop or staging ground for much of recorded history – ancient imperial capitals, like Rome, Kyoto, or Tenochtitlan, and, later, restless centres of commerce, like Venice, Timbuktu, London, and New York. In some cases, like medieval Florence, the inflow of vast amounts of capital and the emergence of rich merchant clans somehow sparked (or at least underwrote) periods of intense cultural or inventive activity. Others, like the contemporary Bay Area/Silicon Valley region, function like hothouse incubators for digital technologies that have changed just about everything.

Today, in most developed countries, more than 80 per cent of the population lives in cities. Globally, that figure surpassed 50 per cent in 2008. But until the nineteenth century, most of humanity did not inhabit urban areas. Indeed, the vast majority of cities, which had evolved from trading posts, ports, fortifications, oases, or hubs for the marketing of agricultural products, were hardly desirable places to live, except for those with means or some kind of ancestral privilege.

Deadly epidemics regularly tore through cities, killing or dispersing the inhabitants. Even in wealthy metropolises with extensive infrastructure, like Rome at the height of its influence, the vast majority lived in squalor. 'Rome,' writes historian Peter Hall, 'was a city of contrasts: on the one hand, the rich who could spend vast sums on banquets and all manner of luxuries; on the other, the poor who depended on the notorious *panem et circenses* (bread and circuses) and who survived under the bridges or in small, dark, cold, rat-infested slums' (Hall 1998, 626).

Thomas More, the English social philosopher, coined the term *utopia* in his 1516 treatise envisioning a just society. Long before More, Socrates, in Plato's *Republic*, examined similar philosophical questions. But urban utopianism per se emerged much later, as one of many responses to the chaotic forces that gave rise to the modern city, namely the Industrial Revolution that began in England in the eighteenth century and the cotton mills of Lancashire.

Rapid industrialization gave rise to the emergence of a new urban underclass, people drawn to cities to work in factories and relegated to overcrowded slum districts. Yet industrialization also created new forms of urban affluence, and the emerging capitalist and bourgeois classes began to retreat from the crowded and dirty inner city to proto-suburban enclaves characterized by private homes and green spaces – in other words, delineated domestic/residential outskirts suited for families.

In response to the harsh urban world of the nineteenth century, social reformers proposed solutions, some of which were explicitly utopian. Cities and their common problems could be abstracted from specific histories and geographies, and thus became the objects of the work of critics, artists, and inventor-entrepreneurs, as well as emerging technical disciplines, like planning, architecture, and transportation engineering.

For well over a century in fact, metropolitan regions have become the stages upon which these competing ideas have played out. They encompass the various strands of utopian city planning advocated by thinkers like Ebenezer Howard, Frank Lloyd Wright, and Le

Corbusier, but also successive political and technocratic programs that yielded enormous infrastructure schemes, top-down land-use planning and urban redevelopment schemes.

Critics like Jane Jacobs pushed back against the authoritarian dictates of modernist urban planning; her observations and brand of advocacy have been taken up by countless neighbourhood activists, local politicians, and land-use planners seeking – perhaps ironically – to replicate the organic urbanism she extolled.

Many others have followed, identifying trends (Edge Cities), promoting neo-traditional, climate-conscious planning (New Urbanism; Smart Growth), or asserting the economic primacy of networked urban regions in global trade flows. Some academic urbanists explain cities as 'systems of systems' or concentrated hubs that spark creativity and innovation. A few have even sought to explain cities scientifically, arguing, as physicist Geoffrey West does in his 2017 book *Scale: The Universal Laws of Life and Death in Organisms, Cities, and Companies*, that the stages of urban expansion can be predicted using empirical observations about natural/economic phenomena like biological growth and scale.

This copious buffet of urbanist thinking has been taken up differently in different places, with varying results, some of which were utterly unintended and even savagely destructive in their application, such as some modernist public housing schemes. In most big cities, however, the effect is that of a palimpsest – layers upon layers, all of it buffeted by the relentless tides of people, ideas, and capital that wash in and out.

At the same time, there are many big cities that exist with almost no apparent nod to the waves of urbanist advocacy and development that have spread around the globe. Before the pandemic, I spent a few days in Hanoi, a city of relentless, anarchic energy. In its core, there are streets lined with four- and five-storey colonial buildings that completely altered my notion of mixed use. Street entrances pass through small shops to interior foyers in which the tenants park their scooters. Steep switchback staircases pass through apartment landings, small temples, offices, and cafés spread out over multiple floors. There is no obvious order, and yet somehow it all works.

The smart city agenda aimed to impose a measure of rationality on twenty-first-century urbanism, with all its chaotic energy. Certainly, to those charged with governing and administering cities, the technocratic promise of the smart city has been highly appealing. After all, what city wouldn't want to be 'smart'? The phrase, moreover, is malleable enough to mean many things to many people. Does 'smart' connote the type of inhabitant who resides in these places? Is it a reference to rationalist approaches to municipal administration that leveraged technology to overcome daunting urban problems, like congestion? Or perhaps the label has a kind of brand appeal designed to attract companies, investors, inventors – smart people.

'One widely-used definition ... defines cities as smart when 'investments in human and social capital and traditional (transport) and modern (ICT) communication infrastructure fuel sustainable economic growth and a high quality of life, with a wise management of natural resources, through participatory governance,' commented the authors of a 2020 German study on the 'varieties of smart cities' (Drapalova & Weigrich).

Yet, as this study and many others have observed, the tech industry seized on the 'smart city' label as a means of developing and selling new generations of scalable digital systems that claim to be capable of tackling complex urban problems, from climate change to security to mobility. Most urbanists and city planners now accept complexity as a given. In a world of mass migration, instantaneous communication, and environmental crisis, anyone who fails to acknowledge that *everything* is complicated simply isn't paying attention.

The purveyors of smart city tech, which relies on big data, algorithms, sensors, and artificial intelligence, regard urban complexity as both a market opportunity and an engineering challenge. Smart city companies, from ambitious start-ups to multinational tech giants, promote their powerful and highly adaptive systems as being well suited to the messy, overcrowded urbanism of the twenty-first century.

While not the only target markets for smart city tech, municipal and regional governments have proven to be highly responsive customers, amenable to the messaging that better technology will improve services and lower costs, but also prevent them from falling behind. Case in point: an annual global ranking published by a smart city 'observatory' that's run by the IMD World Competitiveness Center, which is based in Switzerland and Singapore. Each city's scores are calculated using conventional economic and quality-of-life indicators, but also the availability of technologies, such as mobility apps or online transit ticketing, as well as public attitudes toward the use of CCTVs and facial recognition in crime prevention. Cities whose residents express more acceptance of these technologies receive higher scores ('Smart City Observatory').

Yet as the Sidewalk saga demonstrated, many people felt deeply uncomfortable about the prospect of fitting out urban spaces with the kinds of technologies that have, in the words of Harvard professor emerita Shoshana Zuboff, enabled 'the wholesale destruction of privacy' (Zuboff 2021).

The global pandemic, however, cast a pall over the sprawling smart city industry as local governments facing economic fallout from COVID-19 put their spending plans on hold. Some firms that had bet very heavily on smart city tech, like Cisco, decided to exit in the midst of the crisis. 'Smart cities are a hard sell,' a former Cisco director told *Connected*, a real estate trade publication. 'The return on investment can be hard to quantify, and stitching together disparate smart city technologies can appear daunting. Even basic things like public Wi-Fi have been difficult.'

Despite such moves by leading tech corporations, society's reliance on digital technology soared during the pandemic, and the consequences of these seismic shifts will have a significant impact on cities in the years to come. Which should come as little surprise: throughout history, infectious disease outbreaks have both ruined cities and triggered enormous changes in public health, social supports, culture, and so on. Digital connectivity, in the form of specific applications such as e-commerce or video-conferencing, was already altering urban space before the pandemic, and there's good reason to believe this process has accelerated. Will cities, downtowns, retail strips, movie theatres, etc., survive? And how will the post-pandemic city ard its institutions look, feel, and behave in the era of climate crisis?

These are the quescions for the next generation of city-dwellers, idealists and otherwise.

The Technology
of Cities

1
Connections

In the Detroit row house that later became the headquarters of *Hitsville USA*, Berry Gordy was always scrambling and hustling to find musicians for the recording sessions he'd orchestrate in Motown's tiny studio. In the early 1960s, a promising singer named Marvin Gaye sometimes filled in on drums. Smokey Robinson, another frequent collaborator, sang and also introduced Gordy to a talented childhood friend – a young woman named Diana Ross who belonged to a girl group called the Primettes. Several of those early Motown musicians – artists whose careers transformed pop music – knew one another socially, having grown up in the same working-class neighbourhood in Detroit.

'We just went down and did everything,' Gordy told *Rolling Stone* in 1990. 'And we all knew how to work the machines. And everybody came and played at everybody's session. The way that people could get into Motown was to get a job there and do something meaningful, and then they could come every day … Diana wanted to get a job at Motown so she could be there, but there was not really a job she could do. But I needed a secretary at the time, so I let her try that out.' Ross manned a metal desk outside the studio door, as had Martha Reeves, who later fronted Martha Reeves and the Vandellas. 'Ross,' Gordy recalled, 'worked for me for a summer, but she was so bad as a secretary that I had to let her go' (Goldberg 1990). He signed her instead.

Like the families of most of those musicians, Gordy grew up in Detroit because his parents had joined the 'great migration' of African

Americans who fled the violence and humiliations of the Jim Crow South to find work in northern industrial cities. In Detroit, automakers employed tens of thousands of blue-collar workers, many at Henry Ford's gigantic factory in Dearborn, Michigan. After a tour of duty in Korea in 1952, Gordy, too, found work at a Lincoln-Mercury plant, but he gravitated toward music, his true passion. Motown, the empire he built, was an affectionate nickname for Detroit's handle: Motor City.

Migration, of course, is never just about the destination. Gordy's family came from Georgia, Ross's from Virginia and Detroit. Reeves was born in Alabama and moved with her parents and siblings to Detroit when she was just an infant. The South's history of slavery and then share-cropping was intimately connected to cotton, as well as the textile industry that had sprung up in places like Spartanburg, S.C.

But slavery was underwritten by consumers and businessmen located on the other side of the Atlantic. In England, Liverpool, London, and Bristol – all major ports – served as one vertex of the triangle of the eighteenth- and nineteenth-century transatlantic slave trade: cotton, tobacco, and sugar from the U.S. South and the Caribbean back to England, with the profits used to finance the kidnapping and brutal transport of hundreds of thousands of Africans to the plantations in the Americas. As of 1800, Liverpool merchants controlled 80 per cent of the British slave trade (Riding 2007).

Those port cities were home to powerful plantation owners, as well as the industries that served these trade corridors: shipbuilding, docklands construction, and, in London, financial services. The city had become a global capital of maritime insurance. As the command centre for the British Empire and home base for chartered colonial trading companies, London was not just a port of call, but a communications hub for shipping news. In fact, merchants in the late seventeenth century began congregating at a coffee house near the Tower of London, owned by a man named Edward Lloyd. 'The place became a favourite haunt of ship's captains, merchants and ship owners,' according to an online history of maritime insurance. 'At this time, there were more than 80 coffee houses within the City of London's walls, each claimed its own specialization. By the 1730's, Lloyd's' –

which later evolved into Lloyd's List and then Lloyd's of London – 'was emerging as the spot for marine underwriting by individuals' ('Corporate History').

Assisted by shipping insurance, English traders imported huge volumes of American cotton to provide raw materials to the textile mills in Lancashire, a Midlands industrial region anchored by the City of Manchester and located not far from Liverpool. By the 1830s, writes urban historian Peter Hall, 'Manchester was without challenge the first and greatest industrial city in the world,' home to almost a quarter of all factory workers in Great Britain. Lancashire was traversed by fast-moving rivers and situated near the abundant coal fields of Sheffield. In Manchester, inventors and boot-strapping entrepreneurs developed and patented a series of weaving technologies that created an extraordinarily profitable industry responsible, at one time, for almost 10 per cent of the British economy.

As its textile mills grew larger and more complex, the Lancashire region attracted even more engineers and investors. 'Manchester then became the main engineering centre in Britain, producing not only textile machinery, but water wheels, steam engines, boilers, railway locomotives, machine tools and a mass of engineering products,' Hall explains (Hall 1998, 341).

In December 1842, a twenty-two-year-old arrived in the city with instructions from his father to learn the techniques of industrial management; the Engels family had investments in textile manufacturing. Yet over the next three years, Friedrich Engels spent much of his free time wandering through the crowded and dirty working-class slums that surrounded Manchester's roaring factories. He discovered dingy back lanes, accessible only by narrow passageways. '[He] who turns in thither gets into a filth and disgusting grime the equal of which is not to be found – especially in the courts which lead down to the [River] Irk and which contain unqualifiedly the most horrible dwellings which I have yet beheld,' Engels wrote in his 1845 book, *The Conditions of the Working Class in England.*

During his explorations, Engels encountered stinking tanneries, privies without doors, and pools of urine and excrement. He coined a strong term for the indifference shown by capitalists, governments, and society in general: 'social murder.' Engels was also a keen observer of built form. He noticed that the city's high streets were lined by well-tended, closely spaced shops – an urban plan that conveniently concealed the horrific conditions from the eyes of wealthy merchants. 'I cannot help feeling that the liberal manufacturers, the "Big Wigs" of Manchester, are not so innocent after all, in the matter of this sensitive method of construction' (LeGates & Stout 1996, 50–51). He published his observations in *The Condition of the Working Class in England* in 1845 – twelve years after the British Parliament voted to ban the practice of slavery anywhere within its colonies. Engels's book became a foundational text in what evolved into a program of radical social and economic reforms espoused by Engels and his friend Karl Marx.

The unspooling thread of Berry Gordy's story, the antecedents of which trace all the way to the satanic mills of eighteenth- and nineteenth-century England, may also be spun forward in time, in equally unpredictable directions.

Engels's commentary about Manchester can be seen as part of the literary headwaters for a genre of socially conscious writing, much of it highly influential, about living conditions for the urban working poor. The tradition extended through several of Charles Dickens's later novels (*Oliver Twist* slightly predates Engels's commentary) to Dostoevsky's *Notes from the Underground* (1864), as well as works by crusading journalists like Jacob Riis, author of *How the Other Half Lives*, an illustrated 1890 exposé on the slums in the Lower East Side, and Upton Sinclair's *The Jungle* (1906), a documentary-style novel about grim working and sanitary conditions in Chicago's slaughterhouses. Sinclair's book caught the eye of politicians like Theodore Roosevelt and prompted sweeping reforms in the meat-processing industry.

Throughout the latter part of the nineteenth century, the plight of the urban underclasses took on an increasingly critical role in the politics in many countries, prompting social reforms and radical cultural movements, and eventually the revolution that exploded on the wide streets of Saint Petersburg in March 1917. That uprising sparked others – in Hungary, Germany, and Austria – and inspired socialist movements elsewhere such as the 1919 Winnipeg General Strike.

The joyless grind of life for the working class, articulated by Engels and later Riis, also became the preoccupation of a generation of urban reformers and visionaries. They sought to redesign cities and buildings in ways that would produce cleaner, healthier, safer, and less overtly Dickensian living conditions. By the turn of the twentieth century, the progressivist tool kit included municipal parks, public schools, child care centres, proper sanitation, leafy suburbs suitable for families, transit services, libraries, and social supports for the poor, including purpose-built subsidized apartments featuring modern amenities, open spaces, and light.

One of the leading design voices to emerge from the radical politics of the post-WWI era was the Swiss-French architect Charles-Édouard Jeanneret, known as Le Corbusier. During the 1920s, he proposed a set of radical changes in urban design and architecture, including the construction of soaring modernist apartments meant to provide housing designed to uplift and equalize the masses. His travels to New York City in the 1930s attracted rapt media attention, and his concept of building a 'tower in a park' in response to poverty and over-crowding in Paris found its way into the plans of American housing authorities and developers, perhaps most notably in Manhattan's Stuyvesant Town (Eschner 2017).

As it happened, Diana Ross, in her teens, lived with her family in Detroit's Brewster-Douglass Housing Project – a very similar cluster of cruciform high-rises surrounded by open space and built in the 1930s. From afar, these apartment buildings looked like they had been designed by Le Corbusier himself. All have since been demolished.

In 1972, Berry Gordy moved his Motown label to Los Angeles, a showbiz city built by and for Southern California's powerful real estate interests. Once served by North America's largest network of electrified streetcars, L.A. in the 1970s had become the poster child for sprawl and congestion. (In the 1960s, the regional transit agency began pulling up the streetcar tracks in favour of buses, allegedly – though not in fact – at the behest of the auto industry.) Detroit had also slipped into a long decline, attributable to the destructive dual forces of L.A.-style sprawl and racial tension, as middle-class whites fled to the suburbs. In the city's core, a dense network of expressways effectively choked off the downtown. Meanwhile, Detroit's automakers were having their own problems, losing market share to the German manufacturers clustered around Munich and Hanover, as well as discount upstarts like Toyota and Datsun, based in Japan's heavily urbanized south.

Over just a few decades, in fact, the technologies of sprawl – mass-produced tract housing, highway construction, and the combustion engine – altered the politics of cities, sparking new types of urban activism. Critics and grassroots groups in some places took aim at the legacy of top-down 'urban renewal' planning and the practice of block-busting working-class and racialized neighbourhoods. In other places, communities organized to fight and stop the highway construction schemes ripping through inner-city areas.

In more recent years, mounting evidence of climate crisis, spurred by fossil fuel consumption across a wide range of sectors, has pushed many cities to attempt to limit or at least slow sprawl by boosting densities, expanding rapid transit, and promoting other ways of reducing carbon. These include measures to incentivize green building technologies and renewable energy systems, some of which rely on smart city software and hardware.

There's an ironic coda to this meandering urban saga. In the years before Henry Ford began mass-producing Model Ts, two other transportation technologies were in ascendancy: bicycles and electric trams. According to Frank Geels, a professor of systems innovation at the University of Manchester, '[they] helped to create many new elements that paved the way for the automobile, for example new mobility practices and user preferences, changing perception of the function of streets, becoming used to vehicles with higher speed, the Good Roads movement for smoother pavements, more power for public authorities in the administration of streets, development of new technical elements. Because of these socio-technical knock-on effects, the bicycle and electric tram acted as catalysts in the transition towards automobiles.' As Geels observed in a 2005 paper, 'The success of the automobile was enabled by the previous transformations.'

As of the 2020s, the failings of the automobile have forced many cities to revisit the role of bikes and electric trams, including the City of Angels. Today, the downtown L.A. intersection where Gordy had located Motown's new head office, Sunset Boulevard and Argyle, is just a two-minute walk from a major underground transit station on one of the city's newer LRT lines.

Gordy's success and celebrity obviously sets him apart from the vast majority of North Americans of his generation. Yet in many ways, Gordy's story exemplifies many features of the mass urbanization that started in earnest with the Industrial Revolution and now accounts for the way the majority of human beings live on this earth.

The city, as a form of human settlement, is an ancient invention. Through recorded history, cities evolved over centuries or even millennia from military outposts, safe harbours, trade route entrepots, oases, and pilgrimage sites. Some became imperial capitals or commercial centres but then disappeared due to disease, conquest, or natural disaster.

Unlike ancient and medieval cities, which generally grew slowly, industrial and then post-industrial cities rapidly exploded in size as upstart manufacturers and related service industries attracted entrepreneurs with capital and rivals and labour. That need for bodies – fed by the promise of money or an escape from the grinding poverty of rural subsistence farming – transformed cities into sites of migration and produced geographical ripple effects, such as the accelerated use of slave labour in colonized regions to produce the commodities that could be exported to those emergent cities.

The influx generated new forms of wealth, new forms of misery, and new sensibilities about class, social status, architecture, and power. As concentrated population centres, cities stoked the demand for consumer goods, gave rise to modern forms of finance and banking,[1] and hastened the demise of the artisanal economy, which had its own legacy of strength through the powerful trade guilds that dominated urban commerce in the Middle Ages.

Indeed, it soon became apparent that cities were much more than just concentrations of human beings thrown together by the weird combinatorics of fate and history. They had evolved into complex ecosystems – hothouses for scientific and commercial innovation, political and social organization, and cultural activity. As Larry Busbea, a University of Arizona art historian and urban scholar, writes, 'urban space came to be seen not as a neutral container but as a conductive medium for the movements and exchanges of people, information and objects,' (Busbea 2012, 10).

Busbea quotes the French philosopher Henri Lefebvre, author of *The Urban Revolution*: 'The urban centre fills to saturation; it decays or explodes. From time to time, it reverses direction and surrounds itself with emptiness and scarcity. More often, it assumes and then proposes the concentration of everything there is in the world, in nature, in the cosmos: the fruits of the earth, the products of industry, human works, objects and instruments, acts and situations, signs and symbols.'

Scholars of urban history and sociology have shown how cities, under certain circumstances, ignited cultural movements and attracted inventors who changed the world. The American sociologist Paul Meadows further argued that urbanization has been powered by technological advancement. 'Urbanization represents the processes by which urbanism emerges and develops out of the interaction of technology and society,' he commented in a 1956 lecture.

In his 1998 treatise, *Cities in Civilization*, planning historian Peter Hall filled out the picture, looking at case studies involving certain cities at

---

1. Many types of financial instruments predate industrialization, including bills of lading, credit or promissory notes, and trade in debt instruments. Merchant banking empires like the Medicis and the Rothschilds also emerged prior to the Industrial Revolution, sometimes helping to finance state actions, like wars. The first stock exchanges, early forms of property insurance, the widespread use of legal tender, and modern banking, however, date to the eighteenth century, and stoked the expansion of new industrial ventures and trade globalization.

moments of pivotal innovation. He points out that Detroit, at the turn of the century, was ripe for the transportation revolution created by Henry Ford – a place on 'the edge of the American heartland,' where someone with risky ideas could spot opportunities that others had missed. Similarly, Hall writes, cities like Florence during the Renaissance, Berlin during the Weimar years, and Tokyo in the post-WWII era, flourished because of a concentration of creative people with ideas, investors with capital, and governments with ambition.

Still others regard cities as communications hubs or places where populist energy may be concentrated and then detonated. Cities can devolve into infectious disease accelerators, incubators of extremism, and zones of grotesque inequity. They are destroyed and rebuilt, expand and contract, liberate and oppress. Fully embracing these paradoxes of urban life, Lefebvre's lyrical description rings true.

Yet the ever-evolving social and economic theories of the city – layered one on top of the other in a seemingly chaotic heap – rest on the sturdy foundation of the civil engineering and architectural technologies that have collectively produced the physical city. Many, in fact, are so ancient and universal that we barely acknowledge their presence, much less their relationships to the creation of the thoroughly urban, digitized world of the twenty-first century.

2
Engineering the City

The physical incarnation of the city is an almost impossibly complex puzzle that consists of tangible elements, such as geography, architecture, and the ebb and flow of people and capital, but also imponderables: the currents of history, the passage of time, and the countless number of small human choices that leave, in the aggregate, their imprint on the cityscape.

Yet cities are also imagined and then conjured – dreamscapes rendered in wood, brick, concrete, and steel. 'As early as the outset of the fifteenth century,' writes Ruth Eaton, a British curator, 'one finds indications that the city was increasingly considered as an object that could be described.'

She points to the emergence, during the early Renaissance, of drawing skills, like perspective and the depiction of schematic ground plans (da Vinci), as critical innovations in the family of technologies that inform city-building. 'The increasing sophistication and employment of surveying and drawing instruments contributed further to the distancing between the architect and the city, while the increasing availability of paper and the introduction of printing rendered his delineations easily distributable in quantity. These developments all contributed to the depiction and objective consideration of the city,' (Eaton 2002, 41).

However, the ambitious projection of cityscapes – whether by rulers and priests or architects and planners – is as much about assembling many prosaic components as it is about the sum of imagination plus capital plus labour. This list is long and universal – bricks, beams, pipes, nails, risers, etc. It includes architectural technologies developed in response to harsh local environments, such as the mud wall domestic compounds constructed in ancient cities in Saharan and sub-Saharan Africa. Alongside building materials, structural know-how has shaped urban space for thousands of years, e.g., lintels, the unprepossessing length of load-bearing wood, masonry, or steel that straddles the top of a door or window frame. These modest slabs serve to transfer a wall's weight away from the gap below, preventing collapse. They were used to construct Egypt's great pyramids and also Stonehenge. Thousands of years later, they remain a basic architectural detail in every contemporary building, including the most modest ones.

Reinforced concrete is another example – concrete reinforced with steel or iron bars is now ubiquitous. It's not an exaggeration to say that without rebar, the modern city would not exist.[2] Concrete – made from gravel, sand, and a limestone binding agent called cement – was widely employed as a building material by the Romans. 'The formula for Roman concrete also starts with limestone: builders burned it to produce quicklime and then added water to create a paste,' The Smithsonian explained in 2011. 'Next they mixed in volcanic ash – usually three parts volcanic ash to one part lime, according to the writings of Vitruvius, a first-century BCE architect and engineer. The volcanic ash reacted with the lime paste to create a durable mortar that was combined with fist-size chunks of bricks or volcanic rocks called tuff, and then packed into place to form structures like walls or vaults.' Roman concrete was weaker than modern concrete but very durable, which accounts for the resilience of monuments like the Pantheon (Wayman 2011).

Concrete fell out of use for centuries, eclipsed by brick and wood. In the 1820s, however, a British bricklayer named Joseph Aspdin patented a powder he called 'portland cement,' which could bind

---

2. Rebar, of course, is not just used in cities, but cities amplify the importance of such basic materials.

aggregates into a durable concrete (Kirkbride 2004). About fifty years later, a California-based entrepreneur, Ernest Leslie Ransome, came up with a way of making concrete even stronger.

Ransome's father ran a cast-stone factory (the process was used to fabricate the ornate masonry widely used in nineteenth-century architecture). Ernest, born in England in 1852 and one of nine children, went to work at the plant as a young apprentice. He moved to San Francisco in 1870, got a job in a firm called the Pacific Stone Company, and eventually set himself up as a consulting engineer. In a 2019 essay in *California History Journal*, historian Stephen Mikesell points out that the practice of inserting iron or steel rods into concrete was well established. What Ransome figured out, however, was that by using twisted rods, the reinforced concrete had greater tensile strength – meaning it could withstand forces that torqued structures such as bridges or columns. 'His twisted rebar,' Mikesell writes, 'was a major advance in that it allowed for the use of much smaller pieces of metal, saving money and materials, particularly when the metal surface was deformed to better adhere to the concrete.' Ransome's rebar went into construction of the two oldest reinforced concrete bridges in the U.S. – both in Golden Gate Park – as well as numerous other buildings designed by his firm. It also paved the way for further innovation in this most basic kind of building material.

Mikesell writes that Ransome built his career in a booming port/gold-rush city – San Francisco in the late nineteenth and early twentieth centuries – that had attracted many self-taught engineers. 'We may never again see the like of Ernest Leslie Ransome, a developer of construction methods and machines and a builder of great structures, who learned his craft through apprenticeship and by experience, not in university study' (Mikesell 2019, 18).

It's safe to say that very few people pause to think about rebar as they move through contemporary cities, and even fewer would be aware of someone like Ransome. But the importance of this type of city-building technology becomes highly apparent when it is missing, as happened when a forty-two-year-old Miami condo building, financed in part by Canadian investors, collapsed in the summer of

2021, killing ninety-eight people. When investigators sifted through the rubble and examined CCTV images, they realized that several rebar-reinforced columns in the main-floor parking garage showed signs not just of corrosion from salt, but also construction that didn't meet design standards. 'Critical places near the base of the building appeared to use less steel reinforcement than called for in the project's original design drawings,' the *New York Times* reported days after the tragedy. Quoting observations by a forensic engineer, the paper noted that 'there were signs that the amount of steel used to connect concrete slabs below a parking deck to the building's vertical columns might be less than what the project's initial plans specified. 'The bars might not be arranged like the original drawings call for' (Glanz et al. 2021).

Beyond the building blocks and techniques that fuelled city-building, the lengthy evolution of civil engineering further reveals the deeply intertwined relationships between cities and commerce, geopolitics, and even the cosmologies that informed urban design.

As far back as the 5th century BCE, Chinese rulers commissioned the construction of a far-reaching network of canals used for agriculture and taxation (paid in grain), but also as a means of connecting rural areas to cities. Canal-building enabled the production and transportation of rice, a staple in heavily populated Chinese urban centres. According to a 1998 account of pre-industrial Chinese engineering and technology, the canal networks linking cities and rural areas fostered, or at least accelerated, the development of two other technologies: large-scale printing and iron fabrication. As technology historian Arnold Pacey explains, there was a boom in demand both for books on rice production and plowing equipment, manufactured in ironworks plants located near coal mines (Pacey 1998).

In Kaifeng, one of China's ancient capitals situated in the country's northeast region, canals entered the metropolis through so-called 'water gates' in the city walls. These formidable structures, another fixture of Chinese civil engineering, surrounded many large urban centres, tracing the edges of the rectilinear street grids inspired by Confucian cosmology and other teachings on the layout of political cities, including Beijing. The tower walls and parapets served, obviously, as a form of military defence against invaders, but, as Pacey notes, they signalled something else about urban form:

> The same connection between walls, gates and orderly government is indicated by the following anecdote. Confucius is said to have been in a horse-drawn carriage with one of his disciples when he encountered some children playing in the road. The children had used loose tiles and bricks to build a model city wall across the road and, as the carriage was about to scatter these playthings, one of them stood up and asked Confucius a question: 'Should the city wall be destroyed or ought the carriage to turn round if it cannot pass through the wall-gate?' Confucius apparently recognized an appeal to ideals of civil order and good government and asked his driver to turn the carriage around. (298)

Basic human needs drove yet another category of early civil engineering, geared toward providing fresh water and disposing of human waste at scale. Many ancient cities relied on the provision of latrines, public baths, and drainage pipes. 'The Romans did build many structures seemingly dedicated to improving sanitation – in addition to public toilets, they had bathhouses and sewer systems like the giant Cloaca Maxima in Rome,' explained a 2016 feature on Roman hygiene in The Atlantic. '"They [also] introduced legislation so that towns had to clear away the waste from the roads and things and take all that waste mess outside towns,"' Piers Mitchell, a University of Cambridge paleo-pathologist told the magazine, adding that his research showed such infrastructure didn't actually prevent disease (Beck 2016).

While Romans tend to get most of the credit for early advances in civil engineering, other civilizations recognized how to leverage the underlying principles of physics to build similar infrastructure. In 2010, a team of archaeologists published remarkable findings about Palenque, a Mayan citystate in Mexico's Chiapas region that existed from 250 to 900 CE. They uncovered evidence of a pressurized municipal water system engineered with spring-fed aqueducts and built almost a thousand years before the arrival of the Spanish conquistadors.

'Underground water features such as aqueducts are not unusual at Palenque,' *Science Daily* reported in 2010. 'Because the Maya built the city in a constricted area in a break in an escarpment, inhabitants were unable to spread out. To make as much land available for living, the Maya at Palenque routed streams beneath plazas via aqueducts. "They were creating urban space," said Kirk French, lecturer in anthropology at Penn State. "There are streams in the area every 300 feet or so across the whole escarpment. There is very little land to build on."' The archaeological evidence also showed how the aqueducts help mitigate flooding in the city (Penn State 2010). Several centuries later, in Tenochtitlan and Tlatelolco, the Aztec imperial city located 900 kilometres northwest of Palenque, generations of builders created an extraordinary feat of urban engineering and reclamation in the middle of Lake Texcoco, which once occupied part of the present-day location of Mexico City. With a population of approximately 400,000 when the brutal Spanish occupation began in 1519, Tenochtitlan and Tlatelolco had been built on reclaimed and then elevated islands traversed by canals, with neighbourhoods and adjoining fields linked by hundreds of wooden bridges. At the time, the city – constructed over centuries and financed by an elaborate system of taxation imposed by the Aztecs on nearby regions – had about 60,000 houses built in rows along canals and radiating out from a central precinct of pyramids and temples, all of which were destroyed by the conquistadors. To the Spanish, Tenochtitlan reminded them of Venice.

According to a history of this remarkable Meso-American capital by University of Colorado, Boulder, anthropologist Gerardo Gutiérrez, '[t]he most extraordinary projects … were the artificial causeways connecting the island to the main cities on shore, the aqueduct that brought fresh water to the city, and the dikes that regulated the level of Lake Texcoco. All these engineering projects were formidable tasks that would have been impossible without the forced labor of the conquered polities around the lake' (Gutiérrez 2015).

The elaborate nature of Tenochtitlan's built form serves as a reminder that knowledge about many of the most basic elements of civil engineering did not diffuse, but rather evolved independently in many places, over many epochs, with distinctly urban impacts.

Consider the construction of permanent structures anchored in water, such as the Mnjikaning fishing weirs, located in a narrows at the north end of Lake Simcoe, in Ontario. The weirs, now a national historic site, date to about 3300 BCE and consist of clusters of wooden stakes driven into the clay of the shallow lake bottom. Indigenous fishers strung their nets between the stakes to catch fish.

Maintained over five millennia, the weirs were used in more recent times by the Huron-Wendat and later the Anishnaabeg. Nor were they designed simply to enable fishing. The weirs served as a gathering place imbued with both social and spiritual significance for Indigenous peoples in Southern Ontario and could be described as proto-urban. 'The only other examples known to exist are in the Pacific Northwest, the Canadian North, and the State of Maine in the American Northeast,' according to a 2003 thesis by Kate Mulligan.

Long before the advent of steel-and-concrete spans of the sort that Ernest Leslie Ransome had made possible, bridge engineers understood how to build 'cribs' or 'bathtubs' in fast-moving rivers, creating enclosures made of stones with logs affixed to the bottom. Once these cribs were reasonably watertight, labourers pumped out the enclosure and erected piers that could be securely anchored to the bottom – a technique still used in contemporary bridge construction.

Meanwhile, arched spans, with loads supported and distributed using capstones and trapezoid-shaped blocks, were strongly associated with Roman engineering. Yet similar bridges existed elsewhere, among them the Zhaozhou Bridge in Northern China. Built about 1,400 years ago, it is considered the world's oldest spandrel stone bridge still in active use. (The structure is located in a city of half a million people called Zhao County.)

Bridges, of course aren't inherently urban forms of civil engineering. But these structures enabled urban development by allowing cities to expand across bodies of water, rivers, and ravines, establishing physical connections that enabled commerce, migration new development, and transportation.

By contrast, the evolution of road-building technology follows a somewhat different trajectory. Paths and then roads are as old as human civilization. But for much of early recorded history, they were constructed from flagstones or logs – so-called corduroy roads – or simply existed as beaten ground. The Romans developed sophisticated road engineering techniques that supported an empire extending across Europe. 'Famous for their straightness, Roman roads were composed of a graded soil foundation topped by four courses: a bedding of sand or mortar; rows of large, flat stones; a thin layer of gravel mixed with lime; and a thin surface of flint-like lava,' according to one historical account. 'Typically they were 3 to 5 feet thick and varied in width from 8 to 35 feet, although the average width for the main roads was from 12 to 24 feet. Their design remained the most sophisticated until the advent of modern road-building technology in the very late 18th and 19th centuries' (Sponholtz).

While medieval cities had some paved streets, the game-changing innovation in road-building – and, simultaneously, road financing – occurred in Bristol, England, in the early 1800s. In 1806, a Scot named John Loudon McAdam, who had once worked as a coal tar manufacturer, became the paving commissioner in Bristol, a booming Atlantic port and destination for imports of sugar and tobacco from American plantations. After almost a decade, McAdam took on a post with a far broader scope, and one that would cement his legacy as the inventor of the modern paved highway.

At the time, inter-city highways, known as turnpikes, were managed by trusts and toll keepers. McAdam, who had testified before a House of Commons committee on reforming England's roads, argued for a more professional form of administration and also spelled out design principles that road contractors and surveyors must follow. These included excavating and levelling the roadbed, packing it with layers of crushed stone and gravel, and ensuring a contoured surface that caused water to run off to the side instead of pooling. 'Not only did John Loudon McAdam's design result in a smoother surface and carriage ride, but it was cheaper to build and lasted longer,' noted an essay in *Interesting Engineering*, an engineering blog. 'This "new" roadway surface and construction process have since been immortalized with McAdam's name, often with the Americanized spelling "MacAdam" or "macadam."' (Later innovations involved sealing the surface with tar and eventually asphalt.)

While McAdam (and his sons) had gradually gained control of turnpikes around Bristol, he and other reformers pressed the British government to centralize authority over the country's transportation network, as well as London's metropolitan system. McAdam, who wrote several books about highways and turnpikes, argued that the government should hire surveyors and dispatch inspectors, and allocate revenues specifically for road maintenance. He had public opinion on his side, as travellers complained about the combination of terrible road conditions and high tolls, which were especially prevalent around London.

By the end of his life, McAdam had become not only internationally renowned, but also a verb. '"Macadamizing" was not only, in its literal sense, a practical work of great public utility,' commented a prominent British historian. '[I]t became a symbol of all progress, and was metaphorically used in common parlance for any aspects of the new age where improved and uniform scientific methods were in demand' (Spiro Jr. 1956, 212).

3

Water and Sewage:
The Original Urban Networks

In the middle of the night of September 2, 1666, a fire broke out in a bakery located on Pudding Lane, in the old City of London, just a few blocks from the Thames. By the morning, much of the surrounding area had gone up in flames. Over the next four days, the fire spread relentlessly. 'London in 1666 was a tinderbox, ready to ignite at any time,' write Cathy Ross and John Clark in their 2008 history of the city. That summer, they observe, had been very dry and the warrens of medieval streets were 'crowded with timber houses, which often leant far out into the narrow streets, making it easy for flames to jump between buildings' (Ross & Clark, 112).

By the time it had burned itself out, the Great Fire had destroyed 13,200 houses, eighty-seven churches, the Royal Exchange, and dozens of commercial buildings. While the casualties were modest – fewer than ten people died – the consequences were devastating, with over 100,000 Londoners left homeless. The disaster, moreover, came just a year after an especially lethal plague pandemic, linked to fleas on rats. It killed tens of thousands of people – a fifth of the city's population – with outbreaks spreading to the towns on London's periphery.

State authorities provided a small amount of financial relief after the fire, but the back-to-back calamities forced Londoners to figure out how to build back better, to borrow a phrase from our times. The esteemed architect Christopher Wren drew up an ambitious blueprint that anticipated similar post-fire rebuilding schemes developed after fire consumed Chicago in 1871 and Toronto in 1904. While some of Wren's most famous commissions – e.g., St. Paul's Cathedral – date back to this period, his reconstruction plan was ultimately rejected by landowners.

In fact, the Great Fire's most enduring legacy doesn't involve buildings, but rather the civil engineering systems that serviced them. Over the next century and a half, London became a globally recognized hub for civil engineers and investors, who together invented not only the technical and commercial foundation of modern water and sewage infrastructure, but also the paradigm for the first truly scalable networks – a form that would be replicated in services from gas street lights to rail to modern telecommunications. 'As these networks proliferated, they changed urban life, rendering it more habitable and less hostile,' observes Leslie Tomory, a technology historian who describes the emergence of London's water systems as 'the roots of the networked city' (Tomory 2015).

In 1666, London, with a population of about 200,000 people, had no firefighting services and no centralized supply of fresh water. Most Londoners got their water from wells or fountains, although a small number had it delivered directly into their homes via wooden pipes. A handful of private companies supplied the water to affluent subscribers, pumping it from the Thames, as well as canal-fed ponds situated at higher elevations in the suburbs.

As the city rebuilt, a new financial services industry sprang up: companies that offered fire insurance to property owners. To mitigate their own financial risk, these underwriters also operated their own brigades of firefighters, who – in an intriguing precursor to contemporary corporate branding – wore colourful uniforms that associated them with a particular insurer.

The reconstruction of London attracted many new residents, and the population growth spurred demand for water provided directly to homes. By the late seventeenth century, one water supplier – the

New River Company, whose shareholders included King James I – emerged as a dominant firm, drawing water from two springs and the River Lea at Islington Hill, north-west of the city, then distributing it through a rapidly growing network of mains to tens of thousands of subscribers, mostly in the West End. Tomory points out that London, at the time, had seen an influx of new wealth, and consequently mounting interest in consumer products as well as luxury goods and services, among them water. Other water firms were also competing for customers, and by the 1720s, most homes had lead pipe hookups, but New River, he writes, was by far the most profitable, 'its shares become worth tens of thousands of pounds.'

The commercial success of New River soon threatened to backfire because of the company's chaotic approach to building out its network, explains Tomory. The firm, which still relied primarily on gravitational pressure to send water through its pipe network, couldn't provide a steady supply for its rapidly growing customer base. To compensate, New River provided subscribers with water according to a schedule, to be stored in basement cisterns. The company, moreover, balanced its loads by installing valves within its pipes – known as 'turncocks,' and accessible from apertures embedded in the road surface.

New Company line workers would fan out each day and turn the valves on or off as a means of directing the flow of water to certain districts at specified times. 'After a few hours the valves would be shut again,' Tomory writes. 'The water supply was cycled between the various mains feeding different areas of the city over various days, which meant in practice that houses received water for two or three hours only a few days a week.'

Despite these supply limitations, New River's directors as well as those with competing water companies, took care to provide on-demand free water to the fire brigades of the insurance companies that had started signing up customers after the fire. According to historical geographer Carry van Lieshout, the owners of London's water companies, acutely sensitive to accusations of profiteering, made sure to not only practise this kind of philanthropy but also promote their own civic-mindedness. 'In a social environment where business fortunes often depended on one's reputation,' she observes, 'the maintenance of their company's good name was an essential part of being an eighteenth-century man of business' (van Lieshout 2017).

Yet the rapid growth of post-fire London – and the accelerating demand for piped fresh water – were pressures that couldn't be resolved just with PR and supply management. In the coming decades, New River and its competitors began to develop and invest in a range of new technologies designed to improve and expand service.

The first step in this long transition involved optimizing their networks – a set of calculation-based operational adjustments that would be entirely recognizable to contemporary systems engineers. For example, New River's engineers and advisors, Christopher Wren among them, reckoned that the company should divide up its service areas based on elevation, as measured from the Thames, in order to even out the pressure of the flow for all those dwellings receiving water within a given window of time.

To further standardize the way the network functioned, New River's consultants advised the firm to invest in the installation of secondary and even tertiary pipes so the large-diameter mains that flowed out of its pumping stations and reservoirs could evenly distribute water to smaller and more localized networks, organized by area and street.

New River also began to take steps to ensure that none of the small pipes that flowed into individual houses were connected directly to the water mains. 'Customers,' notes Tomory, 'were not so keen on having this change implemented because being connected to mains meant a much better water supply, since mains produced a higher pressure with regular flow.'

By the first decades of the eighteenth century, New River and London's other water suppliers were making significant capital investments in new reservoirs, canals, and pumping stations, creating a privately owned network of modern infrastructure that put the booming city well ahead of other major European commercial centres. These firms, however, had little choice: as the population surged and the city expanded outward, the water companies could no longer rely only on springs and heights of land to power their networks. They had to build reservoirs at higher elevations, and thus invest in systems to 'raise' the water, initially with horse power or windmills and, later, with new innovations like water towers and the adaptation of steam-engine-driven pumps for these applications.

The earliest steam-engine pumps had been invented in 1698 and were used for removing water from mines. A coal-fired furnace would heat water, producing steam, which was injected into a cylinder fitted with a movable piston. The steam forced the piston to rise, with the motion transferred to an attached pump arm. Using a second injection of cold water, the steam condensed, producing a vacuum in the cylinder and drawing the piston down again. The up-and-down motion cycle produced the pumping action.

In the 1770s, James Watt, a Scottish inventor, designed a much more powerful, energy-efficient version, marketed through Boulton & Watt, an engine manufacturer and foundry based in Birmingham. While the Boulton & Watt steam engine had many industrial and transportation uses, London's water companies began purchasing them to pump water into their expanding pipe networks. By the end of the eighteenth century, most of the city's fresh water supply was being moved around with steam-driven pumps, and almost all of the city's buildings had fresh water hookups. (In response to the recommendations of a royal commission, the whole system, encompassing the networks of nine companies, was consolidated and removed from private ownership in 1903 with the establishment of the Metropolitan Water Board.)

The massive expansion of fresh water service helped stoke the fortunes of a city whose growth was being fuelled by urbanization, industrialization, and the inbound spoils of the British Empire. Little more than a century after the Great Fire, London's population had hit a million people, and would double again by 1840. Then, as now, burgeoning cities were marked by extremes of wealth and poverty. The palatial mansions and estates of London's newly affluent mercantile elite coexisted with overcrowded Dickensian slums and debtors' prisons.

While the provision of fresh water did improve quality of life, a city the size of London produced unimaginable quantities of garbage, sewage, and human waste (a.k.a. night soil), most of which drained into the Thames or leached into wells, triggering outbreaks of highly infectious water-borne diseases like cholera.

Several decades earlier, Alexander Cumming, a Scottish mathematician, had invented a small device that rendered city life somewhat more palatable, but within the confines of private homes. The so-called 'S-bend' pipe created a small reservoir of clean water in the drain beneath toilets, sinks, and tubs. It's raison d'etre couldn't be more straightforward: the S-configuration prevented smelly methane gas from wafting back into homes and buildings tied to municipal sewer infrastructure. Cumming patented the S-bend in 1775, and his invention ushered in the era of the flush toilets – initially known as Crappers – but their adoption in England was slow, at least initially.[3] Nor did flush toilets, or S-bends within them, effectively confront the enormity of London's sewage problem. Indeed, municipal rules promulgated in the 1840s requiring homes to drain toilets into sewers instead of cesspits vastly exacerbated the crisis.

Early nineteenth-century London, in fact, was focused on three interconnected preoccupations – the plight of the burgeoning ranks of the poor, their potential rebelliousness, and the need to confront infectious diseases through 'sanitation reform.' Throughout the 1830s, Edwin Chadwick, a Manchester-born journalist turned social reformer, emerged as an outspoken advocate for changes to the antiquated welfare system, including the introduction of poor houses for the destitute, laws that incentivized able-bodied people to work, and improvements in living conditions at the societal level, particularly those that affected public health. 'In 1842 Chadwick's three-volume

---

3. Flush toilets remain a work in progress. 'More than 170 years later,' noted a report by the BBC in 2017, 'about two-thirds of the world's people have access to what's called "improved sanitation," according to the World Health Organization, up from about a quarter in 1980 … But that still means two and a half billion people don't have access to it, and "improved sanitation" itself is a relatively low bar' (Harford 2017).

report "An Inquiry into the Sanitary Condition of the Labouring Population of Great Britain" became a landmark in social history, with its graphic descriptions of how the filth in air, water, soil, and surroundings was a major factor in the spread of disease, especially in urban areas,' according to one biographical account ('Sir Edwin Chadwick' n.d.). He was eventually appointed to head up a new board of health for London.

Though Chadwick wasn't an engineer, he had strong views on certain civil engineering matters, such as a new approach to building sewers so they wouldn't collapse. But in terms of sorting out London's sewer crisis, the heavy lifting fell to the city's chief municipal engineer, Joseph W. Bazalgette (1819–91), the official tasked with eliminating the Thames' stench, which was considered, in that period, a source of infection.

Using funds allocated by the national government, Bazalgette embarked on an epic works project: completing a 3,200-kilometre network of underground sewers so they would all flow into five giant drains, to be constructed along the banks of the Thames, called interceptors (Douet 2021). With the assistance of four mammoth steam-driven pumps, the interceptors would shunt waste way downstream, past the tidal low-water mark in the Thames estuary, thus ensuring the sewage couldn't be swept back into the city at high tide. The interceptors, in turn, were constructed behind stone river walls and capped by embankments that have functioned ever since as some of London's pre-eminent public spaces.

Though the scheme was unprecedented in scale and ambition, Bazalgette and his task force of civil engineers brought plenty of know-how to the endeavour – perhaps not surprisingly, given the fact that London had been a proving ground for engineers for decades. Many had gained experience with tunnelling and steam-driven pumps while working on railway, canal, or mining projects. This venture, moreover, produced key technical innovations in the use of steam-engine pumps, which had never been previously used to move sewage. As industrial archaeologist James Douet relates in his account of the project, Bazalgette's team invited, screened, and subsequently rejected several proposals from England's leading steam-engine designers, including firms that built locomotives. But in the process of analyzing the strengths and weaknesses of the various designs, Bazalgette and his engineers teased out a design they considered to be optimal for the task, and then awarded the contract.

It was an exacting and rigorous evaluation process, and one that yielded a new engineering solution that would become standard in the municipal sewage-pumping systems that proliferated in England and elsewhere. Comments Douet: 'It would have been a surprise had they been other than cautious in planning the world's first major steam-powered sewage pumping stations in the great national project to which so much discussion had been directed, and on which the future health and well-being of the citizens of the capital depended.'

The powerful sewage pumps were housed in a series of impressive pumping stations, whose ornate architecture expressed the ambition of a transformative works scheme. His achievement altered not just London, but industrializing cities everywhere, including cities like Toronto, whose interceptor sewers date to the 1910s. 'Bazalgette was an engineer – with no medical background – "of small stature and … somewhat delicate health,"' adds G. C. Cook in a paper in the *Journal of Medical Biography*. 'This man arguably did more for the health of Londoners in the mid-19th century, than anyone before or since' (Cook 2001). In fact, his legacy as one of London's pre-eminent city-builders is commemorated at the Crossness sewage pumping station, an extravagantly designed structure that is now a museum.

The long history of toilets and sewers is not only well documented but holds a considerable fascination, the inspiration for numerous books, studies, and websites enumerating the development of this most prosaic but fundamental feature of urban infrastructure.[4] However, what's particularly notable about the evolution of London's water and sewage systems over a century and a half is that these expanding networks emerged from a confluence of many seemingly disparate forces: the relentless problem-solving ethic of industrial

---

4. Among the most comprehensive is a site called Sewer History, maintained by the historian of the Arizona Water Association (Schladweiler et al.).

engineers, the enabling role of profit-minded entrepreneurs willing to bet on technological innovation, and the raw political energy ignited by concentrated adversity. It's worth noting that after years of cholera outbreaks and sewage-filled streets, British parliamentarians finally approved the funding for Bazalgette's destiny-altering sewer plan because the stench from the Thames, which flows directly beneath the windows of the House of Commons, had become intolerable. Also worth pointing out is that these changes did not emerge from a singular or idealistic vision of some urban future, but rather the serendipitous process of trial and error that informs all innovative processes.

For both fresh water and sewage infrastructure, the balance of the nineteenth century saw more critical engineering innovations layer on top of these existing systems. Emerging scientific insights about the true vectors of microbial infection (Victorians wrongly believed in miasma, or the transmission of illness via bad smells or night air) would be translated into technological and public health advances, such as chlorination, pasteurization, meat handling, and sewage treatment as an alternative to dumping raw human waste into rivers and oceans.

Yet the development and construction of London's physical infrastructure, by both private and public investors, represented the true turning point. These intricate networks of pipes, drains, sewers, pumping stations, and valves created the baseline conditions under which large numbers of people could survive within dense urban areas. Drawing on engineering and mechanical advances developed for entirely different industrial applications, the water and sewage networks both encouraged urbanization and enabled its acceleration.

London, by 1900, had a population of 6.7 million people – a milestone that simply wouldn't have been possible without these two foundational forms of municipal infrastructure. The resulting concentration, of course, gave rise to the modern city, with all its social, cultural, and economic dynamism, as well as its distinctively urban politics, hardships, and opportunities.

The invention of the scalable network, moreover, provided a formula for expansion, meaning that cities could grow outward, and beyond their pre-industrial geographical constraints. Those insights, as Tomory argues, also laid the groundwork for other families of urban innovations, including those that would reveal and then illuminate the spaces of cities in an entirely new light.

4

City Lights

Billboards went up all over, but especially along main streets in the rapidly developing residential neighbourhoods pressing out from countless nineteenth-century downtowns. The ones in Toronto were designed by E. L. Ruddy, an ad firm; often erected in front of vacant lots, the billboards promoted the latest home appliances: water heaters, fridges, stoves, devices that delivered on the heavily hyped promise of new technology in the service of middle-class domesticity.

Despite the economic depression of the 1930s, these marketing messages resonated with Toronto consumers and homeowners. Unlike the nightmarish visions of city life rendered in films such as Fritz Lang's *Metropolis* (1927) and Charlie Chaplin's *Modern Times* (1936), and in stark contrast to the receding frenzy of the Roaring Twenties, the ads posited a safe and comfortable urban future anchored by the nuclear family and enabled with labour-saving devices.

The advertiser behind these billboards, as well as a series of opulent showrooms, was Consumers' Gas, a pillar of Toronto industry that traced its roots to a sprawling complex of gothic gasworks on the eastern edge of the downtown that dated back to the 1860s. Indeed, what all those appliances had in common was that they were gas-powered. Homeowners enticed to purchase them could hook up their dwellings to the expanding network of gas lines running under city streets and then pay a monthly fee to source their fuel from Consumers'.

Interestingly, when James Austin, a Northern Ireland–born financer, first invested in the fledgling gas company in 1859 and oversaw its rapid expansion, Consumers' had an entirely different market in its sights: gas lighting, a technology that was sweeping rapidly through industrializing cities in Europe and North America, transforming the very experience of living in those cities. After all, gas lighting illuminated the public and commercial spaces of the night-time city in ways never before seen. According to historians of that period, gas lighting gave rise to the forms of nightlife (theatre, restaurants, cafés, clubs, etc.) that we have long taken for granted. Improved street lighting also helped police control crime.

Yet gas lighting as a transformative urban technology collided head-on with the emergence of a rival lighting technology powered by electricity that was produced in coal-fired generators and hydro-electric stations. In fact, the competition between gas and electricity companies raged fiercely for several decades in virtually every big city. In Toronto, Austin pushed to improve the reliability and quality of Consumers' gas-producing network, then sought to consolidate the firm's hold on the illumination business by attempting to expand into his rival's turf – a move blocked by Toronto aldermen, who seemed to prefer electricity (Armstrong 2003).

By the 1920s, electric light was clearly winning the light wars, despite the efforts of the gas industry to retain its position as the dominant player. In many city regions, including San Francisco, the gas and electric utilities merged and morphed into sprawling energy monopolies like PG&E, but not in Toronto. In 1910, the Ontario government decreed that hydro-electric power should be considered a public good and removed from the private market. Consumers' Gas, in turn, pivoted, staking its commercial future on appliances, industrial customers, and heating – a decision that paved the way for the emergence of Enbridge as one of North America's gas and pipeline giants.

The story of the technology of urban light can be traced, oddly, to the invention of fireworks in China almost 2,000 years ago. These tiny explosives turned up in Europe in the 1200s, likely with the goods carried back by traders travelling the Spice Route. In the next few centuries, the popularity of fireworks displays, or 'illuminations,' spread from capital to capital, and finally to North America, employed for a wide range of celebrations and demonstrations of power by everyone from emperors to popes, mayors, political parties, and victorious armies.

These elaborate and entertaining pyrotechnical demonstrations served to illuminate grand buildings and public squares, drawing mass audiences to witness multicoloured rockets lighting up city streets normally sheathed in darkness after sunset. According to a 2018 history of urban lighting by David Nye, a professor emeritus of American studies at the University of Southern Denmark, 600,000 Parisians showed up to watch a display marking the marriage of Louis XV's sister. Another, held on November 4, 1825, marked the completion of the Erie Canal, featuring fireworks and a spectacular light show from the roof of New York's city hall.

During the 1860 U.S. presidential election, Republicans set off fireworks and held torchlight parades. 'Every night was marked by … tumult, shouting, marching and counter-marching, the reverberation of explosives and the rush of rockets and Roman candles,' said one observer quoted by Nye, a leading technology historian.

Between such festivities, of course, most people got their light from candles, fireplaces, or oil lamps. Some cities also had a few oil street lamps, but they cast little light, and certainly nothing like the ephemeral brilliance of grand fireworks displays. Those illuminations, in fact, whetted the public's appetite for urban spaces that could be seen and enjoyed after sunset.

Which is not to say that city dwellers simply slept once darkness fell. As Nye points out, all sorts of things happened at night, from doctors' visits to the collection of waste. People went to taverns to drink, cooks rose well before dawn to begin preparing meals, and watchmen, the predecessors of municipal police officers, patrolled streets. 'Darkness partially leveled society and loosened social controls, and those who were subservient by day enjoyed greater freedom during the night,' he writes. 'Secret societies, protest groups, homosexuals, and persecuted religious sects commonly met under the cover of darkness' (Nye 2018, 16).

The advent of gas lighting in the early decades of the nineteenth century drastically altered this picture, recasting the way city dwellers dealt with darkness. As with many technologies, the advent of gas lighting involved technical ingenuity and opportunistic investors, but mainly it emerged almost by accident, as the by-product of an entirely different process.

The rapid industrialization of the late eighteenth century was driven by the proliferation of steam engines fuelled by coal. In the 1770s, a young Scottish engineer named William Murdoch went to work for Boulton & Watt, the Birmingham-based manufacturing powerhouse that later produced the engines used to pump water and sewage in London. He realized that when coal was burned to heat water to create steam, it gave off a flammable gas and left a residue of coke. Murdoch figured out how to capture that waste gas and pipe it to a narrow nozzle, where it could be ignited, creating a continuous flame. Boulton & Watt's managers reckoned they could sell this new technology to their industrial customers, the first being a textile mill in Manchester. As Murdoch recounted a few years later, 'The peculiar softness and clearness of this light, with its almost invarying intensity, have brought it into great favour with the work people' (Murdoch 1808). He added that gaslight was safer to use in the combustible atmosphere of a cotton plant because it didn't throw off sparks the way candles did.

Boulton & Watt began building and selling the equipment for producing gas, mainly to its industrial customers. The assembly involved ovens, retorts, and other devices designed to purify the gas by removing tar, and gas containers to store the end product. The company soon faced a commercial rival, an upstart firm called the Gas Light and Coke Company (GLCC), which had been founded by an elbows-out German entrepreneur named Frederick Albert Winsor. He had seen early demonstrations of gaslight in Paris in 1802 and reckoned this new technology represented a huge opportunity. He moved to London, rounded up investors with deep pockets, and began to recruit customers, such as theatres, public buildings, and finally signed street-lighting contracts with local authorities.

In his 2011 account of the early days of the gaslight industry, Leslie Tomory observes that the inspiration for Winsor's most important innovation came from the network of sub-surface mains constructed by London's water companies. 'The growing presence of water companies piping water under streets to homes … presented Winsor with a legal model, as well as one way to imagine the distribution of gas – via pipes running under the streets,' he wrote. 'Water supply and gas provision were treated by Parliament and public opinion during this period as any other sort of business venture, to be placed in private hands, with the assumption that competition would protect the public interest.'

During the 1810s and 1820s, Boulton & Watt and GLCC squared off in a very public war of words and intensive lobbying that would have seemed very familiar to anyone who has watched rival tech firms attack one another. The two companies traded accusations about safety issues – gasworks plants had a tendency to explode – while British parliamentarians debated whether the gaslighting business should be regulated. As Tomory explains, other upstarts joined the fray, some of them long shots and others offering potentially disruptive alternatives, like whale oil. In an attempt to refute damaging allegations about safety, GLCC hired chemists to review its processes and propose improvements. Winsor's firm also agreed to a political compromise designed to ensure that GLCC would stay in its lane, i.e., limiting its commercial activities to laying down mains and selling gas, and not expanding into the business of manufacturing the equipment, which was Boulton & Watt's turf.

Despite all the controversy, the technology itself was proving to be extremely popular – a bona fide solution to the problem of dimness. 'The demand for gaslight, driven by its illuminating power proved to be vast, with GLCC constantly receiving requests from shops, homes, and public buildings,' Tomory notes, adding that the company often struggled to deal with leaks and other technical service problems relating to its rapid expansion.

Within a few decades, gaslighting had spread rapidly to cities across Europe, pushed forward by Winsor's innovative approach to building a distribution network, as well as the growth of industrialization and rail. After all, the gas business, with its dependence on coal, could only expand to cities where coal could be shipped.

First movers like Winsor's firm scaled rapidly, to borrow a phrase from twenty-first-century tech. 'Gas Light and Coke Company's success in solving the many problems it faced in constructing a large, urban gas network is demonstrated by its rapid growth,' Tomory concludes. 'In mid-1814, it had four paying customers and £180 in annual revenues … [B]y 1820, its 122 miles of mains were supplying gas to about 30,000 lamps and its revenues had reached £101,785.' The steep revenue growth shows GLCC had tapped into a large and eager market.

The public's appetite for gas lighting jumped to the U.S. and Canada. By 1853, New York's two gas utilities had built 246 miles of gas mains that served businesses and residences, and 9,000 street lamps, according to Nye. Hundreds of other U.S. cities soon followed. The sheer momentum of the dispersion of this technology can be seen as a preview for how other types of networks – transit, telephone, cable TV, internet – would scale within urban settings.

The technology dramatically altered city life. Theatres shifted their performances from the afternoon to evenings. Streets seemed safer at night, and the bright new light also drew crowds outside in the evenings. Cafés opened to cater to this new activity. 'The custom of taking a walk at the end of the day became more common, and the French invented the word *flanêur* to describe a fashionable person sauntering through the city streets,' observes Nye.

Yet the spread of urban illumination proved to be socially illuminating as well. In Paris, the advent of this new evening leisure activity was enabled by Baron von Haussmann's extensive reconstruction of the city – a process that involved levelling dense and crumbling slum districts and replacing them with wide boulevards lined with elegant gas lamps.

As the prominent American political theorist Marshall Berman pointed out in *All That Is Solid Melts into Air: The Experience of Modernity*,

his 1982 account of urbanism in the age of modernity, '[T]he boulevards, blasting great holes through the poorest neighbourhoods,
enable the poor to walk through the holes and out of their ravaged
neighbourhoods, to discover for the first time what the rest of their
city and the rest of life is like. And as they see, they are seen: the vision,
the epiphany, flows both ways. In the midst of the great spaces, under
the bright lights, there is no way to look away. The glitter lights up
the rubble, and illuminates the dark lives of the people at whose
expense the bright lights shine' (Berman 1988, 153).

The urban world teased out of the shadows by gas lighting, with its
soft warm glow, did not survive the ethos of invention and capitalism
that prevailed in the late nineteenth century. Just as file sharing and
then streaming killed CDs over about two decades of sustained, albeit
fitful, technological advancement, electric lighting completely van-
quished gas within a generation. By the 1920s, when Consumers' Gas
was trying to sell gas-powered refrigerators to housewives, electricity
was extending its dominance from lighting to communications and
consumer goods.

The first electric light was invented at almost the same time as
Winsor began marketing gas lighting in London. But 'arc lights,' which
worked when a charge jumped between two electrodes encased in
glass, produced a harsh white light. What's more, the heat generated
by the current caused the electrodes to burn out frequently. However,
throughout the nineteenth century, German and English inventors
steadily expanded the science and engineering of electricity, which in
turn gave rise to practical applications, such as electric motors. In the
1870s, a growing number of cities began installing arc lighting in
public spaces – typically spherical glass street lamps on poles well
above the sidewalk, to spare pedestrians from staring directly at these
intense light sources.

The effect, according to Nye, was transformative. 'Where gaslight
provided a narrow range of muted colours, the arc light replaced this

sepia landscape with one where fabrics and flowers retained their daylight appearance,' he observes. 'Gaslights had made the city recognizable and navigable, but electricity made possible a wide range of nocturnal behaviour once only possible during the day' (Nye 2018, 46).

As is well-known, the world of nineteenth-century electricity was fraught with technological schisms, and in particular between low-voltage direct current (DC) and alternating current (AC). The Croatian-born engineer/inventor Nikola Tesla had been working on street lighting in Paris and moved to New York in the 1880s, where he went to work for the U.S. super-inventor Thomas Edison. (Their clash over the dominance of AC or DC as the standard for electricity generation has become the stuff of legend.)

After an extensive process of trial and error at his lab in Menlo Park, New Jersey, Edison in 1878 announced the invention of an alternative to the arc lamp: an incandescent bulb that produced light using a very fine filament stretched between two electrodes. Its glow was softer than that of an arc lamp, and it consumed less energy. Edison also realized that he had to build an integrated manufacturing and distribution network to support his invention – an engine-driven generator to produce the power, circuits to transmit it, and outlets for the bulbs themselves.

According to historian Thomas Hughes, who wrote extensively about the evolution of major American technological systems, Edison 'announced his brainchild with fanfare in the *New York Sun* on October 20, 1878 … [H]e told the reporter of his plans for underground distribution in mains from centrally located generators in the great cities; predicted that his electric light would be brought into private homes and simply substituted for the gas burners at a lower cost; and confidently asserted that his central station would "light to all houses within a circle of half a mile."' As Hughes points out, Edison's brash instinct to hype his scheme preceded his ability to actually build and integrate all the necessary elements (Hughes 1979, 126).

As proof of concept, he tested his incandescent lighting with a single industrial company – a New York City printing company – but then began laying the groundwork for a more extensive deployment based on the gaslight industry's business model: a central source of power, distributed through an underground network to end users who would pay a fee. Edison tested the model in London, but his big play was the construction of the Pearl Street Station, which opened in lower Manhattan in 1882 – the world's first electrical generating plant and the corporate ancestor of the energy giant Con Edison.

The four-storey structure, built on a pair of adjacent 25 by 100 foot lots, housed four huge boilers in the basement, which powered six twenty-seven-ton generators, dubbed dynamos, that were based on a design by Werner von Siemens, founder of the electrical engineering powerhouse ('Detailed Biography' 2016). The upper storeys held devices to monitor current and test lamps. About 80,000 feet of cables snaked out from the station through a network of underground conduits accessible through manholes. The choice of location, a few blocks from Wall Street, was not an accident: Edison wanted his station to be in close proximity to an area with a dense concentration of potential customers ('Milestones: Pearl Street Station, 1882'). Among the first was the New York Times, which published glowing reviews of this new light source.

To whet the appetites of potentially obstructionist municipal officials, one of Edison's well-connected collaborators invited New York's mayor and several aldermen to visit Menlo Park for a demonstration. Edison led a late-afternoon tour of the labs and then summoned the guests to a darkened second-floor space. 'Lights suddenly went on to disclose a lavish "spread" from famous Delmonicos,' Hughes recounts. The shock-and-awe display allowed Edison to secure a franchise agreement with the city to bury cables beneath public streets.

However, as he points out, Edison wasn't just an inventor and promotor; he paid very close attention to the underlying economics. He meticulously calculated the cost of electric light relative to gaslight, a process that meant working backwards from the most fine-grain elements of this technology, such as the cost of filaments and the physics of electrical current.

The gaslight industry, moreover, had a very firm grip on its market by the 1880s, with substantial investments in production and distribution infrastructure, as well as arrangements with municipalities to run the mains under city streets. '[G]as remained a formidable competitor, as domestic customers were accustomed to it, and the gas system was literally built into their architecture,' Nye notes. 'Over 1,000 miles of gas mains beneath New York's streets supplied factories, theatres, office buildings, and homes as well as streetlights' (Nye 2018, 52–53). In 1892, he adds, gas lamps outnumbered arc lamps by twenty-two to one.

A year later, the Chicago World's Fair – a.k.a. the Columbian Exposition or the 'White City' – provided what could be described as an explosive marketing push for electric light. Throughout 1893, over 27 million people visited the fairgrounds, which featured elaborate domed buildings, esplanades, and waterways, extravagantly illuminated, inside and out, with electric light. 'Beneath the fountains, spotlights fitted with colored filters permitted operators to create symphonies of color to the accompaniment of the band music,' Nye writes. 'The electrical engineers thought these fountains in the Court of Honor "taught the public the possibilities" electricity offered for inexpensive improvements to city parks' (Nye 2018, 121). Similar demonstrations occurred in many other major cities on both sides of the Atlantic.

Over the course of the next two decades, Edison and several of his most trusted lieutenants, who brought engineering, managerial, and financial savvy to the enterprise, built the necessary foundations of what would become the standard architecture of electrical infrastructure – networks of massive generating stations, which fed high-voltage transmission lines that were linked to substations, local grids, and finally consumers. This process of commercialization pivoted on the development of numerous other technological and engineering innovations, such as the eventual transition to Nikola Tesla's AC power, which proved to be far more manageable than the DC Edison had originally used.

Electrification took North America by storm. To put the speed of this evolution into a contemporary context, the two decades following the 1994 introduction of the first commercial browser, Netscape, encompassed the wholesale transformation of internet access from a network of generally static websites and analogue connectivity via a phone line to the advent of high-bandwidth fibre-optic cable, readily available wifi, and the full deployment of streaming video. They were comparably transformative.

Yet, as Nye explains, the transition from gas to electric light wasn't a linear process, and required, among other things, the development of entirely new ways of financing energy. In cities like Chicago, several different lighting technologies were still in use prior to World War I, and incandescent bulbs had a relatively small market share – evidence, he says, that the changeover was influenced by factors beyond cost and superior technology. In this case, the present-day analogy is to electric vehicles, the consumer reluctance toward which has been a function of non-technological factors, e.g., availability of charging stations and 'range anxiety.'

There is one other important point of comparison between the light revolution and contemporary technological systems which has to do with spinoff applications made possible by additional capacity. As electric light gained traction and drove investment in electrical distribution infrastructure, new uses emerged, including one of the most far-reaching from an urban form perspective: electric transit in the form of streets, trolley buses, and subways.

Beginning in the 1890s, electric streetcars, initially operated by private firms, began transporting commuters in urban areas. Inter-city rail was very much a nineteenth-century phenomenon that connected urban regions, opened up rural areas to settlers, and enabled industrial shipping. But electric streetcars expanded the geographic footprint of many cities, allowing new development on the urban edges and enabling the rise of the so-called 'streetcar suburb.' This pattern of moderately dense, pre-automobile development extended linearly along streetcar lines, as homes and small apartments clustered within walking distance of the commercial main streets that served as the spine of these transit networks. The effect was amplified with the advent of subways, which, in early adopter cities like London and Paris, used electric power to solve the problem of running rail service underground without the use of steam engines.

Just as the telecommunications industry's multi-billion-dollar investments in broadband fibre-optic networks gave rise to waves of new data-intensive applications for computers and smart phones, the massive expansion of electrical generating and transmission infrastructure in the late nineteenth and early twentieth century paved the way for city-altering technologies that had nothing to do with lighting.

Finally, the shift from gas to electricity triggered far-reaching political clashes over society's relationship with this new and transformative form of energy. These battles were in stark evidence in Ontario, among other places. At the turn of the century, hard-driving capitalists like Henry Pellatt, the man who built the faux château Casa Loma, were determined to make huge bets on hydro-electric power generation. He, and many other entrepreneurs, reckoned that electricity's future included much more than just lighting and streetcars.

Pellatt's firm, the Electrical Development Company, secured permission to build a monumental generating station at Niagara Falls, with an eye to supplying burgeoning markets in southern Ontario and especially Toronto. The City of Toronto, however, also wanted to secure access to Niagara's hydro power, but through a publicly owned utility, so the municipality wouldn't be beholden to private energy interests. After several years of skirmishes between the city and the various provincial governments, Ontario established a public hydro commission and declared that electricity should be provided at cost to consumers.

In May of 1911, according to an account of the city's power system, 'Adam Beck, chairman of the Hydro-Electric Power Commission of Ontario, pushed a ceremonial button, marking the official inauguration of publicly-owned electricity distributed by the Toronto Hydro-Electric System. With that historic action, Beck launched what would become the largest municipal electricity distribution company in Canada' ('Turning on Toronto' n.d.).

With its assortment of modern appliances and showrooms, Consumers' Gas in the 1920s and 1930s gamely tried to buck the tidal momentum toward electricity, but with limited success. As CDs were to cassettes, or streaming services have been to appointment television, electricity was simply a better and more versatile technology – not just for lighting, but for a very broad range of other applications, many, though not all of which, were urban.

5
Cities, Communications Technology, and the Feedback Dilemma

In the months and then years after a pair of nuclear bombs levelled Nagasaki and Hiroshima, killing hundreds of thousands of civilians, a growing contingent of scientists, among them leading American physicists connected to the Manhattan Project, began expressing their profound unease with the deadly military uses of scientific knowledge. The *Bulletin of the Atomic Scientists* became the focal point of their conversations about what physics had wrought in the service of geopolitical conflict.

One of the early running themes had to do with the future of America's cities: in the context of an accelerating nuclear arms race, what were the social and economic implications of weapons that could wipe out entire urban centres – not just the residents, but also infrastructure and industrial capacity? 'In an atomic war, congested cities would become deathtraps,' opined Edward Teller, often described as the 'father of the hydrogen bomb,' and two collaborators in a 1948 essay in the *Bulletin*. 'A country like the United States ... is particularly vulnerable to the devastating impact of atomic bombs' (qtd in Kargon & Molella 2004, 764–77). The article's title revealed their solution: 'The Dispersal of Cities and Industries.' Others, including leading urban planners, soon widened this discussion, recommending radical de-urbanization strategies that encouraged cities of no more than 100,000 people, highly dispersed and intentionally decentralized. The notion of upending long-standing conventions of urban planning in response to the threat of nuclear war seems incomprehensible today, but was seen then as a rational response to potential annihilation.

Yet Norbert Wiener, a then-prominent MIT mathematician who had coined the word *cybernetics* to describe the complex interactions and feedback loops between humans and machines, had grown uncomfortable with the implications of these planning ideas. He did not participate in the top-secret development of nuclear weapons during WWII but quickly joined the chorus of leading scientists sounding alarm bells in the postwar period, especially as the U.S. government stepped up its nuclear arms program and then entered the Korean War (Kargon & Molella 2004).

Wiener began working on an alternative approach to the threat facing cities with two M T colleagues, a political theorist and a philosopher of science. Their concept, dubbed 'life belts,' called for the creation of radial beltways encircling major American cities, which would contain vital institutions like hospitals, as well as backup infrastructure. They reckoned post-attack chaos would be as deadly as the bombs themselves. 'These networks were designed to control and direct the flow of traffic towards safe areas at the urban periphery during the hours immediately following a nuclear detonation aimed at the concentration of people, goods, and services in the city centers, while also providing bypass routes for major railroads and highways,' Columbia University architectural historian Reinhold Martin recounts in a 1998 essay about Wiener's ideas and their implications for urban space (Kargon & Molella 2004).

In a long feature published in December 1950, entitled 'How U.S. Cities Can Prepare for Atomic War,' *Life* magazine detailed Wiener's proposal. The story included eye-catching visuals, among them photos of brutally congested downtown streets and god's-eye-perspective renderings of this tidily reorganized radial city of the atomic age. 'Life belts around cities would provide a place for bombed out refugees to go,' the article claimed. (Wiener and his colleagues intended to publish their plan in a scientific journal but never got around to it.)

Though perhaps not a household name, Wiener in the postwar era was a well-known and influential academic whose 1948 treatise 'Cybernetics: Or Control and Communication in the Animal and the Machine' laid down some of the most far-reaching ideas behind technologies like artificial intelligence, process control, and computer vision. (His 1950 book, *The Human Use of Human Beings*, wanted to introduce these concepts to a general readership.) Anticipating a future that included computers, Wiener sought to establish a discipline that described the emerging relationship between human beings and machines, including those that might someday be capable of higher-order reasoning – a development he considered theoretically possible.

The acuity of his vision of the future is evident in many realms, not least in the highly individualized ways we use our laptop computers and smart phones. The unique configuration of settings, downloads, apps, online connections, and modes of storing files on our devices that each of us has developed, as well as the countless options provided through operating systems and software, attests to the existence of a symbiotic relationship that is almost as distinctive as a human fingerprint.

Wiener was also interested in feedback loops – iterative processes found in biology, technological systems, and social dynamics. Thermostats, for example, maintain steady heating or cooling levels through negative feedback loops, i.e., by constantly reading ambient temperature and adjusting the furnace or air conditioner accordingly. But positive feedback loops can create highly unstable outcomes – for example when a microphone linked to a speaker picks up its own sound. A handful of people panicking in a dense crowd may prompt a rapidly spreading sense of fear that feeds on itself and triggers a stampede.

Cities also serve as a locus for all sorts of negative and positive feedback loops, such as traffic light controllers that automatically adapt to vehicle volumes. But there are other urban feedback loops that create unintended outcomes. Consider the 'discovery' of an out-of-the-way and interesting neighbourhood. As word about its value as a hang-out or tourist destination spreads, the area attracts new restaurants, bars, and shops, and then more visitors, more selfies, more Yelp reviews, etc. The dynamic causes rents to rise, gentrification to accelerate, and 'incumbent' residents to move away. This negative feedback loop, in other words, gradually and then rapidly obliterates the neighbourhood's perceived authenticity.

As he laid out cybernetic theory and considered the Cold War risks facing dense urban regions, Wiener saw analogies between biological processes such as the human circulatory system and the ways in which information moves through cities. 'We have conceived the city as a net of communications and traffic,' he and his collaborators wrote in their 1950 paper on lifebelts. 'The danger of blocked communications in a city subject [to] emergency conditions is closely analogous to the danger of blocked communications in the body.' If a nuclear attack was akin to a massive stroke, they argued, the city had to take preventative measures, such as ensuring that its residents could disperse quickly. As technology historians Robert Kargon and Arthur Molella noted in a 2004 account of that *Life* article's impact, 'Wiener's attempts to extend cybernetics into civil defense policy and urban planning may seem an act of scientific arrogance, but it was a genuine expression of his commitment to an interdisciplinary outlook.' They add that he, like some other Cold War scientists, had become 'skeptical that technological advancement would improve humanity's state.'

Wiener wasn't the only one thinking about nuclear warheads and cities. The Eisenhower administration launched its extensive interstate highway-building program in part to create transportation corridors that could be used for civilian defence or military purposes. Military contractors working for organizations like the RAND Corporation were also busy consulting municipal officials on how to use the so-called scientific management techniques employed in the armed forces to plan for not just civil defence, but other 'domestic security challenges,' such as the growth of inner-city slums, according to MIT sociologist Jennifer Light, author of *From Warfare to Welfare: Defense Intellectuals and Urban Problems in Cold War America.*

'If at first they used the language of cybernetics and scientific approaches to urban problem solving, soon their justifications would expand to include the language of military attack,' writes Light, who notes how municipal officials in the postwar period also learned to employ aerial reconnaissance photo interpretation techniques developed for military uses in their land-use planning (Light 2005, 64).

Yet perhaps the most intensive effort to safeguard American assets from attack involved information technology. By the late 1950s, every home had a telephone; radio and television were mass communications media; and a growing number of large organizations, including universities, governments, and the military, had invested in mainframe computers, many of which were set up to share information and software through rudimentary networks.

'In 1960, the RAND Corporation commissioned a study of methods for protecting telephone and data links between U.S. military bases and their command and control centres, in the event of a nuclear war,' explained Philip Steadman, a professor emeritus of urban studies at University College London in a 1999 anthology entitled *American Cities and Technology: Wilderness to Wild City* (Roberts & Steadman, 251).

With the prospect of an unmanageably large bill for hardening all that communications infrastructure, a RAND electrical engineer named Paul Baran proposed a workaround. His idea involved breaking electronic messages into many smaller 'message blocks,' each of which would include what today would be dubbed metadata: their point of origin, their destination, and instructions for reassembling all the other blocks to reproduce the original message.

Baran, Steadman wrote, also devised a technique that would direct these blocks through telecommunications networks along a myriad of possible paths – a deliberately nimble approach. At almost the same time, a Welsh computer scientist named Donald Davies came up with a nearly identical system, which he called 'packet switching.' In both cases, the goal was to leverage the dispersed architecture of a network of computers to mitigate the risk to the entire communications system if any individual node was damaged or destroyed – i.e., it had survivability. Their ideas, in some ways, offered a mirror image to what Wiener had proposed for making cities more resilient in the face of a calamitous attack. These solutions, taken up first by the military and later by leading research universities, laid the groundwork for ARPANET, which would eventually evolve into the internet.

For most of recorded history, information, with a few exceptions, travelled only as fast and as far as humans could propel themselves. In other words, communications technologies were, by default, transportation modes and technologies: horses, Roman roads, caravan routes, carriages, ships, and eventually railways. The modes of communication themselves ranged from letters or books to diplomatic pouches and commercial or financial documents, such as bills of lading, bearer bonds, promissory notes, or letters of credit.

Information, of course, had a very broad range of uses including strategic purposes. In the early 1800s, members of the Rothschild family, which operated a far-flung banking and trading network throughout England and Europe, developed tactics for accelerating the pace at which they received the commercially sensitive information – e.g., decisions of foreign governments – that they needed for transactions. Instead of depending on mail service, they employed their own couriers and ships in order to further hasten the speed of their inter-company communications. The firm also used carrier pigeons to transmit stock prices, and colour-coded envelopes to signal shifts in exchange rates. Anticipating the resilience built into digital communications networks, the Rothschilds also sent multiple versions of the same message through different routes as a hedge against the risk of intercepted notes (Ferguson 1999).

In the 1840s, the commercialization of the electric telegraph rapidly altered long-distance communication. As Steadman points out, the earliest British customers were railway companies, which deployed telegraph service along their networks and used it to transmit information about schedules and even tips for police pursuing escaping suspects. In the U.S., earlier adopters included news wire services, like the Associated Press, and stock exchanges. The Boston police department set up an internal telegraph network to connect precincts and allow beat cops to send messages to headquarters from police boxes located on city streets.

By the 1860s, tens of thousands of kilometres of telegraph cable had been laid, including transatlantic lines. Within cities, thousands of bike couriers physically delivered telegraph messages to recipients, meaning, as Steadman points out, that 'communications *between* cities was at this stage much faster than communications *within* cities.'

Alexander Graham Bell upped the technology ante with the invention of the telephone in 1876. While his first public call was a long-distance one, between Brantford and Paris, Ontario, Bell envisioned a means of providing local service that was inspired by the underground networks built in previous periods by water, gas, and electricity utilities. 'In a similar manner,' he explained to his investors in an 1878 letter, 'it is conceivable that cables of telephone wires could be laid underground, or suspended overhead, communicating by branch wires with private dwellings, counting houses, shops, manufactories, etc., uniting them with a main cable to a central office where the wires could be connected as desired, establishing direct communications between any two places in the city' (Roberts & Steadman 1999, 243). But as it happened, interest in telephone service was keener in remote rural areas. 'This confounded the telephone companies, who anticipated only urban markets,' says Steadman. Those differences soon evaporated. By the 1920s, he notes, telephone service had more or less eclipsed the telegraph to become the dominant form of interpersonal communications technology.

One can certainly argue that the intervening century, from a technological perspective, has been defined, if not utterly dominated, by rapid and relentless advances in information and communications technology (ICT) – from radio, TV, and record players to digital switching, fax machines, cellular service, personal computers, the World Wide Web, high-speed internet, smart phones, fibre optic cable, Wi-Fi, e-commerce, CCTV, GPS, artificial intelligence, the internet of things, 3-D printing, 5G mobility, cryptocurrency, etc., etc., etc.

As is also true for air travel and the private automobile, these technologies have all served to collapse distance, whereas the civil engineering advances that emerged in earlier periods, and particularly during the Industrial Revolution, responded to the challenges posed by the perils of urban proximity: fire, infectious disease, waste, extreme overcrowding.

From the first days of the telephone, examples of the device's particular impact on cities and urban form soon surfaced. Telephones seemed to be very well suited for large office buildings, both during the construction process, when they allowed crews working high up to communicate with site managers, and once the building was in use, so office employees on different floors could connect with one another. Steadman offers other early 'use cases,' such as room service in high-rise hotels, although he and others caution that telephone technology alone didn't spur the development of high-rise buildings: the emergence of building technologies such as steel frame construction, curtain walls, and automatic elevators all played a critical role.

In the 1960s, American planners and defence analysts sought to adapt another Cold War–inspired technology, coaxial cable TV, for urban (i.e., civilian) applications, namely the creation of widely accessible communications networks that would connect poor inner-city residents to education and local government services via two-way video as a means of improving social welfare. As Jennifer Light comments of three lengthy government discussion papers that considered this ultimately stillborn idea, '[C]able was never discussed as the money-making entertainment system it eventually became. Rather, each report imagined an urban infrastructure developed to provide a variety of services to users in their homes or in neighbourhood telecommunications centres, an infrastructure with capacity for two-way communication as well as instruction' (Light 2005, 181). The high capital costs, however, worked against this model for community-access cable, and the nascent cable industry pivoted to mainly commercial programming by the late 1970s.

The much wider question is what role ICT has played in shaping urban regions over the past fifty years, and whether the influence of one extremely powerful family of technologies can be prised apart from other city-shaping forces, from the Baby Boomers' suburban exodus to mass migration, trade liberalization, and geopolitical conflict over natural resources. It is a puzzle that has preoccupied sociologists, geographers, planners, and policy makers for several decades. These problems, moreover, have also given rise to big-bang theories, such as the central role of networks in the Information Age and the cumulative impact on society of the so-called third and fourth industrial revolutions.[5] Some analysts describe the modern, wired city as, essentially, a communications hub.

Long before Zoom and shared cloud-based files, Norbert Wiener recognized that there would come a day when professional services wouldn't need to be co-located with more mechanical forms of labour and production. In *The Human Use of Human Beings*, he describes how an architect in Europe could work remotely on a building in the U.S., using existing technologies like a 'teletypewriter' and 'ultrafax' to transmit facsimile images of blueprints 'in a fraction of a second' to the construction manager. 'The architect may be kept up to date with the progress of the work by photographic records taken every day,' he mused. 'In short, the bodily transmission of the architect and his documents may be replaced very effectively by the message transmission of communications which do not entail moving a particle of matter from one end of the line to the other' (Martin 1998, 113).

Wiener's prescience is remarkable, yet it skips ahead several steps in the emergence of the digitally connected city states that now dominate the global economy – mega-regions like Shanghai, Seoul, and Manila, whose eight-digit populations and economic heft rival those of small countries. From 1970 to 2021, for instance, metropolitan Jakarta's population soared from about 4 million to 30 million people.

Many forces have driven the eye-popping growth of these places, including the waves of trade liberalization that encouraged manufacturers

---

5. Coined by Klaus Schwab, the German engineer and economist who founded the World Economic Forum, Industry 4.0 describes the global move toward advanced automation and technologies like 3-D printing. It succeeded the third industrial revolution, which marked the widespread use of computing and digital technology.

to relocate to low-wage, low-regulation regions, especially since the end of the Cold War. But a handful of pivotal developments in the way multinationals organize themselves and market their products served to turbo-charge the growth of megacities in the global south.

Beginning in the 1970s and accelerating in the 1980s, Japanese carmakers started adopting two transformative changes in their manufacturing processes: a new approach to ensuring quality control, and what would become a revolution in the way they managed inventory and suppliers. The premise of 'just-in-time' (JIT) manufacturing was that large industrial operations, like auto assembly plants, shouldn't warehouse the myriad parts they used to make products. The practice of storing inventory represented a cost and could be pushed back to parts suppliers, which were told to deliver components only when the assembly plant needed them. Those components, in turn, had to satisfy the automakers' exacting quality control standards. These process engineering changes meant higher expectations and increased competitive pressures for the suppliers, who could lose customers if they didn't perform.

By the 1980s, the Big Three U.S. automakers were rapidly losing market share. German carmakers, with their long history of precision engineering and collaborative labour relations practices, retained their position, but Japanese and Korean manufacturers saw dramatic growth in their fortunes, including in North America, the birthplace of the private automobile. U.S carmakers had to scramble and play catch-up, and soon began building their own JIT systems.

Much more than conventional manufacturing, JIT depends on markedly improved communications, especially between firms. The system only works if a manufacturer knows precisely what it needs and when, and can then transmit this data to its suppliers in a timely way. Fundamental to the logic of this approach is seamlessly efficient information-sharing and highly efficient distribution. JIT also had a pebble-in-the-pond effect. Parts suppliers began to push their own suppliers to adopt the same outlook, and so on down the line, meaning that the ethic of just-in-time manufacturing and distribution spread rapidly through the automotive food chain and then beyond, into virtually every other industrial sector.

The parallel development involved a seismic shift in corporate thinking about brand. As journalist Naomi Klein first explained in *No Logo: No Space, No Choice, No Jobs*, consumer-products giants recognized that branding meant far more than logos and other marketing communications. They could be used as a way of organizing production, with global brands like Nike reinventing themselves as decentralized postmodern corporations in which product design, strategic marketing, and promotion were managed centrally, but the actual production could be outsourced to suppliers operating in low-wage countries – a highly scalable formula that generated huge margins.

These disruptive changes in manufacturing occurred alongside – and by no means independently of – the equally dramatic upheavals in ICT: the introduction of desktop and then laptop computers, the rapid uptake of email and other intra-company digital networks, and finally the commercialization of the internet in the mid-1990s. Business software tools proliferated, as did both advanced manufacturing and corporate technologies, from robots to bar-code scanners, data mining algorithms, wifi sensors, secure electronic funds transfers, biometric devices, logistics software, and all the other building blocks of what would become a highly optimized global economy driven by torrential flows of commercial and financial data.

In many post-industrial city regions, robust economic growth has come with increasing social disparities, income inequality, and housing shortages. Urbanization in the global south has produced vast slums, such as the favelas encircling some Latin American cities, as well as the rise of truly Dickensian forms of economic activity generated by global trade, such as teeming recycling depots sustained by the importation of mountains of consumer, packaging, and electronic waste from developed nations.

At the same time, many big cities, especially those anchored by diverse regional economies, post-secondary institutions, and major cultural facilities, have become magnets for what University of Toronto geographer Richard Florida dubbed the 'creative class' – a broad category that includes professionals, knowledge workers, and artists. Cities with a large number of 'creatives,' Florida found, tended to be more tolerant, denser, and walkable, and they also could offer quality-of-life amenities, from theatres to trails to high-quality schools. These kinds of cities also fuelled the growth of so-called edge cities – satellite suburbs that attracted high-tech manufacturing in part because local municipalities made sure to equip these places with all the digital and mobility needs that such employers sought (Audirac 2022).

These city regions, as it turns out, have tended to attract the highly skilled people who work in the nerve centres of major financial institutions or global companies, as well as tourists and other categories of travellers, such as those attending trade conventions in the pre-pandemic era. Consequently, so-called creative class cities are also places that have been particularly susceptible to accelerating gentrification and real estate speculation.

While international trade is nothing new, Columbia University urban sociologist Saskia Sassen has argued that game-changing advances in information and communications technology have unleashed these huge transformations in cities, characterized by the dispersal of manufacturing, the ascendence of international professional services and financial behemoths, and the concentration of capital and power in global cities – a widely used term she coined in the mid-1990s (219).

Since then, many urban experts have sought to come up with ways to name, characterize, and classify these new types of cities. The University in Leicester, in the U.K., maintains a detailed ranking of global cities based on a wide range of metrics; Sassen is one of the project's founders. Another, the Spanish sociologist Manuel Castells, has charted the global growth of networks and information cities. Some groups have promoted notions such as 'intelligent communities,' 'innovation clusters,' and even 'mega-regions.' Yet in the 2010s, a new label, meant to express the ethic of the digitized, cosmopolitan metropolis of the near future, began to gain currency. As an urban brand, it was at once descriptive and aspirational:

Smart.

The Dream of the
Smart City

1
Smart City Tech:
A Primer

Far from the disorderly world of big-city streets, Mart Suurkask, the CEO and founder of Bercman Technologies, demonstrated a working prototype of the firm's 'smart pedestrian crosswalk' before a small crowd of onlookers gathered in a trade show booth in November 2019. The booth was hosted by the Government of Estonia at the sprawling annual smart city trade show that was held in Barcelona each year until the pandemic forced the event to go virtual.

I'd travelled to the Catalonian capital to spend the week talking to presenters, listening to smart city sales pitches and checking out demos. The event took place in Barcelona's cavernous suburban convention centre, a three-hall affair with breakout rooms, snack bars, and theatres. Like most industrial trade shows, the floor felt a bit like a mini indoor city, the brightly lit aisles crowded with lanyard-wearing attendees carrying tote bags full of brochures. Like a modern-day souk, touts worked the edges of their booths, encouraging people to sit for a presentation, test some gadget, take a business card. The logos of the big sponsors – for 2019, Cisco and Mastercard – were festooned on walls and way-finding maps around the convention centre.

Given the particular focus of this event, the organizers and demonstrators had doubled down on the urban motif. The event had its own neighbourhoods, complete with 'cafés' and street furniture. Several regional and state governments had their own districts. Tel Aviv's booth was designed to look like a bar, complete with pulsing EDM and free beer. I noticed that besides an appearance on one panel discussion, Sidewalk Labs was nowhere to be seen.

Bercman's device looked exactly like crosswalk signs throughout Europe: a post supporting a square sign with the universal symbol of a pedestrian crossing a street. What makes it 'smart,' as he explains, is an assembly of digital devices stowed inside the sign: high-tech motion detectors aimed in all directions that are programmed to calculate the velocity of vehicles approaching the crosswalk to determine whether they are slowing safely when someone is crossing.

The software included a 'machine-learning' algorithm that allows the detector to learn and then anticipate traffic patterns so it can 'optimize' for cars moving through a particular location. Bercman's smart crosswalk was also fitted with wireless transmission capabilities that will someday automatically send notifications to fast-moving, connected vehicles, alerting them to brake right away. When the crosswalk signal detects danger, it flashes and beeps.

The start-up, which is based in Tartu, Estonia's second-largest city and a hub of tech development, wanted to find solutions to rising pedestrian fatality rates, as well as the eventual advent of self-driving cars. 'We thought these vehicles might need some help from smart infrastructure,' Bercman said in his presentation.

As of 2020, the smart crosswalk was still in development. Suurkash told me that in real-world testing, about a third of the warning signals turned out to be false alarms.

As it happens, the company's device was also fitted with sensors measuring air quality, traffic flow, and pedestrian volumes, as well as digital cameras designed to identify licence plates. The sign, he said, 'is just one part' of a smart city 'ecosystem.'

Since the 1960s, the ICT revolution – from early mainframe computers and cable TV to 5G smart phones and high-bandwidth fibre optic cable – have transformed cities into densely networked hubs where digital interactions are woven virtually into every facet of urban life.

Smart city technology, a by-product of the ICT revolution, is a broad and amorphous catch-all category. One common denominator is that these technologies are designed to gather and synthesize digital data generated by all sorts of urban activity – GPS-equipped transit vehicles, hidden patterns in huge databases of building inspection records, power consumption trends, online resident feedback to planning approvals, and so on. Some experts advocate for 'intelligent civil infrastructure,' which proposes extensive deployments of wireless sensors attached to everything from roads and bridges to water mains, and which are designed to detect system failures even before they can be noted by inspectors (Goldsmith et al. 2021). The ostensible goal is to put all that data to work to address a range of urban problems – 'optimizing,' as smart city tech insiders say.

One can think of smart city systems as technologies that watch or listen to what's happening in urban areas and then transform those observations into action. However, while we live in a hyper-accelerated world of high-speed communication, smart city technologies, to be effective, must overcome both the so-called latency problem – the lag between gathering ground-level information and acting on it – and the bugs or viruses that invariably find their way into any computer-driven system.

These systems, Eric Miller, a professor of civil engineering and director of the University of Toronto's Transportation Research Institute, tells me, 'are about creating more and better feedback loops, on the assumption that it will lead to better outcomes.' But, he adds, cities are highly complex 'systems of systems' filled with human beings who don't necessarily respond rationally or predictably to the world around them. 'The central question,' Miller observes, 'is the interaction between technological systems and people systems.'

Smart city systems are built with a diverse and ever-growing range of technological building blocks: hardware, software, cloud-based data warehouses and cellular networks, artificial intelligence algorithms, etc. The components run the gamut from smart phone apps and cheap sensors to multi-million-dollar transportation control hubs. Some observers have used the term *everyware* to describe their ubiquity. While a lot of smart city tech is designed for and purchased by local or regional governments seeking to digitize a wide range of services, these systems can also be found in health care, education, and utilities, as well as private sector environments, such as smart office buildings.

Many are focused on security and urban mobility applications, while others – e.g., mapping, short-term rental, or recommender apps – aren't geared at the municipalities per se but turn out to have far-ranging implications for the ways in which cities actually function. Still others are built using various forms of information released by municipalities through open data portals – everything from zoning bylaws and property lines to the GPS signals on transit vehicles.

Sensors

The building blocks of smart city systems, these very inexpensive, compact (fist-sized or smaller) devices can be installed on all manner of objects, ranging from utility poles and buses to water mains and bridges. They can be designed to gather readings on air quality, vibrations, passenger loads, traffic volumes, or leaking pipes.

Sensors are fitted with small radio transmitters to send readings wirelessly, with the signals ultimately shunted to control centres that monitor water systems or local utilities and use this real-time data to manage problems.

For example, in 2009 Philadelphia installed 'BigBelly' waste bins equipped with GPS-enabled sensors that detect when they need to be emptied. Carlton Williams, Philadelphia's street commissioner, told me the devices allow the municipality to route garbage trucks more efficiently – i.e., they pick up only from full bins – and have slashed the number of crews on some routes, with a $650,000 per year savings. The reduction in the number of trucks has also reduced congestion. 'We think it's a huge success,' he says in an interview.

Tiny sensors are now embedded in all sorts of privately purchased consumer goods and electronics, such as smart thermostats, wearable continuous glucose monitors, or fitness trackers in products like Fitbit or Apple Watches. These devices are creating entirely new types of data-driven relationships between the private realm of the home or a business and the wider public realm of the city.

The sensors in smart thermostats, for example, provide continuous temperature readings that are sent wirelessly to a central control device. But some smart heating systems are also tethered electronically to local utilities, which aggregate all this information and use it to manage their energy output or even remotely adjust heating or cooling levels in customers' homes in response to peak-period demand.

Some health sensors wirelessly connect people with conditions like diabetes to medical practitioners as well as with smart phone apps that can predict changes in insulin levels. A 2018 research study of more than 33,000 diabetics, some with continuous glucose monitors and others without, showed lower health care costs and fewer hospital admissions among those fitted out with these wifi-enabled devices.

Fitness trackers, in turn, reveal another type of interplay between personal health and public amenities. The enormous popularity of the 10,000-steps fitness regimen has prompted many people to begin taking regular walks in their neighbourhoods or local parks. The additional pedestrian (and cycling) activity is unquestionably a positive development and could even serve as a prompt to local governments to build out pedestrian/cycling infrastructure, perhaps even, as some researchers have argued, by leveraging the GPS data generated by these trackers (and smart phones generally) to determine where they could be adding or expanding sidewalks or creating new trails.

Yet such applications also raise hard questions about privacy protections and the potential misuse of such sensors for surveillance or marketing purposes.

Digital Video and Facial Recognition

The presence of hundreds of thousands of closed-circuit television (CCTV) cameras on city streets around the world, as well as all sorts of buildings and other public spaces, is nothing new, but these devices have become smaller, cheaper, less static, and more prevalent in a range of settings. For example, digital doorbells with digital cameras, some made by Google and Amazon, allow homeowners to use their smart phones or even laptops to watch for porch pirates or keep an eye on what's going on on the street.

The use of facial recognition systems, as well as related software that can identify an individual's gait, has become increasingly prevalent in some regimes. In China, ubiquitous CCTV surveillance and advanced facial recognition software have been extensively deployed as part of the Communist government's security and intelligence operations. Some of these are developed by private firms like Clearview AI, a smart phone–based facial recognition system, and SenseTime, a Chinese AI company whose investors include Alibaba Group and Qualcomm, a U.S. chip maker.

In many North American cities, police are equipped with body-worn cameras and dash cams that record interactions and upload video for temporary storage. Drones, increasingly inexpensive and deregulated, are fitted out with high-res video. These can be used for everything from real-estate listings and the monitoring of cracks or energy losses on the outsides of high buildings to missing person searches. In the U.K., police drones use facial recognition software to assist with such missions.

Specialized cameras are also being affixed to vehicles for use in mapping applications that go well beyond Google's Street View. For example, Mobileye, a publicly traded Israeli firm owned by Intel, works with vehicle manufacturers to install specialized cameras on the front windshields of trucks and buses. The cameras record whatever is on the street, with the streaming video continuously uploaded to a cloud-based mapping database. These maps can be accessed wirelessly by autonomous vehicles that need real-time information about what is on the road.

But a rapidly spreading backlash against surveillance-oriented technologies, including those embedded in popular social media platforms, has prompted some global technology firms to halt or discontinue their facial recognition programs, among them IBM, Microsoft, and Meta/Facebook, which deleted facial data on a billion users in late 2021. 'The many specific instances where facial recognition can be helpful need to be weighed against growing concerns about the use of this technology as a whole,' a senior Meta artificial intelligence executive wrote of the decision on the company's blog.

The Internet of Things

The collection of objects and sensors with wireless connections to the internet constitutes the 'internet of things' (IoT) and includes devices as diverse as Bluetooth-connected electric toothbrushes with accompanying app, electric water heaters, smart fridges, etc.

In recent years, tech giants like Cisco and IBM have estimated the number of such devices, which includes cellphones. The figures, according to Barcelona-based IoT privacy and information policy researcher Gilad Rosner, are staggering: 8.74 billion globally, as of 2020, although the numbers vary widely depending on what's included. The actual figure, he tells me over Zoom, 'is difficult to pinpoint.'

Smart city systems are increasingly built on a digital foundation that includes an extensive deployment of wifi-enabled sensors that are connected to the IoT. These networks may allow works officials and structural engineers to remotely monitor vibrations on major bridges or property managers to track mechanical systems in smart office buildings.

According to an August 2020 survey of fifty global cities by IoT Analytics, the most prevalent urban applications include connected public transit, traffic, flood, and weather monitoring, video surveillance, street lighting and air quality sensors.

Yet IoT in public space raises critical issues about security – are these tiny and inexpensive devices linked wirelessly to extensive digital networks vulnerable to hacking? – as well as privacy, or what Rosner describes as the 'right to obscurity.' 'The issue is surveillance,' he says. The more sensors, the more surveillance.'

Enterprise-Wide Platforms

Global tech giants like IBM and Cisco were among the first to use the 'smart city' branding as a pitch when they marketed their enterprise systems, notably to the hundreds of thousands of local and regional governments around the world.

While these large firms promised their customers more cost-effective operations or outsourced technical services like payments processing (e.g., Mastercard), their messaging often seems like a confection of progressive urbanism and ominous warnings about the pressures of mass urbanization, from congestion to pollution.

In some cases, the pitch to municipal IT managers is that if they have invested heavily in the backbone system, it then makes good sense to get the most out of it by adding functions that cut across a range of city divisions. The payback improves if customers invest in multiple applications, such as a smart lighting network *and* a street parking app, Del White, Cisco's then global managing director for smart and connected communities, told a small audience at the firm's Smart City Expo booth in Barcelona. 'Every time you add a use case, your ROI gets better.'

Other firms go even further, telling municipalities how these enterprise systems will enable core urban functions, from traffic control and transit to energy consumption and air quality, to operate at peak efficiency. 'There are ways we can optimize a city going forward,' said Roland Busch, president and CEO of Siemens AG, the German engineering giant, which promotes the creation of a centralized city 'operating system' capable of integrating all sorts of urban infrastructure into a single 'ecosystem.'

Some cities have made this leap. The northern English municipality of Hull invested in an AI-driven 'smart city platform' that included parking space detectors, air quality sensors, smart trash bins, traffic counters, and digital video to track road quality, with the data travelling over a 5G network. Furqan Alamgir, CEO of Connexin, which was contracted to install and operate all this technology, describes the firm as an 'enabler.' 'We're not data owners. The data belongs to the people and the city.'

Yet some critics have warned that so-called 'vendor lock-in' provisions in the service agreements have made some smart city companies' proprietary systems difficult to remove or augment with open-source software. 'The basic concern is to avoid cities or districts becoming self-contained, "locked-in" islands, captive of a single company that holds all the enabling technology,' a European Commission urban regeneration think tank cautioned in a 2016 blog post.

Data Analytics and Artificial Intelligence

Smart city technology generates extensive collections of raw data that can be analyzed in different ways to generate insights and detect patterns.

Increasingly, that analysis involves artificial intelligence and the use of highly sophisticated algorithms trained to make predictions. AI, which can be traced to the 1950s and research by computer scientists with ties to the U.S. military, has many non-urban applications, from Siri and other voice recognition systems to recommender engines on movie streaming or e-commerce sites and even apps that can identify skin cancers. AI algorithms are 'trained' on large collections of labelled information – e.g., images – by predicting what the image is and then comparing that guess to the label. Coders continuously refine the algorithm until each prediction has a high degree of accuracy. At that point, the algorithm can be used to make predictions on new data.

In the case of smart city applications, AI has been used, for example, to identify and predict traffic patterns, so city officials can use the algorithm to optimize traffic signals. There are many other emerging applications in fields like planning.

In 2017, for instance, a Harvard-MIT research team published a study about an experiment using Google Street View, itself a vast trove of urban data. Using 1.6 million images of street scenes in five U.S. cities, taken first in 2007 and again in 2014, the researchers amassed a database of paired photos of the same places, from the same perspectives, at two different points in time. The investigators then developed an algorithm to assess 'perceptions of safety' based on a 'crowd-sourced study' of street scenes in New York and Boston, and used this formula to rate the perceived safety of the images they had gathered. Finally, they cross-referenced the street-level safety scores with census and other socio-economic data and concluded, not surprisingly, that denser areas populated by more affluent residents were less likely to experience physical and social decline.

Open Standards, Open Source Software, and Open Data

The principle of technological openness can be viewed as a kind of holy grail for smart cities, and not just those applications that relate to municipal services. With open standards, software, and data, the core idea is that the benefits of emerging technologies and other smart systems don't just flow into private coffers, as has been the concern about vendor lock-in.

The concept of open standards is often used to characterize a democratizing approach to networks and software platforms, but can also be understood when applied to some of the most basic features of daily life, such as ordinary light bulbs, electric plugs, or USB memory sticks. Regardless of who manufactures them, these objects are designed to satisfy common publicly available standards, and therefore they are interchangeable. A bulb works in any ordinary light socket, a thumb drive works in any USB port. (When Apple altered its ports and made them proprietary, there was an outcry because that inter-operability had suddenly disappeared.)

In the world of hardware and software, there are open standards, or specifications for languages such as HTML mark-up code and digital images, like JPEGS, as well as protocols for the architecture of digital networks connected to the internet. Advocates of progressive smart cities say that municipalities, regions, or other institutions must employ an open-standards approach to provide interoperability – the light bulbs – and ensure that tech vendors don't create monopolies for themselves.

The use of open-source software is also regarded as an essential principle in the development of democratic smart cities. In Barcelona, which has been a pioneer in progressive smart city policy, municipally designed software used for various smart applications is intended to be open source and available for other cities to use.

Finally, open data describes government information that is released to the general public through so-called 'open data portals.' The information, however, isn't just the boilerplate that governments routinely produce: reports, documents linked to public education campaigns, etc. Rather, the data in open data repositories is typically raw, complex, and constantly updated – for example, streams of GPS readings showing the precise location of transit vehicles, or databases showing the frequencies of parking tickets written in certain locations. Public sector institutions sit on vast storehouses of such data, and open-government advocates have, for a number of years, argued that when such information is collated and made publicly available, it will provide the raw material for citizen-driven innovations for identifying, analyzing, and solving local problems, e.g., apps that provide up-to-date water quality readings on local beaches.

High-Speed Fibre Optic Cable and 5G Wireless Networks

In big cities around the world, the utility tunnels beneath streets are filled with the kind of broadband fibre optic cable that enables data-heavy applications, from multi-player online gaming to real-time streaming video.

As well, telecommunications giants are installing so-called 5G (or fifth generation) wireless networks in a growing number of large urban regions. 5G technology – which has produced both geopolitical tensions (over Huawei) and pandemic-fuelled conspiracy theories – uses lower radio frequencies, allowing networks to accommodate far higher data volumes than currently possible. The trade-off is that 5G networks need a much denser concentration of cell towers and transmitters.

For many smart city applications, 5G will be a game-changer because these networks enable huge volumes of raw data to move rapidly across wireless networks with what's called 'low latency,' meaning very little time elapses between the detection of a signal and the response to it generated in a remote computer system.

A case in point: Verizon and TomTom, the digital mapping and navigation giant, are testing 5G for busy intersections. The idea is for traffic cameras and connected autonomous vehicles to be in constant communication, via 5G, as a means of reducing the risk of collisions. 'If each vehicle passing through an intersection is able to relay and receive information from other vehicles and streetlight-mounted cameras, that information can be used to notify connected devices when lights turn red or vehicles ahead come to a sudden stop,' explained *Traffic Technology Today*, a trade magazine, in October 2019.

Widespread arrival of 5G also provides less benign applications, such as facial recognition cameras that have been deployed in many Chinese cities as part of the state's security policies. According to a report in *Foreign Policy* Magazine, China is home to sixteen of the top twenty most surveilled cities in the world. Shanghai, which achieved full 5G coverage in its downtown area and 99 per cent fibre-optic coverage across the city, is blanketed by a veritable thicket of video surveillance. 'Identity collection devices are commonplace, having exploded across public and private spaces … A combination of satellites, drones, and fixed cameras grab over 20 million images a day. The bus, metro, and credit cards of local residents are also traced in real time' (Muggah & Walton 2021).

Video Conferencing

When the World Health Organization declared a global public health emergency in March 2020, forcing millions of people to work remotely, video-conferencing platforms, once used almost exclusively for business meetings, saw a dramatic surge of traffic, with countless new users creating accounts.

As we all know, the heavy reliance on platforms like Zoom, Google Meet, and Microsoft Teams wasn't limited to work/office uses and is likely to trigger long-lasting changes – both good and bad – in the way cities look and function.

Local governments for example, took to streaming video from not just council meetings out also a range of other public meetings and consultations, thus increasing accessibility, at least to those with computers. Arts companies pivoted away from live performances in front of audiences to livestreaming performances in front of cameras. Schools and universities also had to transition to online learning, a pivot that saw the emergence of new pedagogical techniques and a boom in education tech. Yet for all the innovation, the depersonalized experience of virtual learning left much to be desired for both teachers and students.

Health care, however, has been a very different story. Telemedicine, long seen as a service mainly of use in remote communities, enjoyed a massive resurgence as a wide range of medical appointments transitioned to secure video links, especially in the mental health field. Even as they dealt with a sharp increase in demand for services, some psychiatrists and therapists reported a decline in missed appointments, suggesting that video conference sessions produced a more consistent course of treatment.

'The pandemic has dramatically sped up the slow adoption of tele-health visits, and increased knowledge of what technology can offer,' concluded a 2021 literature review conducted by University of Saskatchewan researchers and published by the U.S. National Institutes of Health (Li et al. 2021). 'This forced uptake has clearly demonstrated the potential in virtual healthcare service delivery during COVID-19 and the future. Telepsychiatry has been shown to be feasible and appropriate for supporting patients and healthcare providers during COVID-19. Furthermore, geographical barriers to delivering mental health services have been broken in terms of physical distance and its associated financial burdens.' Not surprisingly, many start-ups and wellness tech firms have raced into this burgeoning field, including several that managed to raise hundreds of millions of dollars in equity through initial public offerings in 2021.

Yet the convenience of work-related video-conferencing, combined with the persistence of some pandemic distancing practices and the reluctance of many people to return to their workplaces full-time, produced short-term and possibly medium-term implications for cities and their suburban satellites. Office districts, largely abandoned during the worst parts of the crisis, have been slow to rebound, and that dynamic has produced a domino effect for transit usage and the viability of retail and restaurants located in the vicinity of office districts. Some companies also moved to downsize the amount of office space they lease, anticipating that many people will continue to work from home either full-time or part-time. Other companies, especially in tech-intensive sectors, widened their recruitment net in the expectation that there will be newly hired people who will never need to come into the office.

Smart Energy Systems

Smart cities advocates have long argued that one of the key benefits of these technologies involves improving urban sustainability, and reducing and shifting energy consumption from carbon-intensive sources to renewables. A growing number of utilities use technologies, such as smart meters, peak-period pricing, and load management systems, that allow large consumers, such as office buildings, to automatically make slight adjustments to heating and air conditioning levels as a means of reducing overall energy consumption.

Many municipalities, in turn, are investing in centrally controlled smart street lights. These devices, mounted on utility poles, use low-energy LED instead of conventional bulbs. They have lower maintenance costs because they last longer, and some systems are programmed to adjust automatically to ambient light, which also reduces energy consumption. Some commercial models have other sensors and even video built in, transforming them from static emitters of nighttime illumination to disbursed data-gathering tools.

In regions that promote the use of photovoltaic solar panels, two-way electricity meters allow energy generated on a rooftop to flow into the grid. Growing numbers of homeowners are installing smart thermostats that use sensors to continually readjust heating or cooling levels. These devices are wifi-enabled so they can be managed from a smart phone app. Smart thermostat firms like Ecobee also allow users to wirelessly 'donate' their energy-use data to scientists studying building performance.

Intelligent Transportation Systems

Some of the earliest smart city systems were traffic control centres developed by IBM and other firms for municipal customers. These computer systems combine video, traffic flow readings from weight detection 'loops' built into the pavement, and, more recently, GPS information about public transit vehicles to generate a real-time view of road conditions and congestion.

These so-called 'intelligent transportation systems' – e.g., the Sydney Coordinated Adaptive Traffic System, which was developed in New South Wales, Australia, in the early 1970s and has since been deployed in gridlocked cities around the world – automatically control traffic signals in a dynamic way that responds to conditions on the road.

Many start-ups have flocked into this market. Miovision, a Kitchener, Ontario, firm, in 2015 raised $30 million to develop and deploy automated traffic counters, which are installed in boxes near signalized intersections to measure vehicle movements. Using digital cameras that can interpret road conditions, the devices are fitted out with AI algorithms designed to automatically adjust signal intervals and coordinate with adjacent traffic lights, based on a municipality's road policies. Co-Founder and CEO Kurtis McBride tells me that improved efficiency in traffic flow can cut travel times and reduce emissions related to idling.

Other transportation-oriented technologies have also proliferated in recent years, and include everything from transit smart cards (e.g., London's Oyster) to licence-plate readers, apps showing transit routes and real-time schedules, parking and navigation apps, demand-based micro-transit, and a wide range of vehicle-sharing systems for cars, bikes, and scooters, all of them accessible via smart phones.

A 2018 analysis by McKinsey Global Institute concluded that transportation-related smart systems yielded the greatest gains for cities. 'We found that these tools could reduce fatalities by 8 to 10 per cent, accelerate emergency response times by 20 to 35 per cent, [and] shave the average commute by 15 to 20 per cent.'

Visualization

While architects have long used sophisticated modelling software to design buildings and public spaces, urban planners are turning to related applications that use data visualization tools developed by smart city start-ups. Some firms have created software that aggregate a wide range of big data sets gathered by sensors and other sources to generate so-called 'digital twins': highly detailed 3-D representations of an urban region that allows users to zoom in and out, pivot images, and drill down to find even more detailed data – for example, about the zoning rules that apply to a given location.

The simulation tools permit planners, politicians, businesses, and residents to visualize various future planning scenarios. For example, AugmentCity, a fifteen-year-old Norwegian firm, has created a simulator that looks at how Ålesund, a city of about 70,000 in the country's north, can reduce emissions using a range of strategies, from introducing more electric vehicles to altering the mooring practices of the cruise ships that stop in the harbour. The simulator is designed to graphically depict how different planning decisions impact the city's carbon emissions overall. 'Humans understand data in visual formats,' CEO Joel Alexander Mills said during the 2019 trade show. 'We need humans to interact with technology to make decisions.'

❖

Although some smart technologies – video-conferencing, for example – have solved practical problems and seem to have become permanent fixtures in our society, others are still in development, promising easy solutions that don't quite fit the untidy reality of busy cities.

Shoshanna Saxe, an assistant professor of civil engineering at the University of Toronto, cites an infrastructure monitoring system developed jointly by NASA and the University of Bath. The idea is to use remote wireless sensing devices on satellite radar to detect subtle structural vibrations on bridges that could indicate the presence of worsening weaknesses. Officials and control systems can monitor the sensors for signs of trouble. But, as she notes, the problem with this idea is its reliance on digital devices, wireless networks, and the electrical grid. What would happen, she asks, if the power goes out or the sensors fail to pick up the vibrations created by a potentially catastrophic crack? Other smart city watchers have also warned about the risks of what Anthony Townsend describes as 'buggy and brittle' technologies.

Smart cities, Saxe wrote in a widely shared 2019 *New York Times* column, 'will be exceedingly complex to manage, with all sorts of unpredictable vulnerabilities. There will always be a place for new technology in our urban infrastructure, but we may find that often, "dumb" cities will do better than smart ones.'

She observed that ordinary consumer electronics – e.g., cell phones or kitchen appliances kitted out with some kind of digital functions – become obsolete rapidly, and smart city tech will be no different.

'Rather than chasing the newest shiny smart-city technology,' Saxe warns, 'we should redirect some of that energy toward building excellent dumb cities – cities planned and built with best-in-class, durable approaches to infrastructure and the public realm ... Tech has a place in cities, but that place is not everywhere.'

2
Smart Cities and the Origins of Utopian Urbanism

While the global smart city industry trades in the digital technologies enumerated in the previous chapter (and many others), it has also embraced and promoted (without irony) a utopian vision of the twenty-first-century metropolis – the tech sector's rebuttal to *Blade Runner*, Ridley Scott's dystopian thriller set in the hellscape of the Los Angeles of 2019.

Sidewalk Labs was by no means the only company to promote the notion that the technologically hyper-advanced city could solve many of the world's most intractable urban problems, from carbon emissions to traffic congestion and public safety. Thousands of firms of all sizes have crowded into this fast-growing tech subsector, whose revenues could grow to anywhere from US$300 billion annually to over US$2 trillion, according to various estimates.

Many of these companies have employed, in their marketing materials, the visual and promotional language of cool urbanism and science-fiction futurism. The aisles of smart city trade shows are filled with glimmering digital maps, god's-eye renderings, and mesmerizing data visualizations, all meant to entice customers – most of whom work for cities or regions, or for property developers – to imagine that the city, for all its chaos and complexity, can actually be optimized, like a machine.

The idea has a beguiling simplicity at its core: that with enough connected sensors taking the city's pulse, and with sufficiently powerful information processing capacity for digesting all that raw data, smart city technology can not only 'see' what's happening in urban space at any given time, but also automatically adjust the dials, so to speak. A brain responding to the body's signals. A car engine tweaked to run at peak efficiency. A company whose products align perfectly to its customers desires. The utopian fantasy is that cities are potentially knowable, thanks to the omniscience of technologies that also purport to play the role of oracle, predicting the future, in all its granularity, and ordering up the necessary course corrections along the way.

Yet the relentless serendipity of cities is, as the joke goes, a feature, not a bug – the messy energy that spurs social movements, scientific breakthroughs, cultural achievements, and so on. In places with millions of people living in close proximity, all of them making countless choices each day, there's more than a little hubris in the hegemonistic assumption that the bewilderingly tangled networks and systems of the city can somehow be mastered.

The neo-liberal smart city agenda, however, addresses itself to the flip side of the disordered urban world – to the institutions and commercial or political forces that want cities to be not only ordered and livable, but also attuned to the needs of business.

The practical justifications that inform city planning are familiar to anyone who's followed a neighbourhood development fight or the complicated approvals processes required to create some new amenity, like light-rail transit or a park. Cities seek to regulate growth because they also have to manage infrastructure, like sewers and roads, while providing adequate housing and services. Some types of buildings interfere with others, which is why factories tend not to be next to residential neighbourhoods. Public spaces are necessary for livability, but they can also add or detract from private property. Cities need areas where people work, raise families, shop, play. For all these reasons and many more, modern cities plan, and are planned, to manage growth, to provide quality of life, to promote economic activity, etc.

For thousands of years, cities weren't 'planned' in any way that we'd recognize, and certainly not with the aid of information-gathering technology. Rather, they spilled out of castle walls, huddled on the crests of hills, or sprang up around the port areas situated near ship-friendly harbours. Monarchs commanded the construction of large communal or ceremonial zones, like agoras or temples, while high priests advised on laying out cities in patterns that would please a deity. 'In many ancient cultures,' writes architectural historian Spiro Kostof in *The City Shaped: Urban Patterns and Meanings Through History*, 'the city on earth was supposed to represent a celestial model which it was extremely important to reproduce accurately.' Features like orientation, symmetry, and dimension 'had to be observed,' he adds. 'Which in turn meant an artificial layout, often of some geometric purity' (Kostof 1991, 34).

For example, in Beijing, which became the capital of the Ming Dynasty in 1421, the emperor relied on an ancient Chinese text known as the 'Kao Gong Ji' – a compendium of technologies described as the oldest municipal planning document. That juncture marked the development of the Forbidden City, the 180-acre walled enclave that marks Beijing's political centre of gravity. 'It was a means of legitimising their rule,' Toby Lincoln, lecturer in Chinese Urban History at the University of Leicester, told the *Guardian* in 2016. 'By explicitly drawing on this ancient manual of rites, their new capital city used divine numerology and ritual to express the power of the ruling elite in physical space' (Wainwright).

Other pre-modern instances of municipal land-use regulation sought to control urban populations. In 1516, for example, Venice's administrative council designated a 'ghetto' – the first of its kind – specifically for Jews, who had long been present in the city. Venetian administrators over three centuries had already segmented the city into districts organized around uses, including wards specifically for ship-building, glass-making, and other proto-industrial activities. '[T]hese were the first large scale industrial areas to be set apart from the mixed uses of the ordinary medieval city,' wrote Lewis Mumford in *The City in History*. '[T]he Venetians, no doubt inadvertently, invented a new type of city, based on the differentiation and zoning of urban functions, separated by traffic ways and open spaces' (Mumford 1961, 323).

The law that established the Jewish ghetto, however, was anything but inadvertent. It decreed that Venice's Jews could live and work only within a newly designated enclave, where they could engage in commercial activities like moneylending and pawnbrokering, and that would be locked at night. The move, according to a 2017 history by Dana Katz, allowed the city to profit from the presence of Jewish financing activity while segregating Jews from Venice's Christian majority. 'According to the senatorial decree,' Katz writes, 'ghetto enclosure was necessary to avoid the improprieties and illegalities that surfaced when Jews spread throughout the city.'

Meanwhile, imperial powers like England and Spain exported urban design schemata to colonial outposts in the Americas and Asia. 'When the Spaniards settled in Manila [in 1571],' according to an overview of planning and development in the sprawling Philippine capital, 'they evolved ideas for town planning based on the Italian Renaissance theorists that emphasized the plaza complex in city development. The idea of town planning was codified in ordinances promulgated by King Philip II whereby guidelines for site selection, layout and dimensions of squares and streets and other land uses were provided.'

Surveyed street grids continued to serve as an organizing principle for centuries and can be understood as a technological process for the production of urban space, sometimes imposed by colonial authorities. In New York, the 1811 Commissioner's Plan carved up rural Manhattan (north of Canal Street) into a vast cross-hatching of streets and avenues in anticipation of future development and commercial activity. As Kostof points out, the commissioners didn't envision open spaces; Central Park came several decades later, when landscape architect Frederick Law Olmsted made the case that working people living in crowded conditions required access to natural outdoor spaces for health.

Until the late nineteenth century, planning as currently practised simply wasn't part of urban life or municipal governance, much less recognized as a profession. But then something changed.

❖

In many cities around the world, two types of urban development became ubiquitous in the decades after World War II, initially in North America and Europe, and then in many other regions in the thirty years since global trade replaced the Cold War as the dominant framework of international relations.

One was the mass production of the high-rise apartment building, often modernist slab towers situated in the midst of an apron of open space. These apartment complexes sprung up within and on the edges of many big cities in North America, Western and Eastern Europe, and parts of Asia from the 1960s onward. Dense, yet often dehumanizing because of their scale, 'slab' apartment blocks were constructed in some cases by public housing agencies to provide subsidized accommodation. They also became destinations for millions of migrants, both from rural areas in search of economic opportunity and as immigrants or refugees fleeing strife in their home countries. Dubbed 'arrival cities' by journalist Doug Saunders, they replaced the overcrowded immigrant or working-class ghettos that characterized many industrial cities in the nineteenth and early twentieth centuries.

The second form enabled the growing middle class to move into suburban enclaves. Low-density, low-rise subdivisions consisting almost entirely of single-family homes on spacious properties with front and backyards, setbacks, and winding streets. Residential suburbs, served by arterial roads and shopping malls, included a wide range of dwellings, from modest bungalows to extravagant mansions. Yet they shared some basic characteristics: organized around private property, they tended to be situated away from industrial or commercial centres and, for the most part, required residents to own private vehicles to access almost all types of public and commercial services. In many parts of the world, exclusive suburban subdivisions are sometimes gated to protect their exclusivity and support the property values of the people who live inside the walls.

The rapid spread of both of these types of urban forms depended on the emergence of a handful of technologies: steel-frame construction, elevators, the mass production of inexpensive building materials, and private automobiles, as well as the maturation of civil engineering techniques that allowed municipal services to extend outward into the hinterland at the edges of older urban areas.

Neighbourhoods in many global cities, from Istanbul to Copenhagen to Rio de Janeiro, are a mishmash of smaller dwellings alongside low- to mid-rise apartment blocks that hug the street grid, coexisting with commercial activity. Yet the proliferation of towers and subdivisions can be traced to the utopian ideas of a handful of reformers who sought to remedy the social and health crises of the nineteenth-century industrial city and the extreme congestion of its early twentieth-century descendant. Utopian urbanism anticipates the emergence of the smart city movement, with its rationalist promise of using technology to eradicate the ills of the city while optimizing its economic and social prospects.

Le Corbusier developed the template for a tower-in-the-park in response to his deep dislike of the chaotic environment of crowded Parisian neighbourhoods. Enumerating his impressions of Manhattan in his 1947 book *When the Cathedrals Were White*, he bemoaned the sight of hundreds of traffic lights during his highly publicized visits to the city in the 1930s. 'I was irritated, depressed, made ill by them,' he wrote. 'There can be no salvation – no more for New York than for Paris – if measures are not taken soon which take into consideration the scale established by the automobile' (Le Corbusier, 69).

To architects, Le Corbusier was one of the twentieth century's pioneering designers, known for sleek modernist homes and apartment buildings, as well as the dramatic concrete chapel known as Notre Dame du Haut, in Ronchamp, France, completed in 1955. He described his residential designs as 'machines for living in' in his 1927 manifesto, 'Towards a New Architecture.'

Beyond architecture, Le Corbusier's influence stemmed from his ideas about urban redevelopment, particularly in Paris. As an alternative to the warren-like streets of the Right Bank and the overwhelming traffic on Paris's wide boulevards, Le Corbusier formulated, during the early 1930s, a manifesto for a 'radiant city.'

It featured soaring cruciform apartment towers set out in mega-blocks and delineated by a grid of superhighways. The apartment complexes would each be surrounded by green space with the pedestrian realm separated from the highways that would traverse central Paris. His famous sketches, widely circulated during the 1930s, are rigorously symmetrical, evincing not only the god's-eye perspective, but also his mistrust of the disorderly, organic realm of the city street.

The context is critical. Le Corbusier developed and energetically promoted his utopian vision of the Radiant City at a time when radical social movements had taken hold in many places beyond the Soviet Union. In Berlin during the Weimar Republic, which held power precariously in Germany from 1919 to 1933, left-leaning politics intersected with socialist design movements, such as Bauhaus, the rise of avant-garde art, and the release of zeitgeist films, like Charlie Chaplin's *Modern Times* and Fritz Lang's *Metropolis*, both dystopic cinematic renderings of the mechanistic city of the future.

In Vienna, meanwhile, a slate of Social Democrats, backed by trade unions, had taken control of city council in 1919 and pushed through an ambitious program of public housing, which came to be known as 'Red Vienna' and was financed by taxes on the rich. The city developed tens of thousands of units of subsidized apartments in large blocks, all equipped with socialized amenities like daycares, libraries, recreation centres, theatres, and even city-run cafés. The Red Vienna program was a response to critical housing shortages, poverty, and overcrowding that festered as the city industrialized.

'Though only one of several institutions designed to reshape the social and economic infrastructure of the city along socialist lines, the housing, as a locus for so many of the municipality's communal organizations and facilities, was the nexus of Red Vienna's institutions and the spatial embodiment of its communitarian and pedagogic ideals,' wrote Harvard urban and planning historian Eve Blau in her 1999 survey of the architecture of Red Vienna (Blau, 44).

Le Corbusier's planning ideas were grounded in two basic assumptions about urban planning: one, that automobile traffic had to be rigidly segregated from other forms of street life and urban forms; and two, that autocratic administrators would be able to wield the power needed to impose drastic changes that would sweep aside the clamour and poverty of the older city. (Later, his sympathy for the Vichy regime in occupied France and the authoritarian cast of his thinking caused some early adherents to reject his ideas.)

In Paris, the focus of his attention, there was precedent for sweeping, *dirigiste* redevelopment. Beginning in the 1850s, von Haussmann embarked on an extremely ambitious reconstruction of central Paris. 'The key to Haussmann's success lay in his relationship to the emperor, with whom he was in almost daily contact,' writes planning historian Peter Hall in *Cities in Civilization* (716). He ordered the demolition of sprawling tracts of medieval housing in favour of the grand boulevards lined with elegant apartments that give Paris its distinctive look. The program involved extensive investment in public works like sewers and watermains. Hall characterizes the scale of von Haussmann's plan as 'unprecedented' in human history.

Unlike von Haussmann, Le Corbusier didn't see his Radiant City plans for Paris adopted as he had envisioned, although in the post-WWII era, large-scale demolition in central Paris and the construction of high-rise social housing projects in the suburbs ('banlieue') suggest the influence of his ideas. Le Corbusier also found receptive followers in Brasília, the new capital of Brazil that was built (from scratch) according to the kinds of modernist design and planning ideas that formed the core of his top-down utopianism.

Critics have pointed out other ironies in the way that Le Corbusier's urbanism found expression in the real world. As David Pinder comments, 'Ideas that were intended to rush in a new space and way of life now became, through a tragic twist, a means to bolster the prestige of corporate and bureaucratic clients as well as to provide predominantly cheap and mass-produced solutions to meet pressing housing needs' (Pinder 2005, 140).

The twentieth century's other profoundly influential utopian planning ideology predates Le Corbusier, although the two philosophies worked together and were enabled by the emergence of transformational technologies. Together, they altered the course of post-WWII urban development in many parts of the world.

The Garden City movement was the brainchild of a British planner named Ebenezer Howard. His eponymous 1898 treatise outlined the conceptual thinking behind a set of urban planning reforms that he saw as a means of confronting the alienation of industrial cities, with their slums, noise, and pollution, among many other ills. Howard argued that the remedy to urban overcrowding was the development of new and meticulously planned suburban satellites, where residential and industrial uses were strictly separated from one another, with civic amenities – parks, libraries, etc. – situated at the symbolic and physical focal point.

'Howard asserted that his programme was not anti-urban but rather based on a "balanced" way of living,' observed University of London geographer David Pinder in *Visions of the City*, a 2005 study of urban utopias. 'This involved building anew on fresh ground. He wrote: "Order and beauty rather than chaos and ugliness: the needs of the whole people rather than the supposed interests of a few will be the governing elements in determining the ground plan of the city"' (36).

Howard was by no means the father of suburbanization; as Pinder points out, Howard acknowledged earlier sources of inspiration, including Thomas More's *Utopia* as well as the ideas of other nineteenth-century social reformers. Emerging real estate trends also played a role. By the early decades of the nineteenth century, the members of the newly affluent merchant and industrialist classes had begun to decamp from centres of dense cities like London, where rich and poor had lived and worked cheek by jowl for generations. Those who could afford it built large homes and estates on the outskirts, with the (male) breadwinner commuting into the commercial centre. While these exurban villas were initially used as weekend or vacation retreats, they evolved into full-time residences for the families of the well-to-do and then the striving middle classes. The out-migration by those with means, writes historian Robert Fishman in *Bourgeois Utopias*, represented an organic response to the stresses of city life, yet it also suggested other social dynamics, such as the assertion of class.

The new suburban mansions, for example, were often adorned with gothic details, he observes. 'This appropriation of aristocratic symbolism by the industrial bourgeoisie is not surprising if one considers that suburbia was not "a retreat from urban society and its problems" but a new way of expressing dominance within that society.'

The accelerating spatial segregation served as a physical manifestation of the class divides that industrialization had sparked, Fishman continues. 'As workers and their factories were thus confined [in the core], the modern factory zone came into being. Once the "breezy heights" were firmly in the possession of the middle class, factories and their workers were increasingly crowded into the zone between the high land values of the core and the privileged residential zones at the outskirts' (82).

Both Howard and Le Corbusier actively promoted their respective philosophies of the city through international networks of architects, social reformers, political organizations, and the media. Prescriptions from other utopian-minded thinkers also surfaced. In 1932, for example, architect Frank Lloyd Wright proposed 'Broadacre City,' a radically decentralized and agrarian conception of modern life that explicitly rejected urban and suburban forms, as well as the coarsening influences of big-city capitalism. (His architectural oeuvre included modestly scaled 'Usonian' houses geared toward middle-class families, which heavily influenced suburban residential design in the post-WWII era.)

The adherents of the early 'town planning' movement, which gained momentum after the turn of the century, drew their inspiration from sources like the Garden City advocates, as well as related 'progressivist' campaigns to improve public sanitation and purge corruption from municipal government. Some of the first municipal planners, in fact, subscribed to a collectivist, radical vision of government and rejected the voracious types of laissez-faire capitalism that had produced enormous banking, railroad, and manufacturing fortunes.

By the 1920s and 1930s, planning had become an established function of municipal government. Modern cities, in turn, no longer resembled the nightmarish factory towns that had outraged (or inspired) earlier generations of radicals and reformers. Grade-separated highways were built in response to the growing popularity of the privately owned automobile as well as downtown traffic congestion. Sanitary conditions had improved, as had public health practices, like pasteurization. Skyscrapers were sprouting in downtowns while railroad and streetcar suburbs had grown up around the stations of the commuter rail lines radiating out of downtowns. As well, the earliest purpose-built Garden City suburbs – places like Letchworth, in England outside London, and Radburn, New Jersey, both featuring tree-lined, curving streets and stately homes on large lots – had spurred a new type of real estate speculation focused on the domestic needs and consumer desires of middle-class families.

The writer H. G. Wells, as Fishman points out, had anticipated these dynamics as early as 1901. In an essay entitled 'The Probable Diffusion of Great Cities,' he commented that urban society was 'in the early phase of a great development of centrifugal possibilities.' The outward push of cities, Wells observed, was directly connected to the emergence of new modes of transportation that allowed people to travel ever farther afield for their daily routines.

'Wells' and Wright's prophecies constitute a remarkable insight into the decentralizing tendencies of modern technology and society,' Fishman comments. 'Both were presented in utopian form, an image of the future presented as somehow "inevitable" yet without any sustained attention to how it would actually be achieved' (189).

While the rapid evolution of transportation technology clearly played a major role in the growth of twentieth-century cities, so too did some of the ideas deeply embedded in the thinking of Howard, Le Corbusier, and others. They rejected the chaotic world of the old city in favour of orderly urban areas – both in the core and on the periphery

– where land uses could be strictly regulated and separated from one another, linked by networks of roads and highways.

The notion of separating uses wasn't entirely new: ancient and medieval cities had areas set aside specifically for military, ceremonial, or commercial activities. But in the modern context of the democratic nation-state, zoning laws became the practical tool for implementing the utopian ideals expressed by Howard, Le Corbusier, and others. Indeed, zoning as a mode of municipal rule-making is scarcely a century old, and evolved from the administration of public works. Zoning policies allowed city officials to impose order on disorderly urban environments and therefore to translate the reformers' high-level principles into regulation. The resulting ordinances, bylaws, and official plans demarcated what could happen with a particular piece of land – its uses, the allowable heights and densities of buildings, the size of lots, the setbacks from streets or property lines, and so on.

Despite the egalitarian values espoused by utopian urbanists, the earliest land-use rules did little to improve the lives of the working class or the very poor – quite the contrary. By codifying what would *not* be permitted – e.g., apartment buildings or small lots – zoning regulations served to exclude racialized minorities and played a devastating role in isolating poor Black and Hispanic neighbourhoods in American cities. Such land-use tools could further be deployed as instruments of social engineering, e.g., effectively ensuring that low-rise residential areas were highly gendered/domesticated zones that contained housing and services exclusively for families with children.

Other scholars have pointed out the contradictions inherent in municipal planning. As Rutgers University urban studies scholar Michael Lang observed in a 2010 paper, 'It has been noted that modern town planning, once a nexus of radical and progressive theory and practice, has been transformed to a means of developing and delivering a series of professional techniques appropriate to the maintenance of the prevailing capitalist system' (Lang 2010).

During the post-WWII decades, municipal officials overseeing suburban development and the construction of greenfield subdivisions embraced the principle of rigorously separating industrial, commercial, and residential land uses. By that point, urbanist critics like Jane Jacobs and Lewis Mumford were attacking the technocratic orthodoxies of modernist planning, which depended heavily on cars and the demolition of working-class neighbourhoods to make way for dehumanizing public housing complexes – the cheaped-out offspring of Le Corbusier's Radiant City – and highways linking subdivisions to central business districts.

Since the 1960s, in fact, a previously unknown form of urban conflict and politics surfaced in big cities, revolving around disputes over land-use policies. Jacobs fronted grassroots movements against highway construction and top-down slum clearance programs packaged as 'urban renewal.' Meanwhile, the backlash to seemingly limitless suburban sprawl, which had been driven by demographics, postwar prosperity, and, in the U.S., 'white flight,' exported congestion and car dependence to the urban fringes while ratcheting up the cost of municipal infrastructure.

Beginning in the late 1970s, as artists and young people began to reclaim hollowed-out downtowns and abandoned industrial buildings, gentrification and NIMBYism came to define the contours of land-use planning politics – a dynamic that persists to this day.

Fast-growing cities have responded in many ways, enacting regulations meant to contain sprawl, investing in rapid transit infrastructure, up-zoning residential areas to allow for more density and approving intensification policies for core areas. Along the way, municipalities that had, for decades, rigorously enforced the separation of uses began to approve 'mixed-use' development, a somewhat new term for a very old urban idea, which is that people can live in the same areas where shops, businesses, and offices are located, as is the case in the mega-cities in the global south as well as most of Europe.

Yet intensification and mixed-use planning have posed tough questions for cities that were accustomed to a more orderly approach to land use. Planners have to show that the additional growth won't overwhelm existing urban infrastructure systems. Some residents will balk at the prospect of change and uncertainty, while others demand access to better housing and services. The proliferation of sophisticated digital planning tools is a technological response to the political and bureaucratic friction generated by the trend toward denser and more vertical urban neighbourhoods.

There's a certain irony in the way this story has evolved. Many cities had sought to banish or severely limit the mixing of land uses in part to address the environmental and social crises of overcrowded industrial cities. In so doing, postwar metropolitan regions swapped out the problems associated with extreme density for the problems that flow from extreme sprawl.

The utopian urbanism of the late nineteenth and early twentieth centuries may have had more influence because most societies at the time were not predominantly urban, so architects and planners and critics had the latitude to conjure up the ideal future metropolis.[6] However, the great waves of urbanization that began in the early twentieth century and continue into the twenty-first have produced cities and mega-regions with no historical precedent whatsoever. Mass migration is dramatically reshaping the social and cultural fabric of cities of all sizes. And torrents of highly mobile global capital have rapidly altered urban form and development around the world, forcing booming cities and their planners to look to land-use regulation as a means of managing growth in ways that are socially and environmentally sustainable.

In this context, the prevailing ideas around contemporary urban growth have tended to be anything but utopian, focusing instead on more grounded goals like promoting 'creative cities,' economic 'clusters,' or social housing programs designed to reduce income inequality. Some planners, like Denmark's Jan Gehl and New York's transporation commissioner Janette Sadik-Khan, fought to create more pedestrian-friendly spaces and bike lanes in recognition of the twinned demands of density and climate change. Others predicted that so-called 'edge cities' – suburban satellites that attracted not just home builders but all kinds of economic activity – would define the

---

6. According to the U.S. census, fewer than 20 per cent of Americans in the 1890s lived in cities. The proportions were similar in industrialized European countries like Germany.

urban future. For a brief time in the early 2010s, an American management professor had some success promoting his concept of an 'aerotropolis,' which envisioned cities rearranging themselves around major hub airports linked to adjacent business parks filled with companies that made and shipped goods. In the years since, smart city advocates and tech firms, as we'll see in later chapters, have sought to solve the problems of twenty-first-century cities with digital tools.

Urban utopians, however, haven't abandoned the intellectual playing field. In the 1990s, a school of American architects and planners led by Peter Calthorpe and Andrés Duany set to work promoting 'New Urbanism,' an approach to town planning that more or less explicitly evoked Howard's ideas. But when New Urbanism found its way into the plans of real estate developers, it quickly degenerated into little more than high-end neo-traditional residential architecture in exclusive new-build communities.

In the fall of 2021, an e-commerce billionaire named Marc Lore unveiled plans to build a 'utopian megalopolis' on 50,000 as-yet-undeveloped acres somewhere in the U.S. southwest. Dubbed by one academic as an example of 'unicorn planning' for its tabula rasa approach to city-building, 'Telosa' will be fitted out with smart technology and eventually grow to 5 million residents. Lore also wants it to be governed by a non-profit foundation that would reduce inequality by reinvesting taxes on rising land prices into social services.

'If you went into the desert where the land was worth nothing, or very little, and you created a foundation that owned the land, and people moved there and tax dollars built infrastructure and we built one of the greatest cities in the world, the foundation could be worth a trillion dollars,' Lore told *Bloomberg BusinessWeek*. 'And if the foundation's mission was to take the appreciation of the land and give it back to the citizens in the form of medicine, education, affordable housing, social services: Wow, that's it!' (Brustein 2021).

Meanwhile, in Europe, the concept of the 'fifteen-minute city' – first introduced in 2015 by a Franco-Colombian academic named Carlos Moreno – has gained currency among some urbanists and can be described as a utopian response to the stresses of twenty-first-century cities in the era of climate change. Moreno's idea, popularized via a seven-minute TED Talk, is that all city-dwellers should be able to access the majority of their needs – markets, health care, schools, recreation, culture, etc. – within a fifteen-minute walk or bike ride of their homes as a means of building local communities and reducing car dependency. Moreno's thinking – which has been attacked as elitist – was widely discussed during the early months of the pandemic, when many people were working from home.

The fifteen-minute city's best-known disciple is Paris mayor Anne Hidalgo (as of 2022), who moved to severely restrict car traffic during the COVID-19 crisis. Moreno's vision, however, has found adherents beyond the French capital, including the international network of climate-focused cities that calls itself the C-40. As the online architectural publication *Dezeen* reported, 'Moreno's framework, which can be adapted to suit local cultures and needs, has already informed urban planning in cities such as Buenos Aires, Chengdu and Melbourne.'

Moreno, like Le Corbusier a century earlier, regards cars as anathema to healthy and livable cities. In his view, there are, or should be, four core principles underwriting the development of the fifteen-minute city: ecology, proximity, solidarity, and participation. Every bit of urban space, Moreno argues, should have multiple uses, all in the service of reducing traffic and creating calmer, cleaner, and more human-scale neighbourhoods. 'The fifteen-minute city,' as he says, 'is an attempt to reconcile the city with the humans that live in it.'

His brand of urban utopianism is less mechanistic and grandiose than the prescriptions of dreamers like Le Corbusier, Howard, and Lore. But like theirs, Moreno's vision is built on a foundation of sweeping assumptions about how cities should yield to a set of tidy planning ideals that have little to do with the messy ways in which city-dwellers actually live their lives.

3
Planning Smart Cities

In 2018, after years spent working in Toronto's development and infrastructure sectors, Monika Jaroszonek and Erin Morrow decided to open a small consulting shop whose mission was to inject some twenty-first-century data visualization and computer modelling magic into the practices of municipal planning.

Anyone who has worked in land-use planning understands that it is a highly bureaucratic profession tasked, unenviably, with taming or at least containing the torrents of capital that flow in and through cities, reshaping the way they look, function, and are experienced.

Planners both produce and consume thickets of geographical information: official plans, maps, zoning regulations, land-use policies, surveys, schematics, just to name a few. They have to understand everything from land-use economics to transportation demand patterns to the reasons why pedestrians may not follow a paved path through a park. In most cities, planners serve as a kind of buffer between developers, architects, and landowners on one side, and the general public and local politicians on the other. They exist in the modern world because, in the past, the messy realities of cities became intolerable, inspiring both radical politics and utopian reforms – an iterative dynamic that persists to this day in planning fads like the fifteen-minute city movement.

As an architect who dealt extensively with planners, Jaroszonek was interested in how complex planning policies contribute to built form. Morrow, a planner and Ratio City's Chief Product Officer, wanted a better feel for 'the underlying system, the bones of the city,' as he put it to me in 2021. 'Those are really hard problems. You need a lot of data, and it's shocking how unavailable it is.'

What they did was combine huge existing databases of public information to create a set of web-based mapping software that layers regional and local land-use policies and zoning rules for every address, as well as density allowances, property lines, geographic features, and even the locations of heritage buildings. They fed all this location-specific detail into a software system programmed to create highly granular maps and 3-D schematics of any neighbourhood, allowing users to game out how various types of projects may alter a community.

Ratio City's platform – a quintessential smart city technology – generates nifty visualizations, checks to see if projects conform to existing zoning bylaws, and estimates how changes in the number of proposed units, for example, might affect the form of an apartment complex. It also allows users to swoop around these models electronically, like they were video games, studying projects from different angles and scales.

Eventually, Jaroszonek and Morrow want to layer on estimates of how projects will affect traffic or transit use. Because it draws on historical data, the company's software can depict trends in how neighbourhoods have changed in response to new land-use policies. However, there are no plans to use it to predict future trends. 'It offers a complete view of what's going on,' says Jaroszonek. Adds Morrow: 'We can see all these different policies impact a particular site.'

The firm's clients are developers, but its goal is to remove public ambiguity in the approvals process by providing residents and municipal officials with accessible depictions, showing how their neighbourhoods will change. 'A lot of the problem in the development process is information asymmetry,' says Morrow. 'People assume they're not being told everything.'

Ratio City has a formidable competitor: Esri, an international firm that virtually invented spatial analytics and the wide array of geographical information systems (GIS) mapping software tools employed by planners working for governments, large corporations, and entities like busy container ports.[7] The company – which is based outside Redlands, California, and has offices around the world – describes its service as 'the science of where.' Its website even contains a gallery of 'maps we love.'

Founded in the U.S. in 1969 by Jack and Laura Dangermond, Esri is one of those rare tech companies to have successfully navigated the rapids and shoals of the computer industry. 'Esri is now being used by some 350,000 businesses, government agencies and NGOs around the world who collectively create some 150 million new maps every day,' according to a 2015 profile in *Forbes* magazine. 'Over the years, the company embraced computer workstations, PCs, servers, the Web and mobile devices. As it surfed wave after technological wave, Esri also managed to defy predictions that it would be crushed by Google, whose multi-billion dollar investments in "geo" technology made it synonymous with digital mapping.'

Since the early 2000s, the company has effectively locked up the Canadian public sector market for GIS software, which is used for all sorts of applications, from emergency management to mapping municipal infrastructure and, during the COVID-19 pandemic, mapping the trajectory of the outbreak and then vaccinations. Another example: online interactive mapping tools that show the locations and dates of pedestrian and cyclist fatalities and injuries over time, and that can be used to support traffic safety improvements, such as calming, speed reductions, or the installation of bike lanes. The idea is that this kind of time-series data should not only inform decision-making, but also make it possible to determine whether the actions taken have produced a benefit in terms of road safety.

As a 2021 City of Toronto staff report noted in its recommendation to extend the company's licence, 'Esri software is used extensively

---

7. Originally·conceptualized by Ottawa geographer Roger Tomlinson, GIS are densely layered digital maps that contain a wide range of information associated with a particular place – natural features, buildings, boundaries, infrastructure, businesses, land-use and zoning rules, census data, aerial photos, pollution sources, etc.

across the City for business support and service delivery. Other vendors in the market do not have the same software service offerings that meet the scale and complexity of the City's use' (City of Toronto 2021).

The software developed by Esri and Ratio City can be described as 'smart' in the sense that these companies – and others like them – have devised innovative ways to compile and visualize technical data so it can be used to support policy or operational decisions that run the gamut from land-use planning to public health.

These kinds of analytical tools have become essential for cities seeking to deal with the fallout of other digital technologies that have severely disrupted city planning.

The case of Airbnb offers a vivid illustration. Originally conceived as a convenient app that would provide travellers with a broader array of accommodation choices, the evolution of Airbnb – and its imitators – revealed the staggeringly disruptive power of the digital platform economy. At its pre-pandemic peak, Airbnb was driving developers' marketing plans, stoking the financialization of the global housing market, accelerating gentrification, and distorting, in some cases, local retail scenes in 'authentic' neighbourhoods that had become destination hot spots – a dynamic stoked by social media and amplified by the viral spread of traveller selfies. The traffic incentivized merchants, landlords, and retailers to reorient themselves to tourists with money to spend, thereby pricing out their traditional customers.

In some destination cities, like Barcelona, municipal officials banned or severely limited Airbnb because it was destabilizing older working-class neighbourhoods. In other places, such as Toronto, city officials were forced to respond to the rise of the so-called 'ghost hotel' – apartment buildings overrun by units purchased for short-term rentals, some of which served as party palaces. Before Covid struck, the platform's popularity also ratcheted up rents as condo owners and landlords discovered they could earn more in a month with short-term stays than from leases signed with long-term tenants.

With municipalities struggling to get ahead of these market distortions, Esri has promoted its 3-D mapping tools to visualize how changes in short-term rental rules and zoning could impact affordability. In a 2019 blog post, the company demonstrated how its platform could generate graphics depicting how these regulatory changes could impact development in Honolulu, a city that was struggling to figure out how to protect housing affordability given the runaway popularity of short-term rentals. The post explained,

> According to a 2015 report, 66,000 housing units will be needed in Hawaii by 2025 to meet demand, with nearly 26,000 of those dwellings required in Honolulu. A number of proposed zoning changes aim to address this looming housing deficit. [These] include restrictions on the square footage of residential units to combat monster homes; an easing of height restrictions on low-rise apartments to allow five-story walk-ups rather than the existing three-story limits; and a proposal allowing home owners to build and rent accessory dwelling units.

Interestingly, Esri is working both sides of the short-term rental street; the company also promotes another of its software products, ArcGIS, to investors looking to purchase Airbnb apartments in optimal locations. As it explains in a 2020 'storymap' posted on its website, the company scoped out a potential strategy that someone with $1 million to invest might undertake with its software. Using Yelp data on restaurants, GIS information on proximity to desirable neighbourhoods, and rental rate data from a website called Inside Airbnb, Esri's software could direct clients to optimal locations in San Diego, which, it noted, was 'the most profitable city for 2-bedroom listings.'

The short-term rental sector is just one of the balls that city planners must now juggle as they seek to manage the so-called 'wicked problems' of twenty-first-century urban regions. Migration and the provision of affordable housing are dramatically out of sync. Sprawl and sprawl-fuelled congestion drive up both the cost of living (due to driving expenses for homeowners) and municipal services while pumping carbon into the atmosphere. Yet the moral imperative to confront climate change using planning tools such as intensification and green building techniques is easier said than done, and meets resistance in multiple forms.

Orbiting all these more policy-oriented matters are tenacious questions about uprooting the income inequality and racism that became so embedded in municipal governance; intense debates over the importance of architecture, urban design, and green space in civic life; and deeply conflicting views on how to accommodate children and seniors in a bustling metropolis. In the 1960s, Henri Lefebvre, the radical urban philosopher, asked: Who has a right to the city? We must also ask: Who plans? Who governs? And what constitutes sustainable, equitable planning in a complex urban world that's constantly being redefined by capital, migration, and climate change?

These are the problems that pile up relentlessly on the desks of city planners.

Even before the advent of state-of-the-art mapping software, municipal planners had to synthesize all sorts of information: census data, maps, surveys, real estate values, statistics on communicable diseases, and so on. Transportation planners conducted traffic counts or built statistical models predicting road usage. Transit authorities used data such as labour market statistics as well as economic models to test the relationship between fares and ridership rates to make decisions about new routes and frequency of service, among others. According to MIT science and technology historian Jennifer S. Light, planners learned how to combine census and household survey data with aerial photography and military satellite sensing to map growth, housing conditions, and urban 'blight.'

Beginning in the 1960s, municipalities began investing in costly mainframe computer systems to perform tasks like monitoring traffic. By the mid-1970s, Light wrote in her 2003 book, *From Warfare to Welfare: Defense Intellectuals and Urban Problems in Cold War America*, analysts working for the City of Los Angeles were developing mathematical models that combined information from databases of digitized aerial images, census statistics, and building inspection reports to make predictions about future housing development scenarios – a precursor of today's smart city analytics.

Cities gradually started adding more devices or systems capable of providing a wider array of real-time data, including automatic licence plate readers, closed-circuit TVs, and intelligent transportation systems (ITS) that could automatically adjust traffic lights depending on the volume of traffic sensed by electronic loops, or sensors, in the pavement. Local utilities added electronic energy meters. Transit agencies adopted smart cards instead of tickets and tokens. These devices were generating rivers of data.

In 2010, following a devastating landslide that left hundreds dead and thousands homeless, municipal officials in Rio de Janeiro realized they'd have to be better prepared for intensely disruptive events in anticipation of the 2014 World Cup and the 2016 summer Olympics. As the Center for Public Impact (CPI), a think tank supported by the Boston Consulting Group's foundation, noted, the transit system barely worked, violence was rampant, and the tens of thousands of poor residents living in the favelas perched on the slopes of the steep hills surrounding Rio were particularly exposed to natural calamities, especially landslides. Citing the leadership of then mayor Eduardo Paes, CPI explained, 'The city needed an initiative which would help it bring together information concerning the environment, transport, crime and medical services to establish a sense of coordination and control.' In short, an operations centre.

A *New York Times* correspondent visited the newly built hub in 2012 and sent back an admiring dispatch on the eve of Carnaval. 'City employees in white jumpsuits work quietly in front of a giant wall of screens – a sort of virtual Rio, rendered in real time,' Natasha Singer wrote. 'Video streams in from subway stations and major intersections. A sophisticated weather program predicts rainfall across the city. A map glows with the locations of car accidents, power failures and other problems.'

The facility had been constructed by IBM at Paes's request and was touted as a game changer for complex cities like Rio. 'There is nothing quite like it in the world's other major cities,' Singer noted. 'I.B.M. has created similar data centers elsewhere for single agencies like police departments. But never before has it built a citywide system integrating data from some 30 agencies, all under a single roof.' The technology, she added, would dismantle the silos between municipal departments because the operations centres' analysts could use all sorts of software tools to combine real-time data about the city and even predict how development patterns might influence future disasters. As Paes told the *Times*, the act of combining data would help the whole city.

But there was another more corporate objective at play, one that anticipated, by about five years, the goals that Sidewalk Labs had when it launched its ill-fated Toronto smart city venture. IBM was positioning the Rio project as a kind of calling card, a highly integrated and presumably costly investment that could benefit other cities looking to make themselves smarter. The market opportunity seemed huge and had become an integral part of IBM's strategy to boost global revenues to US$150 billion.

Rio's operations centre caught the eye of Rob Kitchin, a professor of geography at the National University of Ireland, Maynooth, who quoted it in a widely cited study entitled 'The real time city? Big Data and smart urbanism.' Kitchin,[8] who has become one of the world's leading authorities on smart cities, noted that similar hubs had cropped up in New York, Dublin, and London, which had created a dashboard. The dashboard, he explains, is a data visualization tool that 'tracks the performance of the city with respect to twelve key areas – jobs and economy, transport, environment, policing and crime, fire and rescue, communities, housing, health, and tourism.' Unlike Rio's facility, the dashboard data isn't updated in real time.

Kitchin pointed out that the network of operations centres, apps, and dashboards can be regarded as a new species of urban information-gathering system in that they collectively 'provide a powerful means for making sense of, managing and living in the city

---

8. Kitchin maintains a clearing house of scholarship on smart cities, available here: https://progcity.maynoothuniversity.ie/2022/01/smart-city-cases-reading-lists

in the here-and-now, and for envisioning and predicting future scenarios.' The benefit for municipal planners in particular is that these technologies enabled evidence-based decision-making. 'Rather than basing decisions on anecdote or intuition or clientelist politics or periodic/partial evidence,' he observed, 'it is possible to assess what is happening at any one time and to react and plan accordingly.'

There is some truth to this conceptualization of the utility of real-time municipal data for planning purposes. For example, when city officials can track cycling activity using apps installed on cyclists' smart phones, they can 'see' where bike lanes are used and needed. Similarly, if transportation or transit planners can track daily traffic or ridership volumes over an extended period, using data from cell-phone signals or tap-on/tap-off fare cards, they can add service or identify areas experiencing increases in work-related car trips. Such insights could lead to planning that informs infrastructure and private investment, as well as choices about programming public spaces.

Nor are planners relying solely on municipally generated data and analytics. Numerous planning apps have also emerged, such as Walk Score, which rates neighbourhood walkability in cities around the world. The website Inside Airbnb 'scrapes' address, rate, and other host details from Airbnb's main site, cross-references this information with housing and rental market data, and then maps it all. The site was created by a handful of New York City affordable housing activists. Visitors can see the density and locations of Airbnb units in any given neighbourhood in any city. The site, in effect, is a data visualization tool that gives planners and residents valuable housing market information (and policy insights) into phenomena such as condo towers that have become overrun by short-term rental investors and ghost hotel operators.

Advances in computing power and coding tools, as well as the long-anticipated maturation of artificial intelligence, are creating entirely new ways of leveraging data in order to observe what's happening in a city. For example, the City of Stockholm, through a research partnership with MIT and Sweden's KTH Royal Institute of Technology, has set up a project to install solar-powered sensors on buses, garbage trucks, and taxis to gather data on noise, air, and road quality. 'Building an opportunistic sensing platform that can be deployed and configured on-demand,' the investigators say, 'we provide cities with denser spatiotemporal data about the urban environment, enabling decision-making and fostering public engagement on environmental issues.'

Some of the most compelling case studies in the use of data for planning involve the combination of new forms of technology and non-digital ways of thinking about the quality of urban spaces.

In the early 1960s, Danish architect and planner Jan Gehl began meticulously documenting pedestrian activity in a new car-free zone in central Copenhagen to prove to area merchants that they weren't going to lose business. Carried out by volunteers, Gehl's 'public life surveys' tracked pedestrian and cyclist activity, bench usage, sidewalk café seating, and so on, with the results painting a picture of how and when people used their streets. Those surveys were carried out by volunteers, not machines, and thus were grounded in subjective observations about the rhythms of city life.

In the late 2000s, New York City hired Gehl to conduct similar surveys and analysis on Times Square and several of Broadway's skewed intersections. The street-life surveys revealed a conspicuous dearth of younger and older pedestrians – a detail non-video sensors wouldn't pick up – while an analysis of the chronically congested intersection showed the road allowance occupied almost 90 per cent of all the open space in the Square.

In 2008, NYC's transportation commissioner, Janette Sadik-Khan, used Gehl's findings to order a radical remake of Times Square, closing large segments of the road and creating public spaces fitted out with tables and chairs. The model has been replicated elsewhere in the city, reclaiming hundreds of thousands of square feet of space in Manhattan from traffic.

In Toronto, the King Street Transit Pilot Project, which launched in 2017, offered a similarly compelling example of how city officials succeeded in integrating technology and planning judgment to improve public services and public space. In 2015, the city set up a big data innovation team to tease out insights from information generated by electronic traffic counters, cycling apps, vehicle detectors, and other sources that produced continuous flows of digitized transportation information.

The plan envisioned significantly restricted private vehicle use on King Street, a downtown arterial, in order to improve streetcar service. The city's data analysts used low-resolution cameras installed in traffic signal controllers at intersections to monitor pedestrian and vehicle volumes, and then drew on anonymized Bluetooth signals from smart phones to calculate how much time riders spent on streetcars traversing the area. Project officials also tracked daily revenues through point-of-sale payment devices to assess how declines in vehicle traffic impacted King Street businesses.

The city published a monthly dashboard of key metrics to demonstrate changes in travel times, cyclist and pedestrian activity, and commerce. Restaurants, in turn, were allowed to build partially enclosed patios extending into the street – a move that laid the groundwork for the city's CaféTO pandemic program, which allowed scores of eateries to expand into cordoned-off street-parking spaces.

The metrics affirmed the experiences of commuters, residents, and local businesses: that streetcars were moving faster, pedestrian and cycling activity was up, and merchants hadn't seen the drop in business some had feared. In 2019, council voted to make King's transit priority corridor permanent.

As with downtown Copenhagen and Times Square, the King Street project illustrated how planners and analytics experts can make innovative uses of granular urban data in order to deliver city-building goals, and that it is possible to do so without compromising privacy or directing scarce funds to expensive smart city tech firms.

Over the course of the decade separating Rio's decision to install its cutting-edge operations centre and Sidewalk Labs' decision to abandon its Toronto venture, the narrative about the novel uses of digitized urban data changed. Increasingly, it seemed as if the technology tail was wagging the planning dog.

In some cases, smart city solutions to planning problems have been dramatically oversold, both by municipal officials and tech giants. In 2012, Eduardo Paes told the *New York Times*, 'We want to put Rio ahead of every city in the world concerning operations of daily life and emergency response.' Rio did manage to deliver both the World Cup and the Olympics, but IBM's much-touted operations centre did not lead to reductions in crime, poverty, police violence, or income inequality, according to a Rio-based watchdog group set up to monitor social conditions in advance of the 2016 games.

In other places, the tech solutions just seem somewhat far-fetched. The party district of downtown Eindhoven, a tech hub of 220,000 people in southeastern Netherlands near the German border, is a case in point. The area, a pedestrian-only street known as the Stratumseind, is about 225 metres long, 15 metres wide, and crammed with bars. On some nights, as many as 15,000 people will stream into this strip, and fights often break out. Rising violence was becoming a significant public safety issue.

In 2015, Tinus Kanter, an Eindhoven municipal official, began working on a smart city solution to the safety issues on that stretch. In partnership with Stratumseind businesses, police, and the lighting giant Philips, which is headquartered in Eindhoven, the city transformed the stretch into a 'living lab' with a range of technologies designed to drain some of the negative energy out of Saturday-night revelries.

Video cameras were installed at each end to track how many people were entering or leaving the area, without capturing facial images. The project team then developed and installed a series of audio sensors programmed to detect aggressive sounds, while an off-site AI algorithm scanned and interpreted social media for posts that mentioned Stratumseind or contained geotagged images of the strip. Software devised by the city and its tech partners combines these data streams and sends red flags when trouble is detected, including to the police. Depending on the signals received about the crowd's behaviour, lighting provided by the company shifts to softer hues when things get ugly.

Kanter comes by his interest in crowd control honestly: before joining the civil service, he ran a heavy-metal music festival. He stresses that the city insisted on 'privacy by design,' so the systems do not capture personal information. The municipality also took more conventional steps, adding planters, terraces, and seating to break up the space. 'What I see now is that the street is becoming nicer and more open,' says Kanter, who adds that Eindhoven has been carefully tracking project data. 'We think that gathering numbers is a good thing because [they] provide scientific proof.'

However, what the data shows in terms of safety isn't especially clear. Kanter insists there's less fighting, although he can't prove the lighting and the sensors are the reason. Albert Meijer, a University of Utrecht professor of public innovation who has studied Stratumseind, says the technology alone didn't markedly improve safety. What did change, he adds, is that media coverage of the area shifted from focusing on the brawling to focusing on the devices, which, in turn, has attracted municipal delegations from around the world, and which may have been the point all along. 'Philips,' he says, 'wanted to show its new street lighting to sell around the world.'

Other municipalities and smart tech firms have gone even further with the use of external sources of social media data and analytics. An Israeli company called Zencity, for example, developed a software-based smart city service using AI. Their platform gathers and assesses citizen feedback on local planning matters – a process it calls 'sentiment analysis.' The feedback comes from online surveys as well as social media chatter, tourist ratings, complaints to the municipal 311 lines, etc. 'It's representing the voices of the silent majority,' says former Zencity manager Nir Zernyak. The company presents its system as a decision-making tool for municipal politicians and officials.

Zernyak cites an Oregon example. Beaverton, a suburb of Portland, has attempted to ban so-called 'car camping' by setting up two 'safe parking' locations for homeless people who live in their cars. The city or partner agencies help the users to access social services. In its marketing materials, Zencity claims its 'actionable, data-based insights' revealed that Beaverton may have to change its zoning rules to allow for these sites and that not all neighbourhoods wanted one – conclusions that may not have required this kind of outsourced data-crunching.

Perhaps the most contentious source of new urban data comes from sensors designed to monitor and manage the use of public spaces. Often, these types of applications seem benign. In New South Wales, for example, Street Furniture Australia, an industry group, recruited academic planners and landscape architects to evaluate street furniture fitted out with wirelessly connected sensors that perform tasks such as monitoring when a trash can needs to be emptied or how park benches are used. Other applications included park-based workstations equipped with wifi and USB ports, as well as tables that can be booked in advance via a smart phone app.

The data generated from these 'smart social spaces' is aggregated on a 'smart asset management dashboard' that municipal officials use to monitor how these hubs are used. The idea behind the pilot, explains Nancy Marshall, a University of Sydney planning professor who is part of the evaluation team, is to find ways to encourage people to use public spaces, but the group also wants to conduct 'behaviour mapping.' She says none of the sensors gather personal information.

How this intel gets used is an open question. Information that flows from park bench or picnic table sensors could prompt planners to add amenities if heavy traffic is indicated. But it's not difficult to imagine less positive applications. For example, if the data shows a lot of late-night traffic, local residents worried about crime might use the information as extra fodder for municipal officials to remove benches, or tips for police to increase patrols. Marshall stresses that the data from the pilot projects isn't shared with NSW law enforcement officials, but such assurances hardly guarantee that the municipalities that eventually purchase these systems will be as restrained.

New York University planning and urban analytics expert Constantine Kontokosta offers another caution. Trash bin sensors designed to monitor when a container needs emptying could, in theory, provide data that allows city officials to apply algorithms to optimize collection routes, by using GPS mapping tools to direct trucks only to full bins, thus saving money on fuel and labour.

But in a 2018 paper in the *Journal of Planning Education and Research*, Kontokosta writes that such analysis might come into conflict with other municipal goals and practices, such as the need to abide by collective agreement rules. 'The computing challenges are solvable,' he notes. '[T]he real uncertainty lies with how to integrate data-driven processes into public sector management.'

4
Smart Cities, Big Data, and a Question of Trust

In January 2019, the Toronto Region Board of Trade floated a trial balloon in an attempt to defuse the controversy that had swirled for a year and a half around Sidewalk Labs' closely watched plans for Quayside, a twelve-acre brownfield site on the city's waterfront.

Google/Alphabet's smart city plan turned on fitting out the entire project, which would include numerous new buildings and public spaces, with thousands of sensors designed to gather massive quantities of data from a heavily wired neighbourhood. That information would then be sliced and diced in all sorts of ways, from specific energy and infrastructure operations to more open-ended applications, such as the management of public spaces.

The company had also promised that independent firms, including start-ups, could have open access to the raw data and use it to manage services and develop apps that could eventually be scaled up and deployed in other cities. Sidewalk Labs called this approach to digital city-building its 'platform' strategy – a business model not unlike Apple's app store, and more than a little open-ended.

Activists and pundits had attacked Sidewalk's proposal, zeroing in on a few fundamental questions: Who would own all that data? How was it to be used? Could Sidewalk's sensors somehow identify individuals and target them for ads ... or worse? Who would profit? And, finally, were Canada's privacy laws adequate for regulating the collection of all this urban information?

During a period when the manipulation or outright misuse of individual data by tech giants like Google and Facebook had provoked a 'tech-lash,' it seemed clear that Sidewalk's pitch would live or die based on how the company's planners addressed these core issues.

The Board of Trade's solution, dubbed BiblioTech, seemed beguilingly elegant and politically benign: entrust all that data to the Toronto Public Library, a well-loved local institution that happens to specialize in managing information. This 'data hub,' according to the board's recommendations, would be overseen by the Information and Privacy Commissioner of Ontario, with the library in charge of developing policies for data collection and use.

Similar but subtly different 'data governance' proposals had also surfaced – among them a pitch from provincially owned tech incubator MARS for a 'civic data trust,' defined as 'a trust that is established to manage the digital layer of a smart city.' According to MARS, this new trust's assets 'may include the physical infrastructure (sensors and data warehouses), code base (database, standards, processing structures, and interface) and data that make up the digital layer. The civic digital trust may also manage financial assets to ensure the sustainable operation of the trust.'

With Sidewalk's plans coming under intense scrutiny from critics who were skeptical about the company's data strategy and its ulterior motives, it was not surprising that the company's local supporters were talking about libraries and trusts.

Data is both the opportunity and the flashpoint in most conversations about smart city technology. Smart city hardware and software effectively soak up all sorts of data and transform it into intelligence that can, in theory, improve urban infrastructure, create new services, or add efficiencies to existing ones. Indeed, the promise of smart cities involves capturing very large tranches of so-called fast data and then applying sophisticated analytics to detect patterns or generate predictions. These findings can be used to make cities more livable or sustainable. That, in any event, is the vision.

As the global tech sector well knows, data has enormous monetary value, especially in large batches – the new oil, as the cliché goes. As importantly, data is the not-so-natural resource that is fuelling the development of lucrative artificial intelligence–based technologies. These run the gamut from voice-recognition algorithms and online language translation services to much more ambitious systems that can generate fine-grain recommendations about optimizing urban transportation networks or deploying police officers so they're working in the areas most likely to experience crime. The development of algorithms that feed off urban data figured prominently in Sidewalk Labs' plans. 'The algorithm is where the value is,' observes Natasha Tusikov, an assistant professor at York University who studies smart cities and data governance.

According to Kurtis McBride, CEO of Miovision, a Waterloo smart traffic signal firm, Canadian policy makers have yet to wake up to an economic reality that global tech giants like Google understand. By the 2030s, he predicts, most urban infrastructure will be fitted out with technology that generates data with significant commercial value. Either private firms will own and profit from it, or the value in those pools of urban data can be used to advance the public good, he says. 'You have a decision about what kind of future you want.' Government officials, McBride continues, 'aren't thinking about this.'

What further complicates the discourse about data is that the term itself is not only exceptionally broad – akin to talking about 'mammals' or 'transportation' – but also somewhat nebulous. Data covers everything from databases of building inspection records, recreation program registrations, and census track statistics to signals generated continuously by traffic monitors, smart phones, and GPS devices.

According to scholar Rob Kitchin, author of *Data Lives: How Data Are Made and Shape Our World* (2021), smart city data is fundamentally different in character from older forms of static information that were commonly used for city-planning purposes. He noted in a 2016 article,

Such data [included] censuses, household, transport, environment and mapping surveys, and commissioned interviews and focus groups, complemented with various forms of public administration records. In general, this data is analysed at the aggregate level and provides snapshots of cities at particular moments. Increasingly, these datasets are being supplemented with new forms of urban big data.

Big data has fundamentally different properties from traditional datasets, being generated and processed in real-time, exhaustive in scope and having a fine resolution. Rather than data being derived from a travel survey with a handful of city dwellers during a specific time period, transport big data consists of a continual survey of every traveller: for example, collecting all the tap-ins and tapouts of Oyster cards on the London Underground, or using automatic number plate recognition-enabled cameras to track all vehicles.

This transformation from slow and sampled data to fast and exhaustive data has been enabled by the roll-out of a raft of new networked, digital technologies embedded into the fabric of urban environments that underpin the drive to create so-called smart cities. (Kitchin 2016)

The idea, as Kitchin has explained, is that the city as a physical space is discernible on a continuous basis using various sensing and surveillance technologies, including devices – like smart phones – that leave a trail of data on someone's movements and that can then be used to support urban systems. 'The instrumented city,' as he puts it, 'offers the promise of an objectively measured, real time analysis of urban life and infrastructure.'

In some cities, raw, real-time information from big data streams – e.g., from air quality monitors, traffic sensors, wastewater flow rates – is gathered and marshalled, with the resulting 'informatics' pressed into service to describe quantitatively what's going on in the city at any point in time.

Municipal officials use this kind of data, and the practice has raised questions about the technocratic nature of smart city information gathering. 'Such instrumentation of the urban environment, however, is not by itself sufficient to have a meaningful impact on the quality, sustainability, and resilience of cities – or more broadly on urban policy and planning,' Constantine Kontokosta, the NYU informatics scholar, observed in a 2016 paper. 'Understanding the social, economic, and cultural dynamics of urban life requires both an appreciation of the social sciences and a substantive engagement with communities across diverse neighborhoods' (67–84).

The installation of smart city sensors, in turn, can create information that didn't exist in the (unmonitored) past. 'The whole idea of the smart city is that every interface is a data collection space,' says Anna Artyushina, a York University PhD candidate who specializes in data governance for smart cities, in an interview.

Case in point: sensors designed to detect if a parking spot is occupied or empty at any particular point in time. If there's no monitoring device, the spot's status – taken/vacant – is knowable only to someone who happens to be passing by. But what if there's a connected digital system that registers the spot's status in real time and makes this information available to transportation officials or anyone with an app? The resulting data could be used to alter parking rules – maybe the spot is always vacant and could be used for some other purpose? – or even generate revenue: after all, if you need to park, you may be willing to pay to find a location.

We already live in a world that's programmed to track our movements, our consumer habits, our online behaviour, and our digital interactions, thanks to smart phones, apps, Google searches, social media platforms, and security devices in private spaces like malls and office buildings. Personal data is harvested, aggregated, analyzed, and then sold or shared, often without our knowledge or explicit consent.

Nor can data be considered neutral or apolitical. With the growing deployment of smart city technology, scholars and critics have raised important questions about the values or biases embedded in seemingly objective information. As Kitchin points out, 'Data do not exist independently of the ideas, techniques, technologies, people and contexts' that produce and use them in urban settings.

For those reasons, the management of personal and operational data gathered by smart city systems in public spaces (streets, parks, etc.) has become a hot-button topic, and rightly so.

Data and Privacy

Many critics of the Sidewalk plan for Toronto expressed grave concerns about privacy. Could sensors identify individuals who just happened to be on the street, or in a park, for example? There were also privacy questions about other types of systems, such as smart condo buildings that continuously collect energy consumption readings from individual apartments. Could that data be used to make inferences about the occupants' habits? While Sidewalk initially retained former Ontario privacy commissioner Ann Cavoukian to evaluate its plans using a 'privacy by design' approach, she eventually resigned, citing concerns that Sidewalk would not live up to its pledges.

In most big cities and especially in high-traffic core areas, public spaces have long been monitored by public and private CCTVs. In China, the government has installed widespread surveillance networks that extend from smart phones to the widespread use of facial recognition systems and, with the pandemic, location-based tracking apps. As the *New York Times* noted, 'officials in some places are loading their apps with new features hoping the software will live on as more than just an emergency measure.'

At the other end of the spectrum is the European Union's General Data Protection Regulation (GDPR), which is considered to be the world's 'strictest' privacy legislation, according to Anna Artyushina. California legislated a comparably strict consumer privacy framework that went into effect in early 2020, and the GDPR has influenced privacy reforms in other countries, including Canada. While the GDPR has broad applications in the private sphere (e.g., the law regulates the use of cookies and establishes the legal right for individuals to 'be forgotten'), its core principles are also highly relevant for smart city applications.

Traditionally, privacy laws were constructed around the principle of consent, which means that entities collecting information on individuals had to obtain their agreement – a cumbersome process that involved the kinds of legal language found in the fine print of many forms of software.

Some of the most progressive versions of privacy law have rejected the consent approach and instead pursued a different way of framing legal privacy. According to an analysis by Artyushina published in 2020, the GDPR is centred on four pillars of data protection: purpose specification, data minimization, automated decisions, and special categories. As she writes,

> The requirement of purpose specification states that personal data must be collected for a 'specific, explicit, and legitimate' purpose and cannot be further 'processed' in a way which is 'incompatible' with the original purpose. Data minimization means keeping data collection to the bare minimum required for data collectors' operations. The notion of automated decisions grants European citizens the right to opt out of automated decision-making. The provision on special categories prohibits companies from gathering and processing data 'revealing racial or ethnic origin, political opinions, religious or philosophical beliefs, trade union membership, and the processing of data concerning health or sex life.' Additionally, the GDPR makes it a data subject's right to transfer their information to another service provider or to require the data controller to delete certain information about them.

Outside the EU, some cities have adopted similar principles in their smart city strategies. The City of Boston, for example, says it 'collect[s] as little data as possible to solve a particular problem' and has solicited privacy advice from the American Civil Liberties Association.

Aspects of the GDPR can be found in Canada's privacy legislation, including some recent amendments to national privacy laws (provincial governments also enact privacy laws that apply to municipalities). 'However,' Artyushina notes, 'the Facebook/Cambridge Analytica scandal in 2018 demonstrated that the country's privacy protection laws may be ill-equipped to deal with technology companies.' York's Natasha Tusikov adds that Sidewalk Labs' plans for collecting what it called 'urban data' – i.e. all the various types of information gathered by sensors installed in public spaces and the buildings within the Quayside areas and then used to operate infrastructure or services – exposed a gaping hole in Canada's privacy laws.

Data Bias

The best-known and best-publicized instances of data bias involve facial recognition apps. Because of the way the algorithms were developed, facial recognition systems were more likely to fail when asked to identify Black or Asian faces. The reason? The systems were 'trained' to make matches by using huge collections of images of faces that were predominantly white – an example of what's known as 'algorithmic bias.'

But data bias manifests itself in more subtle ways, too, and even within urban systems that aren't normally considered to be political. For example, when cities across North America began setting up 311 call centres, they weren't positioned as smart city systems. Rather, proponents saw 311 as a means of improving both citizen engagement and bureaucratic accountability. Over the years, 311 services have become increasingly tech-enabled, with social media accounts, apps, and the release of machine-readable complaint-tracking records through open data portals.

Municipalities now sit on huge troves of 311 call data – hundreds of thousands or even millions of requests per year – that can be mined and analyzed, and then used to inform municipal planning and budgeting. After all, a proliferation of calls about basement floods, missed garbage pickups, or dubious odours from a nearby factory can give officials important clues about what's happening in a neighbourhood, as well as the performance of city departments. If scanned carefully for longer-term patterns, 311 calls may also offer predictions about future problems.

These call records certainly qualify as 'big data.' But the ways in which this information is or can be used also offers important lessons, both positive and negative, about applications for other large urban data sets that might be generated by smart city technologies, sensors, and other systems.

One obvious question: How do municipal agencies make decisions on how or when to respond to residents' requests for service? Researchers who study 311 data have found that with many municipalities, such decisions tend to be made in a black box, with little transparency (e.g., first come first served, a triage system, etc.).

These data sets also contain important patterns that could assist in making service delivery either more efficient or more equitable (which aren't necessarily the same thing). The wrinkle is that cities need to understand the conditions that motivate residents to call 311. 'We know that people don't complain at the same rate,' says Constantine Kontokosta. '[A]n individual accustomed to seeing rodents in their building may be less likely to complain than someone seeing a rodent in their apartment for the first time. In addition, individuals may have different levels of trust in government, differing expectations that the government will actually respond, and socio-cultural traits that make them more or less likely to report a problem.'

Another pattern, noted by a New York State Health Foundation/ Harvard research team in a 2020 study, found that spikes in calls about a particular problem may actually be orchestrated community campaigns meant to force municipal officials to address an issue. The study described the practice as a 'misuse' that could lead city officials to 'erroneously' conclude that an area was seeing some kind of decline.

A further evaluation, published by Kontokosta in 2017, looked at complaints by New Yorkers about hot water problems in their buildings. 'We wanted to assess where bias was occurring, and to what extent,' he says. Drawing on 311 data, inspection reports, census tract information, and other records, the study found that neighbourhoods with high rents, higher incomes, better educated residents, and larger non-Hispanic white populations 'tend to over-report.' 'Based on these results, we find that socioeconomic status, householder characteristics and language proficiency have a non-trivial effect on the propensity to use 311 across the city.'

Still other analysts have mined 311 data sets to show how they correlate to broader trends, such as the spread of urban blight. Those patterns, according to a 2016 analysis by NYU and the Center for Urban Science and Progress, could theoretically be used to predict future real estate prices.

For planners, mining 311 call records holds out the potential to forecast service demand and also correct for biases that might lead city officials to be more attentive to complaints from more affluent or vocal communities. In 2017, a team of geographers and artificial intelligence scholars at the University of Illinois Urbana-Champaign used six years of Chicago 311 sanitation service requests (e.g., overflowing garbage cans) to develop what they said was the first algorithm capable of generating accurate predictions to help guide decisions about scheduling and routes.

Yet Kontokosta, in a 2018 study on biases in Kansas City's 311 service entitled 'Who Calls for Help?,' offers up a caution, given findings that some individuals and communities – women, middle-income families, homeowners parents whose kids attend private schools, households with internet access – were far more likely to call 311 than other demographic groups, as was the case in New York. 'As such, training predictive city service delivery models on these data would lead to an inequitable distribution of service provision, leading to over-allocation of resources to households and neighborhoods that are more likely to report problems' (Kontokosta & Hong 2018).

Open Data

Since the early 2010s, most city governments have taken to routinely releasing certain types of municipal information through open data portals – websites that allow users to download, for free, 'machine readable' databases (i.e., formatted so they can be queried with readily available software) that municipal officials have made public. The information ranges from registered pet names to air quality readings, overnight shelter usage, and the locations of urban objects, from signals and crosswalks to park benches. New York City's huge open data portal even includes a Central Park squirrel census. These data sets are updated regularly. The contents are subject to privacy laws to ensure that no personally identifiable information is released.

Early on, the open data movement was regarded as a cause célèbre among digital open government advocates, who saw it as a way of unlocking public information tucked away in municipal servers and protected by bureaucracies. Cities hosted hack-a-thons for coders and app developers who would figure out how to use this treasure trove of data and create digital services for city dwellers. Some local governments made it a practice to aggressively release new data sets (New York City passed a law in 2012 mandating the disclosure of all municipal data from all departments by 2018) while others did it grudgingly or with little enthusiasm.

Some applications bobbed to the surface – e.g., a transit route app that maps the real-time movement of transit vehicles and can inform users when the next one will arrive. In other cases, the municipal data became the foundation of business ventures. Activists have marshalled large sets of data, often presented in visualizations, to advocate for non-commercial goals ranging from public space improvements to changes in police check practices.

Among the early users of open data portals, in fact, were municipal officials, who could finally gain access to operationally relevant but previously inaccessible information from other departments. For instance, databases of records of citizen complaints coming in to 311 call centres have been used to make service improvements, while data on taxi movements is used to assist in transportation planning.

In recent years, London, New York, and other cities have begun retooling their open data strategies to respond more quickly to requests and allow for the release of streams of live data.

Some players, in turn, have begun to ponder the monetary value of all this publicly generated information and whether municipalities should be giving it away. Miovision's Kurtis McBride says that companies like his use public data streams – e.g, traffic counts – and transform them into a profitable business model. 'The more data I have, the more the data is worth,' he said last year during a public consultation session entitled 'Realizing the Value of Data.' 'The public sector needs to think about whether open data is a lost opportunity.'

Municipal Dashboards

Since they first began to appear in the late 2000s, urban 'dashboards' have become not just de rigueur for cities aiming to position themselves as smart and evidence-driven but also, in the words of one analyst, 'an object of desire' for municipal politicians. On their face, city dashboards serve up a buffet of indicators about all aspects of urban life, from traffic and jobs to investment, housing, safety, and so on. The data on dashboards appears to be constantly updated, and drawn from sources like development applications, economic indicators, crime stats, and even through water bills or transit fares.[9]

While dashboards are publicly accessible and thus available to anyone, the users tend to be civil servants, local politicians, media,

---

9. Toronto's Dashboard, which lives on the City of Toronto website, displays data on sixty-five key performance indicators in six categories: community vulnerability, crime, development and construction, economy, revenue, and services. Each KPI is shown in its own colour-coded box – red, yellow, and green – with the latest year-to-date information, an arrow indicating the trend line, and the percentage change from the previous year. Users can also click on individual boxes to get even more granular information, such as historic data, charts, and explanatory notes.

businesses looking to invest in a city, and other specialized audiences. Produced typically by outside consultants working with teams of municipal officials, dashboards can be seen to contribute to a city's public image in the way that international city rankings do – a quantifiable and apparently objective snapshot of a particular city at a moment in time, the perfect tool in a world where the phrase 'evidence-based decision-making' has become an indispensable disclaimer for a wide range of political choices.

Yet in a 2021 essay in *New Media & Society*, Jathan Sadowski, a Melbourne-based social scientist who studies smart urbanism at Monash University, exposed the backstory of one Australian city dashboard and found it to contain a lot more political messaging and image-making than met the eye.

Sadowski had spent two years working on a revised dashboard for Parramatta, a booming suburb of Sydney that wanted to promote itself as a smart city. The old dashboard, he explained, had 'been left to die.'

Its primary purpose, Sadowski soon discovered, was to provide the city's chief executive officer with ammunition for holding lower-level managers to account. 'People resented being browbeaten with KPIS,' he noted. 'Thus, by extension, their ire was directed at the corporate dashboard; it became a despised tool of control.' A new CEO eventually took over and didn't care about the dashboard's KPIS, which meant the lower-level managers in charge of providing the data simply stopped updating it.

Parramatta officials decided to start from scratch and assembled a working committee of local politicians, municipal managers, and data visualization consultants. A mock-up version with fake data was eventually presented to the committee, whose members, Sadowski notes, became preoccupied with the placeholder data – evidence, he observes, of the power of these visualizations. 'The dashboards are meant to represent reality, but they can influence perception so much that they bend reality,' he explained.

As Sadowski concluded: 'These are not the stories of technological development that we usually hear. Stories of failure and frustration, of delays and dead ends, are extraordinarily typical features of the work done in government and technology. But these stories run counter to the narratives of innovation meant to sell smartness' (Sadowski 2021).

Data Governance

In a light-filled event space in Toronto's historic Corktown neighbourhood, dozens of reporters and Sidewalk Labs officials gathered one sunny morning in June 2019 for the long-awaited release of the company's so-called Master Innovation and Development Plan (MIDP). Monitors were situated around the edges of the room, and Sidewalk's brash CEO, Dan Doctoroff, was holding forth at the front.

Members of the media had been given hard copies of the MIDP – a four-volume, richly illustrated box set of documents weighing in at about ten kilos, with 'Toronto Tomorrow' emblazoned in block letters on the side. Those volumes – also available online – seemed to cover everything one could possibly want to know about Sidewalk's plans, including copious details about architecture, environmental features, and technology, as well as appendices laying out the fine print: how this place would be managed, who would be in charge, what legal exemptions were required, and so on.

By the time the reporters gathered to watch the presentation, many had already been contacted by the media relations officials with Waterfront Toronto, which had brought Sidewalk to town two years earlier, to give them a heads-up that the agency's chair would be rebuffing key elements of the plan.

The most theoretical and legally opaque details involved the governance of this new community – Sidewalk had made it clear that it wouldn't be the City of Toronto – and the handling of all the data that would be collected within its 12 acres. According to the MIDP, that information would become the responsibility of something it called an 'Urban Data Trust.' The trust, the company stated, would be tasked with storing and protecting the data collected within Quayside, ensuring privacy and monetizing the IP created for this futuristic neighbourhood. The trust would also devise data-sharing standards that would be applicable for other smart cities – a hint that information generated in Toronto might not stay in Toronto. But in the spirit of establishing a mutually beneficial partnership, Sidewalk said the city would get a cut of the action.

Sidewalk Labs pledged that this trust would respect Canadian privacy laws, but critics had a laundry list of questions about how the trust would work, its legal obligations, and its ability to meaningfully guarantee privacy while ensuring that people living, working, and visiting Quayside would consent to sharing their information.

According to a critique by Anna Artyushin, 'the term *urban data* was assigned a new meaning: information "gathered in the city's physical environment, including the public realm, publicly accessible spaces, and even some private buildings." The document categorized urban data into four categories: personal information, de-identified data, aggregate data, and non-personal data, with each and every one to be managed by the trust.' She also debunked Sidewalk's claims about the legality of this scheme: 'Of the four types, only personal information is subject to Canada's legislation.'

Other critics questioned the idea that a private entity, like a trust, should be put in charge of information gathered in the public realm. 'Promises to self-regulate must be viewed with skepticism especially because of the way technology companies have expanded their data collection and use practices,' wrote Rutgers University law professor Ellen Goodman in a 2019 review of Sidewalk's plan commissioned by the Canadian Civil Liberties Association as part a lawsuit seeking to block approval.

Goodman co-founded the Rutgers Institute for Information Policy and Law and studies issues such as the ethics of artificial intelligence in smart cities. As she states in her brief, Sidewalk Lab's digital governance plans contained promises about privacy and responsible use. But, she argued, the gaps in Sidewalk Labs' proposal, coupled with Alphabet/Google's history of misusing personal information, raised warning flags.

She cited some technologies envisioned for Quayside – apartment energy schedulers, a system for tracking each apartment's waste to generate 'pay-as-you-throw' bills, and self-driving parcel delivery robots operating in tunnels beneath the buildings. All would gather personal data (i.e., name, address) that could theoretically be used to figure out when, for example, someone was home, what might be in their waste stream, and insights about their consumption habits. The systems, embedded in the design of the Quayside buildings, relied on algorithms fed by data generated by residents themselves. 'These particular algorithmic regulatory systems are likely to be at the core of the Quayside infrastructure, influencing how the built environment is arranged and functions,' Goodman cautioned. 'Once they are in place, it may be difficult to unwind the data flows.'

Sidewalk's proposed digital governance leaned heavily on anonymizing personal data before it is shared. But Goodman noted the growing research that shows how privacy violations – 're-identification' – can occur despite such steps. Transportation information – tap-on/tap-off transit cards or trip data from ride hailing services – can be cross-referenced with other public sources of information to generate inferences based on a user's behaviour (e.g., regular trips to a health clinic). Citing privacy violations by Apple, Amazon, and YouTube (Google), Goodman concluded: 'There are too many examples of technology companies promising to anonymize personal information, but then compromising that anonymity, to rely on assurances of de-identification.'

Smart city technologies are complex, but technical difficulty isn't necessarily an impediment. Natasha Tusikov cites earlier examples of public governance of highly technical systems, such as the Canadian Radio-Television and Telecommunications Commission or the Atomic Energy Control Board. 'It seems that after all these scandals with tech companies, people have reached a point where there's a role for government,' she says.

Sidewalk's decision to pull the plug on Quayside shortly after the World Health Organization declared an international state of emergency in the early months of the COVID-19 pandemic rendered moot the abstruse debate about the urban data trust. Still, says Anna Artyushin, there are lessons to be learned. 'While Sidewalk Labs' plans for data collection were very much in line with the privatization of urban governance and the normalization of ubiquitous surveillance that takes place in smart cities around the world, the idea to put data in a public trust was rather novel. Using trusts to give the public a share in profits and an oversight role in the governance of personal data in smart cities may seem like a viable solution, but there are some significant limitations to this approach,' she notes. The story, she concludes, 'is a cautionary tale.'

5
Smart City Tech and the Promise of Green Cities

During the 2010s, thousands of Rotterdam building owners installed green roofs on their dwellings – about 330,000 square metres in total, almost 2 per cent of the city's 18.5 square kilometres of flat roof space. But where some cities have promoted such projects to improve energy efficiency and absorb carbon dioxide, Rotterdam's green roof infrastructure is all about water and keeping as much rainwater runoff as possible out of aging, overtaxed sewers in order to prevent flooding.

About four-fifths of the Dutch port is below sea level. As Paul van Roosmalen, the city official overseeing sustainable public real estate, puts it: 'The water comes from all sides': the sea, the sky, the river, and groundwater. 'It's always been a threat.' But he also sees an opportunity to use a marriage of technology and green design to elevate the role of rooftops in managing Rotterdam's water pressures.

While typical green roofs function like sponges and look like gardens, Rotterdam is working with public and private landlords to develop a 'green-blue grid.' Instead of simply fitting out roof areas with plants, these spaces can be equipped with reservoirs or tanks to retain excess flow – blue roofs. The tanks, in turn, are equipped with electronic drain valves that can be opened and closed remotely, in some cases via a smart phone app.

'The problem,' says van Roosmalen, 'is that when they're full, they're full.' The city's vision, he explains, is to develop a system for coordinating the water levels in these tanks to help manage sewer capacity. The idea is to link the valve control devices into a grid of blue roofs that function, in effect, like a dispersed network of storm-water reservoirs. When there's rain in the forecast, the reservoirs can be drained automatically. Then, during heavy weather, they can store rainwater, reducing pressure and flooding in the sewer system.

While Rotterdam's blue-green grid is still far from completion, it can be seen as an example of how a set of digital sensing technologies can be potentially harnessed to produce a smart city solution to an urban sustainability problem.

The technological linchpin in Rotterdam's strategy has been the installation of highly sensitive weather radar on the roof of the city's tallest building. The device is capable of detecting rainfall 16 to 20 kilometres away. Remotely operated blue-green roof control systems can be programmed to dynamically respond to those forecasts and release water that sits in the reservoirs. (A similar project, the Resilience Network of Smart and Innovative Climate Adaptive Rooftops, or Resilio, is underway at several Amsterdam social housing complexes.)

As of 2021, Rotterdam officials were testing a pilot version of this grid. To scale it up, the city has to figure out how to coordinate with Rotterdam's water board, which manages the sewer infrastructure, as well as property owners. The strategy potentially complements other water management planning moves, among them retrofitting public squares with 'rain gardens' – i.e., clusters of water-absorbing shrubs and perennials planted in small depressions in the ground. 'Instead of making bigger sewer pipes, we made a choice to invest in redesigning public space in a way that contributes to a nicer, better, more attractive district,' Arnound Molenaar, Rotterdam's chief resilience officer, told Thomson Reuters in 2019.

Van Roosmalen adds that a green roof can absorb about 15 millimetres of rain per square metre, whereas a roof with a reservoir can retain ten times as much. The city's goal is to convert 1 million square metres of flat roofs to include water retention systems and solar panels. Aggregated across even a portion of the city's flat roofs, he says, 'it's a tremendous amount of water.'

❖

Climate change is, in significant measure, a consequence of the twin historical forces of industrialization and urbanization.

The Industrial Revolution, fuelled as it was by steam- and coal-powered mass production technologies, drew people away from rural areas and small towns and set in motion a complex dynamic that persists to this day. Swelling of urban populations gave rise to poverty, public health crises, and urban pollution, which in turn spurred social reforms, outward expansion of cities, rising incomes, and the commercialization of combustion engines. Mass consumerism and environmental degradation caused by car-oriented sprawl accelerated fossil fuel dependence, plastic waste, and the overuse of carbon-intensive city-building materials, like cement, concrete, and asphalt

Yet post-industrial cities, with their economies of scale and concentrated populations, have also generated a wide range of sustainable innovations, products, and approaches to planning and development. In some places, these have boosted building energy efficiency, improved air quality, increased transit use, and encouraged non-motorized transportation. What's more, some cities, like Vancouver, have stoked the cleantech sector by attracting entrepreneurs, venture capital, and scientists, revealing how urban prosperity can be tethered to the transition to a low-carbon economy.

It's also true, however, that in the globalized twenty-first-century, the cast-offs of the inhabitants of wealthy, urbanized nations are shipped to vast waste recycling or landfilling facilities in countries like China and the Philippines. And when inexpensive goods produced in the Global South are purchased by consumers in affluent countries, all that transnational trade effectively allows the North to shift emissions, air pollution, and ecological destruction to coal-dependent megacities in Asia and the oceans that serve as the primary means of shipping goods around the globe.

The warming caused by these and other factors is expressed in the form of habitat destruction, melting ice caps, extreme weather, sea level rise, and so on. But some of the most disruptive effects of climate change will be experienced by the inhabitants of low-lying coastal cities like New York, Mumbai, Shanghai, and Rotterdam.

However, even before climate change became a global crisis, the technologies unleashed by rapid industrialization, combined with abrupt spikes in urban population, gave rise to profoundly polluted cities. The dismal air quality in megacities like Beijing and Delhi is lethal; indeed, in the early months of the 2020 pandemic, when car traffic plummeted, the residents of Delhi found they could see the mountains north of the city, which are normally obscured by a dense haze.

These are not new phenomena. The widespread use of low-grade coal for heating, coupled with an atmospheric condition known as an 'inversion,' had blanketed London in dense smog for generations, leaving in their wake a residue of grime on both buildings and the lungs of the people who lived with the intensity of the pollution.

One of the ironies of industrial and post-industrial urbanization is that the environmental crises triggered by one generation of technologies has spurred the development of new technologies aimed at cleaning up profoundly polluted cities.

The postwar history of Pittsburgh, Pennsylvania, vividly illustrates that paradox, and the implications for one mid-size city. By the 1940s, Pittsburgh was suffocating on the riches it had generated from its giant steel mills, powered, as they were, by coke and coal from the rugged Allegheny Mountains. Pittsburgh steel had helped create America's railways and then its booming car industry. The family-run business empires associated with the industry – Carnegie, Mellon, Frick – generated enormous wealth that allowed them to burnish their considerable notoriety with philanthropic ventures that ranged from art and education to the establishment of the modern public library system.

Yet Pittsburgh paid a steep price, with extreme air pollution from smokestack industries and water contamination caused by the dumping of raw sewage into the rivers that run through the city. 'From whatever direction one approaches the once-lovely conjunction of the Allegheny and the Monongahela, the devastation of progress is apparent,' according to one early-twentieth-century description cited in a recent journal article by Joel A. Tarr, a Pittsburgh historian. 'Quiet valleys have been inundated with slag, defaced with refuse, marred by hideous buildings. Streams have been polluted with sewage and waste from the mills. Life for the majority of the population has been rendered unspeakably pinched and dingy. This is what might be called the technological blight of heavy industry' (qtd in Tarr 2003).

By mid-century, the city's economic future was in jeopardy, and grassroots organizations were sounding the alarm over the link between air quality and health. 'The smoke had many devastating effects on the city and the way people lived,' Tarr wrote in 2003. 'Some of the most famous were the conditions downtown at midday when street lights had to be turned on.' He relates how the county moved to impose emission regulations and treat its sewage. But besides tougher laws, technological innovations – smokestack scrubbers, the rapid conversion of coal-burning locomotives to diesel, and the adoption of natural gas for home heating – ultimately drove improvements in the city's quality of life.

Urban scholars also point out that the story of Pittsburgh's rebirth as a post-industrial tech hub can be traced to a critical decision by municipal leaders in the 1940s and 1950s. Recognizing that they alone couldn't save the city, those officials decided to make common cause with a new civic group called the Allegheny Conference on Community Development. A coalition of business leaders, universities, and other agencies that coalesced in the 1940s, the Allegheny Conference not only supported air quality measures but also sought to figure out how to ensure the city's survival in a post-smokestack world (Allegheny Conference on Community Development).

Over the coming decades, it helped attract new non-industrial development, supported moves to improve public transit, foster cultural activity, expand the scale of the cleanup of the region, and promote higher education and research-focused institutions, such as Carnegie Mellon University. In recent years, CMU has attracted scientists and tech entrepreneurs, emerging as a centre for R&D focused on autonomous and electric vehicles, as well as energy.

Indeed, Pittsburgh is generally regarded as the most successful of the so-called Rust Belt cities in the U.S. and has been cited by urban geographer Richard Florida as an example of the so-called 'creative class' approach to urban revitalization.

Some of the earliest applications of the smart city technology being created in places like Pittsburgh involved sustainability – and specifically distributed, renewable electricity. Conventional electricity grids were linked to large, and often dirty, power sources: coal- or gas-fired generators. But in the early 2000s, as wind power and solar became more economically viable and politically popular, governments ordered public utilities to figure out how to allow smaller and more localized sources of power generation to access the electricity grid. These included homes or flat-roofed commercial buildings with rooftop solar panels that could generate energy.

In Ontario, the provincial government's 2007 pledge to phase out coal forced a push for renewable alternatives. Inspired by a German policy approach to incentivizing investment in clean electricity (the so-called 'feed-in tariff'), Ontario sought to attract sustainable energy investors, large and small, with attractive subsidies guaranteed over twenty years. Besides these financial incentives, the transition turned on the deployment of smart grid technology, including sophisticated algorithms that could track power consumption and 'smart meters.' These devices allowed utilities to manage energy drawn from a decentralized set of producers, among them private property owners with solar panels that could feed power back into the grid.

Those investments, in turn, paved the way for other conservation-oriented energy-policy shifts, such as time-of-use pricing, which provides ratepayers with a financial incentive to reduce consumption during peak periods and, in some jurisdictions, programs to encourage 'fuel-switching' for residential space heating, with electric air-source heat pumps replacing furnaces powered by natural gas or fuel oil.

The long-term vision for smart grids and distributed renewable energy is cities where individual homeowners and property managers can install a range of technologies – from rooftop solar panels to battery energy storage systems – that can provide low or no carbon energy to the local electrical grid, which traditionally distributes power supplied centrally, by large hydro, gas, or coal-fired generating plants.

Some electric vehicle (EV) companies are aiming to get involved in this market as well. Many firms are racing to develop so-called 'vehicle-to-grid' systems that would allow EV owners to plug in their vehicles and feed surplus energy from their cars' batteries into the electrical grid in exchange for a fee or a rebate on their hydro bills.

The concept is built on the assumption that most private vehicles spend most of their time parked, in driveways or garages. When they're stationary and not in use, the electrical charge stored in their batteries can be put to use in other ways, such as supplying additional power during peak periods, e.g., work hours, very hot days, or very cold days. In effect, the eventual deployment of vehicle-to-grid systems is akin to tapping into a massive storehouse of local, clean, and inexpensive power.

At those times when electricity is expensive, it could be possible for an office building owner to 'buy' electricity stored in the batteries of the EVs parked in the parking garage. If those batteries had been charged at night, when rates are low, the building owner can reduce its dependence on purchasing high-cost power from the local utility. Similarly, the building owner can power up a set of stationary batteries at night when rates are low, and then use the electricity during the day, when it is expensive.

Ultimately, smart grid proponents want to build cities where electricity is distributed not like cable television – in one direction, from a single provider – but rather like the internet, with power flowing in many different directions within an extended urban network. Households and businesses will not only consume electricity but also produce it via solar panels, stationary batteries, and EVs, all of which are set up to export power into the grid using specialized meters and other equipment.

As of 2022, this version of the future of electricity in smart cities remains unrealized, an aspiration with many moving parts. The EV market is growing quickly, but represents only a fraction of the overall vehicle sector. Governments and property managers are still figuring out how to deploy charging stations, while tech companies and EV component manufacturers are racing to build longer-lasting batteries.

Perhaps the most daunting impediment has to do with the management of this new distributed energy system and the complex demands that urban grids will face in the future. As EVs become more commonplace and building owners reduce their reliance on natural gas for space heating, the demand for electricity in big cities will soar, meaning utilities will have to bring in additional sources of generation, generated using low-carbon technologies like wind, hydro, or nuclear.

A portion of that new power will come from local distributed renewable sources: rooftop solar panels, stationary batteries, and EVs. For utilities, however, the task of managing both conventional and distributed sources of power is highly complex from a technical perspective and far less predictable than the conventional approach. Specialized electricity software companies have emerged with digital smart grid platforms designed to do this kind of load-balancing.

But even in forward-looking cities, the transition to distributed energy smart grids remains a work in progress. According to the International Energy Agency, utilities around the world are spending hundreds of billions of dollars upgrading aging electrical grids, but so far only a portion of that is going into smart grid ventures, although those investments are expect to grow in coming years as governments around the world race to meet net zero emission targets for 2050.

The sleepy, monopolistic world of local electrical utilities will be unrecognizable. The emergence of decentralized smart grids will eventually create new local energy markets that eclipse the publicly owned utilities, like Toronto Hydro, that have supplied electrons to urban ratepayers for well over a century.

Innovations in urban energy won't just come from the world of electricity. Some cities, for example, are experimenting with mechanical energy transfer systems that collect and recycle waste heat in municipal sewer mains. In many parts of Europe and a growing number of North American cities, municipalities have invested in 'anaerobic digestors,' which siphon methane created by organic household waste. This so-called biogas is then purified and used for electricity generation (in place of conventional fossil fuels) or to power low-emission vehicles.

Climate-focused architects, meanwhile, have developed techniques for reducing energy consumption in buildings by up to 90 per cent. The so-called 'Passive House' school of design – which was invented in the early 1970s but popularized in northern Europe in the early 1990s – is grounded in a handful of core architectural principles: massive amounts of exterior wall insulation; construction methods that eliminate leaks and so-called 'thermal bridges,' which allow heat to escape; triple-glazed windows and heat-recovery devices attached to drains and exhaust vents; and orientations designed to optimize the use of the sun's heat. Most of the components used in Passive House projects are not especially high-tech, but rather rely on basic physics – that if a building's design prevents heat or cooling from escaping, it will require less energy.

Air quality monitoring, by contrast, has attracted considerable attention from smart city technology firms and researchers, largely because this kind of activity can be significantly expanded with the deployment of wireless air quality sensors. These include monitoring devices attached to lampposts and other urban infrastructure, an expanded network of air quality monitoring stations, and low-cost mobile sensors affixed to rental bikes and even pigeons. Other projects involve cross-referencing anonymized cellphone mobility data with air quality readings taken in various urban locations to assist in determining where exposure to ultra-fine pollutants was highest (Bousquet 2017).

Smart buildings, typically new office towers or commercial complexes, offer a much more involved application for wireless sensors. These buildings are fitted out with networks of thousands of IoT devices – temperature and motion detectors – that feed readings to automated control systems. These use artificial intelligence algorithms to continuously adjust HVAC equipment in order to optimize a building's internal climate, thus reducing operating costs related to energy consumption. By contrast to the more speculative world of roving air quality sensors, the market for smart building tech is highly developed and competitive, and includes multinationals like Siemens or Schneider Electric that focus on giant property management firms.

As was true in a previous era with the emergence of scrubbers for smokestack industries, the adoption (and therefore efficacy) of new sustainability technologies – smart or otherwise – can't be seen in isolation from broader political or policy developments, such as the introduction of strict air quality standards in response to mounting public alarm about pollution.

Indeed, regulation has been consistently shown to drive innovation. A case in point: California's low-carbon fuel standard (LCFS) went into effect in 2011 and has since influenced similar policies in Oregon, Washington, and British Columbia. The standard provides incentives to transportation fuel companies to use low-carbon or renewable additives, such as biodiesel, or pay penalties. Since the LCFS came into effect, the carbon intensity of California transportation fuels – a measure of emissions per unit of fuel – has consistently dropped, while cumulative sales of hybrid electric or battery electric vehicles has soared, from 7,500 in 2011 to over 990,000 by 2021 ('Zero Emission Vehicle and Infrastructure Statistics' n.d.).

Another example of smart regulation is so-called 'Energy Step Codes' that set out targets for overall building energy performance – a critically important front in the fight against climate change.[10] In 2017, both British Columbia and the City of Toronto adopted energy codes that establish minimum standards for new buildings, functioning like regulatory escalators that predictably become more demanding over time. Under the Toronto Green Standard, all new projects

---

10. Building-related emissions account for about half of all carbon released into the atmosphere, and the International Energy Agency reported that building-related CO_2 reached an all-time high in 2019.

must meet the basic level, known as Tier 1, while more ambitious developments that satisfy the next-highest performance target (Tier 2) are eligible for financial incentives. The third tier applies to public sector buildings, while the fourth tier lays out the standards for net zero projects (i.e., that any carbon generated by the building is offset in some way – for example, with solar panels that feed green power into the grid). As the TGS is upgraded, the second tier will become the first tier, the third tier becomes the second tier, and so on. The goal, part of the city's long-term carbon target, is for all new buildings to be net zero.

This type of progressive regulation produces benefits that extend beyond emissions reduction, and can be described as part of a smart city agenda. In Vancouver, for example, the Step Code has pushed building component suppliers to develop more energy-efficient products, such as triple-glazed windows – which are commonplace in Europe, where energy standards are high, but are still a premium product in North America. The Step Code has also spurred a development boom in so-called 'tall timber' construction – basically, buildings constructed from highly engineered wooden beams and pillars instead of carbon-intensive materials like concrete and steel.

The upshot is that these kinds of smart environmental regulations reduce carbon, create jobs and economic activity, and provide building owners with financial resilience in the form of reduced long-term operating costs.

Much more than Canada's, the Netherlands' climate policies reflect a great sense of urgency, given its exposure to sea level rise and flooding on rivers that flow into the country from the east. For that reason, both adaptation and mitigation have been central to the country's plans for future-proofing its cities.

Rob Schmidt, a sustainability policy expert with the City of Rotterdam, points out that the Netherlands' nine largest city regions collaborate to develop and test approaches and technologies: 'We learn from each other how to cope with these so-called smart city projects.' Each city has adopted a policy area: Rotterdam is focused on climate adaptation; Amsterdam, circular economy; Eindhoven, low-carbon mobility and energy transition; and so on.

The national government has launched an Urban Agenda that calls for negotiating 'city deals,' many of which involve smart city projects that typically include multiple partners, such as research institutions. 'Our approach is focused on the opportunity and finding everyone you need to get to a solution,' says Urban Agenda program manager Frank Reniers. 'You put them in a room and try to innovate your way out of the problem.'

The Netherlands wasn't always so collaborative. According to Frank Kresin, dean of the Faculty of Digital Media and Creative Industry at the Amsterdam University of Applied Sciences, Amsterdam in the late 2000s and early 2010s 'was doing everything in its power to become "smart."' The city's appetite for tech drove a great deal of private investment in automation and digitization.

But the infatuation with these corporate solutions, Kresin wrote in a 2016 study, 'had some flaws,' including the risk of excessive surveillance and an unquestioning embrace of the idea that the smart city was 'a machine that needs to be optimized, with no consideration or understanding of the organic reality. It wants to maximize efficiency and avoid friction, so it simply and non-negotiably imposes top-down, non-transparent technological solutions.'

Kresin wasn't the only one concerned about this drift. Beginning in the mid-2010s, citizen groups, entrepreneurs, and academic institutions pushed Dutch policy makers and companies to swap out the top-down approach in favour of a more grassroots philosophy that features extensive public engagement, citizen-science projects, and applied research.

'The big threat is loss of autonomy,' says Jan-Willem Wesselink of Future City Foundation, a Dutch network of municipal agencies, civil society organizations, universities, and technology companies seeking to promote a democratic approach to smart urbanism that aligns with a U.N. social development goal (#11) about resilient, sustainable, and inclusive cities. 'Does Google or some other company decide how you use the city?'

Kresin describes one early effort at broadening the conversation. In 2014, Amsterdam Smart City, a tech incubator, distributed several hundred 'smart citizen kits,' which provided rudimentary sensors to allow people to perform environmental indicator tests on water and air quality around the city. Their findings were fed to the city. While the readings fell short of research-grade data, this experiment in citizen science attracted many participants, generated upbeat media coverage, and, in a few cases, led the city to clean up local beach areas. Its popularity also inspired Kresin and some colleagues to establish the Amsterdam Smart Citizens Lab, where civil society groups, academics, and government officials work together to find solutions to other urban problems.

The distribution of the kits 'was a surprisingly successful project,' says soil chemist Gerben Mol, a resilient cities researcher at Amsterdam's Advanced Metropolitan Solutions Institute (AMS), a university–municipal government joint venture established to conduct more formal applied urban research.

In recent years, a growing number of Dutch city dwellers are finding venues to engage in local conversations or projects about putting urban data and technology to work in addressing the problems they see in their communities – in effect, a cultural, as opposed to corporate or bureaucratic, response.

All this grassroots work has had a bearing on AMS's work. While some of its research falls under the heading of smart city tech – e.g., data visualization projects – other research initiatives are focused on parallel policy themes, such as the circular economy. One intriguing example: an AMS project that created a composite out of a glue-like bacterial residue and decontaminated wood fibre culled from septic waste (i.e., used toilet paper). Currently being tested is a potential application to use this composite as a binding agent in road asphalt.

Amsterdam Smart City's community manager Nancy Zikken says the municipality has 'embraced' TADA.city, a network of European organizations that have pledged adherence to six core principles for digital city initiatives (inclusive, locally focused, controlled by residents, monitored, transparent, and broadly accessible).

She also says that Amsterdam Smart City screens applicants, such as start-ups, to ensure their proposals align with broader policy goals and have what Zikken calls 'social value.' As an example, she cites a firm that recently pitched a parking app that was rejected because it would likely encourage car use in a congested city whose residents want the opposite. 'Most of the companies we're working with really do see the value of incorporating citizens and using the wisdom of the crowd,' she says.

In Rotterdam, city officials, who are driving the blue-green grid initiative, are also using public education, open houses, and other engagement tools to promote these projects, many of which will be installed on privately owned dwellings, using private capital, since the strategy is to attain sufficient scale to make an impact.

Rotterdam, interestingly, hasn't created financial incentives. Rather, in discussions with private property owners, Paul van Roosmalen says his team stresses the benefits and explains the options for what's possible – for example combining a rooftop reservoir with solar. 'They can pick what they think would add to the quality of their specific land,' he says. But there's a more urgent appeal, too: 'You can save your city from drowning.'

From the earliest days of the smart city tech boom to its apogee (circa 2018) and the hype around megaprojects like Sidewalk Labs' plan for Quayside, sustainability has been positioned as one of the main benefits for cities thinking about investments in systems such as air quality sensors, electric vehicle charging infrastructure, smart temperature controls in apartments, district energy, and smart grids that draw on renewable power.

While these technologies – on their own, or even assembled into an extended development project – are enticing in that they hold out the promise of a greener form of city-building, some critics have pointed out the flaw in this approach: '"Smart city" technology is steeped in solutionism,' argued Rebecca Williams, a Harvard Kennedy School fellow with the Belfer Center for Science and International Affairs, in a 2021 study on smart city trends. '[I]ts rhetoric and promotional materials are often couched with the promise of what it could solve rather than what it has demonstrably solved in similar instances.'

Other scholars have come to similar conclusions about the hyped benefits of these technologies. A 2019 study by a team of Norwegian and Swedish researchers concluded that energy sustainability smart city projects in three Scandinavian cities, which involved €70 million in funding from the European Union, had been oversold and were in fact older plans that were repackaged. (They included a new energy centre, administrative offices powered by renewable energy, home retrofits, solar panel installations, and smart building systems.) The authors pointed out that while the recipient municipalities foregrounded sustainability in their smart city proposals to the EU, the technologies they used weren't particularly innovative, and the results, in terms of energy savings, proved to be 'almost impossible' to measure.

'The way we understand and measure energy sustainability in a smart city needs reconsideration,' the authors concluded, pointing out a long list of X-factors, including pre-existing budgets, plans, EU requirements, and the engagement of individual policy makers tasked with delivering on these undertakings. 'By and large, these outcomes are highly contingent, and to a significant extent determined by the implementation of the smart city agenda by policy makers on the ground' (Haarstad & Wathne 2019).

The broader conclusion is that clean/green smart city tech makes sense only when it is embedded in a wider policy and planning framework designed to promote more conventional urban or regional goals, such as intensification, transit investment, and grid decarbonization. EVs and a city fitted out with charging infrastructure won't reduce emissions unless governments reduce the fossil fuels used to generate electricity. A homeowner who spends tens of thousands on state-of-the-art solar panels won't dent their dwelling's carbon emissions unless they first pump insulation into the attic and eliminate the drafts around doors and windows. And no amount of green technology investment can slow the emissions generated by sprawling, car-dependent cities built with vast quantities of concrete, asphalt, and steel.

What's more, new solutions to urban environmental problems need not be high-tech (i.e., technology if necessary, but not necessarily technology). In China in recent years, for example, municipal authorities in sixteen metropolitan regions with water-scarcity issues have pursued so-called 'sponge city' strategies – using native species plantings, wetland construction, permeable surfaces, and rainwater harvesting to reduce runoff and improve water absorption. As one former Chinese official told the *Guardian*, 'A sponge city follows the philosophy of innovation: that a city can solve water problems instead of creating them' (Harris 2015).

Viewed in these ways, the Dutch approach to smart cities and sustainability is, well, smart, with support for tech innovations like blue-green roofs, but as just one element of a national policy framework that promotes urban sustainability through regulation, infrastructure investment, R&D circular economy initiatives, and public awareness.

6

The Quagmire of Mobility Tech

It was an idea that seemed to have all the right ingredients for the tech-saturated world of twenty-first-century urban mobility. In 2015, a Helsinki start-up unveiled a plan for something it called 'mobility as a service,' or MaaS, based on ideas that had been developed in a 2014 master's thesis at a Finnish university. The company, MaaS Global, had built an app that provides city dwellers with a digital one-stop shop for all sorts of travel options – including transit, taxis, ride hailing, and bike sharing.

With Google's online mapping function, commuters can plot the best way to get from A to B and then, through the app, procure or book the transportation modes that fit the route and the users' preferences. Global MaaS sells monthly subscriptions, not unlike cellphone packages, that provide various combinations – up to a given number of transit trips, a certain number of ride-hailing journeys, and so on; the bookings are made through smart phones, and a single transaction covers all the legs of a journey. The 'unified' payment is meant to encourage multi-modal trips. The company's mission is to provide a 'true' alternative to private vehicle ownership. 'MaaS,' according to the firm's website, 'could be the single most powerful tool to decarbonise transport for future generations.'

The idea rapidly caught the imagination of other mobility entrepreneurs, as well as venture capital firms and transportation giants like Siemens. 'We need to make end-to-end trip planning easier,' says deputy CEO Roland Busch.

As of late 2019, Global MaaS had raised almost €54 million ($84 million) from investors including BP and Mitsubishi. Its app, known as Whim, was available in Helsinki, Vienna, Antwerp, and a handful of other cities. Other versions of MaaS had appeared in Stockholm, and trials in North America, India, and Australia were underway. There's even a MaaS industry association.

Yet for all the hype and seeming promise, the concept hasn't taken off. Transportation experts know that individuals' travel habits are difficult to change. Some analysts have enumerated the long list of stakeholders – private, public, and otherwise – that have to be on the same page to ensure that MaaS ventures deliver a benefit. Others have raised questions about what role municipalities should play in the oversight and regulation of these kinds of undertakings.

It also became apparent that in some jurisdictions, municipal transit agencies have not welcomed this innovation – most don't want to relinquish the pricing and distribution of fares to third parties – and consumers have been slow to sign on. According to a recent report by Bloomberg CityLab, some MaaS firms are also facing financial difficulties because the business model isn't especially profitable yet. 'If you're going to disrupt automobiles, one of the biggest industries in the world, it will take a bit of time,' said Global MaaS founder Sampo Hietanen.

The uncertainty orbiting around the MaaS sector reveals much about the promise, risk, and perils of digital urban mobility, which is, arguably, the single most sought-after prize in the sprawling smart city industry. Smart mobility encompasses a wide range of digital technologies and applications, from those already in wide usage (car- and bike- sharing services, ride hailing, transit smart cards, parking apps, electric vehicles, and the steadily expanding array of micro-mobility products on the market) to those that are under development (autonomous cars, buses, and trucks; 'smart' traffic signals; curb mapping; drone delivery vehicles; and even streets where illuminated lane pavers adjust automatically based on traffic levels detected by sensors (an experimental technology dubbed 'Pebble' by Sidewalk Labs).

Many of these technologies will rely heavily on artificial intelligence algorithms and densely layered digital mapping applications, such as Google Maps, TomTom, and Waze, as well as proprietary systems being developed by car manufacturers. They mesh together GPS, satellite images, and cellphone signals along with a rapidly expanding collection of other data streams, from dynamic bike-sharing or transit maps to parking-spot addresses, and eventually, perhaps, the location of potholes. Some of the granular information that drives these services will come from the cellphones of people moving through cities, while other tranches will be harvested from municipal agencies' open data portals.

In some fields, there are enormous opportunities presented by the technologies that fall under the broad heading of smart mobility: more responsive traffic and transit planning; improved accessibility for groups that face impediments in moving around cities (disabled residents, seniors, children); and better low-carbon alternatives to privately owned fossil fuel–burning vehicles.

Yet the disruptive arrival of ride-hailing services like Uber and Lyft – which, pre-pandemic, fuelled congestion and eroded transit usage – serves as a warning that future market-driven mobility innovations will require scrutiny, careful policy planning, and clear-eyed assessments of the costs and the benefits.

Since the dawn of the rail era, transportation technologies have done more to physically shape and reshape cities than any other innovation, except perhaps digital networks. From trains to trams, streetcars, cars, trucks, planes, hulking container ships, elevators, and high-speed rail, the narrative of urbanization tracks the powerful trajectory of transportation technology and its capacity to collapse distance accelerate trade, and alter the global environment.

The digitization, automation, and electrification of transportation heralds the next chapter in this story, and there's good reason to assume these braided forms of innovation will have far-reaching consequences.

Electrification – not just cars, but also everything from planes to e-bikes – holds out the potential for weaning twenty-first-century society from its addiction to gasoline, but the environmental benefits only click in if the electrical grids that support all those new EVs can be both scaled up and decarbonized.

Automation promises to remove driver error from the operation of trucks and cars, and give rise to new forms of urban transportation. But AVs will only come into widespread use once navigation technologies have been thoroughly debugged and cities develop rules and norms governing the operation of such vehicles in spaces they share with pedestrians, cyclists, and other non-automated traffic.

The digitization of urban transportation, which is linked closely to both automation and electrification, encompasses an ever-expanding collection of technologies that are transforming vehicles into wifi-enabled moving computers. Thus equipped, they are linked into intricate networks of mapping software, GPS navigation systems, sharing apps, and digitally enhanced infrastructure platforms that govern the operations of streets, roads, and highways based on continuous readings of traffic flow. Many of these applications already exist, but they tend not to be integrated in ways that allow cities to take full advantage of digital network technology to address congestion. Even more problematically, the prospect of fully digitized mobility also raises critical questions about privacy, surveillance, and security.

In recent years, so-called 'black hats' (i.e., programmers hired to look for bugs) have figured out how to remotely hack into Teslas and commandeer infotainment systems, operate doors, and alter steering and accelerating modes, but not take over control of the vehicle, *Security Week* magazine reported in May 2021 (Kovacs 2021). Stories about hacks on AVs and other electric vehicles have also circulated, raising fears about the potential for weaponizing self-driving cars. Some scholars, in turn, have documented potential security breaches and cyber-attacks against intelligent transportation systems, the highly integrated digital/sensor networks that monitor and control traffic (Paiva et al. 2020).

All these scenarios serve as a reminder that the unfurling future of digital mobility will be radically different than the familiar, congested world of big-city traffic.

Since the late 2010s, new car buyers have been able to choose vehicles with safety features that hint at the dawn of a new era. Automated anti-collision systems developed by manufacturers like Toyota process information from dash cams, GPS devices, tiny radars, on-board sensors with recognition capabilities, and systems that track and adjust the vehicle's position in a lane. The automotive industry, as well as tech giants like Google, have invested billions in these kinds of innovations, and they can be seen as some of the earliest advances in what may lead to fully autonomous vehicles (AVs) – so-called 'level five,' for their ability to guide themselves without a driver.

During much of the decade prior to the pandemic, the investment hype around AVs reflected a feverishness informed by futuristic visions of vast fleets of driverless cars operated by ride-hailing companies. Instead of private vehicle ownership, city dwellers could travel around urban regions simply by summoning shared AVs, which would cost far less to use because there are no drivers to pay.

Some critics, however, find this projected image of urban mobility to be troubling and rife with questions: Where would AVs go when they don't have passengers? Would these services accelerate sprawl or further erode transit ridership, which has already seen drops due to the popularity of ride hailing? What about safety: Despite all the talk about AVs being immune to distracted driving, who is responsible if a cyclist or a pedestrian is hit, as has happened in numerous trials? And finally, are such vehicles, with their wireless connectivity, vulnerable to hacking, satellite signal disruptions, or even power outages?

Other experts point out that the pandemic fundamentally altered the presumed uses for fleets of AVs operated by companies like Uber or Lyft. 'There are huge challenges right now with sharing anything,' says University of Toronto geographer Shauna Brail, who studies the ride-hailing sector. Some of the big players, she notes, have slowed or closed their AV R&D operations.

With fully automated AVs still at least a decade – and more likely two decades – away, it's by no means clear how local and regional governments should proceed. Clearly, there will be implications to the advent of AVs, but no one really knows what a proactive policy response looks like.

The messy, and mostly unregulated, arrival of ride hailing offers important insights. During the early to mid-2010s, tech upstarts like Uber wielded the triumphant rhetoric of disruption: innovators could topple lumbering incumbents that had grown complacent, but such was the way of capitalism. After all, does anyone today fret that a very young Microsoft kneecapped IBM in the 1980s, or that Steve Jobs ruthlessly dethroned Blackberry with the iPhone in 2006?

Yet mobility, and specifically urban mobility, isn't just another consumer good or service; cities are defined, in fundamental ways, by their transportation networks, which create urban spaces, enable commerce, support labour markets, and activate street life, but also require extensive planning and public investment. The notion that mobility is a 'market' isn't wrong, but it doesn't tell the whole tale.

Some cities welcomed Uber et al. and ignored the complaints of taxi companies, which had become complacent over many decades. Others imposed regulations, banned Uber outright, or sought to give homegrown ride-hailing firms a leg up. Over time, however, the policy environment in many places has shifted, including in Toronto. According to a 2018 study conducted by researchers with the University of Waterloo's School of Public Health and Health Systems, safety concerns relating to driver training, background checks, and insurance drove regulatory action in many jurisdictions.

What's missing from that study's list, however, is the non-negligible impact that ride hailing has had on transit, transportation, and land-use planning. For example, a 2018 analysis published by three University of Kentucky civil engineers found that in U.S. cities, each year after the arrival of ride-hailing companies saw rail ridership fall by 1.3 per cent and bus ridership drop by 1.8 per cent. 'The effect builds with each passing year and may be an important driver of recent ridership declines,' the authors conclude. Those losses translate into increased traffic and emissions, as well as accelerating operating shortfalls for transit agencies. Put another way, the profits earned by ride-hailing firms come directly at the expense of the public purse.

The Town of Innisfil, north of Greater Toronto, sought to square this circle by offering subsidized or flat-fee Uber rides as a substitute for bus service – an experiment that garnered international media attention. The problem, as it turns out, was that residents enthusiastically embraced the offer, so much so that the town has ended up spending far more than it would have on a conventional bus service and had to impose a cap on the number of subsidized trips an individual could take. What's more, Innisfil, which plans to develop a walkable urban core over the next few decades, has seen an increase in vehicular traffic as a result of the popularity of the partnership, according to some reports.

More recently, e-scooter firms like Lime and Bird also borrowed from Uber's playbook, rapidly launching their services, in some cases without seeking municipal approval. Like ride hailing, e-scooters can be booked and paid for via a smart phone app. Because e-scooters can move so rapidly, cities that have allowed these devices have also seen a spike in collision-related injuries, in some cases even exceeding those involving pedestrians and cyclists.

Then there's the data aspect. University of Ottawa professor Teresa Scassa, Canada Research Chair on information law and policy, notes that Los Angeles County planners wanted to understand whether dockless scooters made a dent in the so-called 'last mile' problem, i.e., the final stretch between home, shopping, and work where there are few transportation options besides private vehicles. As a quid pro quo, she says, county officials offered to allow the e-scooter companies to operate on city streets, on the proviso that they provide anonymized usage data for planning purposes. But the firms balked and appealed to state legislators for protection.

Cities' experiences with both ride hailing and e-scooters should sound a warning shot for municipal officials. 'The disruption from

AVs is likely to be much more substantial,' Kirsten Rulf, a researcher with the Harvard Kennedy School Autonomous Vehicles Policy Initiative, cautioned on *Medium* in 2018.

'Cities and states need to move into the driver's seat now to set the right course for their constituents,' she said. 'That is why learning from both the scooter wars and the rapid and irrevocable [ride-hailing] implementation is essential for city and state policymakers. They can avoid being on the defensive once again by acting now on AVs.'

While AVs will likely be several orders of magnitude more disruptive than either e-scooters or ride hailing, the prospect of developing AV policy proactively serves up a classic chicken-and-egg dilemma. With the technology still under development, many governments are reluctant to act, beyond enabling AV test projects, such as pilots of automated minibuses. At the same time, AVs, once commercially viable, shouldn't be allowed to use public rights of way in the absence of standards and regulations that govern traditional vehicles.

Which is not to suggest policy makers aren't thinking about AVs: many are. For example, Transport Canada in 2020 released a detailed 'guidance' on cyber-security for 'connected and autonomous vehicles' – an acknowledgement that hackers or terrorists could corrupt these computer systems on wheels, either during the manufacturing process or while they're on the road and operating. The guidance points out that Canada is heavily involved in international standards-setting working groups focused on harmonizing AV regulations.

At the local level, however, it's a different story. A detailed study published in the *Journal of the American Planning Association* concluded that most cities haven't attempted to get out ahead of the eventual arrival of AVs on local streets and highways.

MIT mobility-planning scholars Yonah Freemark, Anne Hudson, and Jinhua Zhao reviewed the transportation plans for 25 large U.S. cities and surveyed another 120. Few, they concluded, had begun planning for AVs. Nevertheless, many transportation officials had formed opinions about the potential consequences. 'Although local officials are optimistic about the technology and its potential to increase safety while reducing congestion, costs and pollution,' the authors found, 'more than a third of respondents worried about AVs increasing vehicle miles traveled and sprawl while reducing transit ridership and local revenues.'

The City of Toronto, interestingly, is an exception – it is one of the few large municipalities to have leaned into the problem of creating a local policy framework for a global technology that has yet to ripen. Approved in the fall of 2019 by city council, the 162-page Automated Vehicles Tactical Plan aims to bridge the gap between the emerging technology and the city's other priorities. The document is nothing if not encyclopedic in scope. It scans the state of the technology, the commercial ecosystem in which AVs are being developed, the weave of federal, provincial, and municipal regulations that apply to vehicles, potential use cases, and even the findings of surveys detailing residents' expectations about AVs

'We're very proactive in thinking about [AV policy],' says Shauna Brail, the U of T geographer. 'But it's unclear how to regulate something that's changing so rapidly.'

The plan's main focus, explains its author Ryan Lanyon, was to force a conversation about how AVs should advance, as opposed to undermine, Toronto's other civic priorities. These include equity and health, sustainability, privacy, integrated mobility, and prosperity. 'We need the technology to move us to those objectives,' says Lanyon, a senior transportation manager with the city. 'The bigger question is, how does the technology get us there? … The vision,' he continues, 'has to accommodate what we want the technology to do.'

The tactical plan lays out a highly detailed menu of small preliminary steps as a means of embarking on a much longer journey. These include measures from ensuring wheelchair accessibility on an automated shuttle-bus pilot project to establishing a testing 'sandbox' for AV prototypes. Much of the work calls for continuing research on the development of AVs, from their impact on surface transit to the way they might circulate when unoccupied. Unstated but evident is the city's intention not to get sandbagged again by a technology that it didn't see coming.

Lanyon's report was informed by a close reading of how early car adoption influenced urban histories. In cities like Los Angeles, critical decision points – e.g., the postwar move to tear up its extensive streetcar network – played a determinative role in the city's fraught relationship with the automobile and the related problems with sprawl and air quality.

His analysis also drew heavily on an influential 2005 essay about the evolution of urban transportation technology between 1860 and 1930, written by University of Manchester innovation scholar Frank Geels. Geels set out to explore the technical and societal 'transition pathway' between the horse-drawn carriage and the automobile. Lanyon says the most important lesson from Geels's work is that there was 'no critical path' that led to the dominance of the automobile; it was never some kind of foregone conclusion. Lanyon also takes the view that we're in a similar period of transition right now. 'As a society, we won't just jump forward' to the adoption of AVs as they are currently imagined (Geels 2005).

Geels's narrative illustrates just how complex that transportation revolution was. The push to rely less on horses was informed by public health concerns – too much manure on city streets – and gave way to the advent of horse-drawn taxis and then trolleys. The inventors of early private cars experimented with batteries and steam as fuel sources, and combustion engines initially didn't catch on because they required a crank. The late nineteenth-century bicycle craze gave rise to specialized precision manufacturing techniques while stoking public interest in individual mobility and the use of bikes for touring. Meanwhile, cities were beginning to pave streets and replace cobblestones with asphalt as the expansion of electricity whet the public's appetite for electric trams.

A Dearborn, Michigan, inventor named Henry Ford borrowed from new bike-manufacturing techniques as he developed what would become the first mass-produced car. But, Geels argues, the 'application' that really fuelled the popularity of private cars was that city dwellers could take them into the countryside to explore. It was a recreational, as opposed to practical, use that produced the demand that allowed the gas-powered private vehicle to eventually dominate. 'The success of the automobile,' Geels concludes, 'was enabled by the previous transformations.'

The learning, Lanyon reflects, is that AVs have to compete with other transportation technologies and uses; the winner is not predetermined just because the auto sector, and tech giants like Amazon and Google, are investing so much money into self-driving electric vehicles. In fact, the pandemic underscored the serendipitous nature of technology adoption in this part of the mobility sector. According to a World Economic Forum analysis published in late 2021, investment in AVs slowed during the pandemic, and the market shifted to the commercialization of self-driving delivery and freight vehicles, as well as more specialized industrial applications such as autonomous forklifts and pallet movers developed for cavernous distribution centres (Laviv et al. 2021).

Smart city watcher Anthony Townsend adds that the car industry's much-hyped investments in AVs have also diverted attention from what he feels will become more impactful applications, such as smaller, nimble autonomous transit vehicles or a range of specialized mobility devices that rely on AV navigation systems, such as bikes capable of rebalancing themselves and next-gen motorized wheelchairs. 'There are so many scenarios for other kinds of vehicles,' he says. 'But that's not part of the main narrative because that's not part of the auto industry's messaging.'

COVID-19 further revealed the ways in which politics and abrupt swings in public opinion can affect the evolution of emerging mobility technologies as much as advances in engineering. Because the pandemic coincided with a spate of severe weather crises and served up bracing lessons about the experience of global catastrophes, many governments stepped up their carbon-reduction plans and established dates for the phase-out of combustion-engine-powered vehicles – something that had never happened before 2020. Those moves, in turn, stoked demand for battery electric vehicles, whose performance and range have steadily improved, and prompted governments to step up investments in charging infrastructure and grid capacity.[11] A growing number of major automakers, in turn, have pledged to move to all electric in coming years – a development that could happen sooner than many expect. According to BloombergNEF, in fact, global EV sales jumped 80 per cent in 2021 and accounted for 7.2 per cent of all vehicle sales in the first half of 2021 (Walton 2021).

Similarly, the market for micro-mobility devices, many of which are battery-powered, saw its own pandemic bounce. With the drop in car traffic and transit use, many cities significantly expanded their networks of bike lanes to accommodate the growing use of conventional bicycles, e-scooters, and e-bikes, including app-based e-scooters and municipal bike-sharing services.

Market research studies have forecast rapid growth in this segment, and some assessments have found that people who rely on micro-mobility devices are travelling longer distances. 'According to a U.S. micro-mobility company that rents e-scooters,' noted a 2020 McKinsey Partners study, 'average trip distances have grown 26 percent since the start of the pandemic, with rides in some cities, such as Detroit, increasing by up to 60 percent' (Heineke et al. 2020).

However, these emerging modes of low-carbon transportation are not free of controversy. In some places, tensions between the users of traditional bikes and faster-moving or heavier e-bikes have flared. Some cities, in turn, have faced a backlash against so-called 'dockless' e-scooters, which can be left anywhere and have tended to clutter up streets and public spaces in early adopter cities, like Edmonton.

A 2020 study in the *Journal of Urban Affairs* by two University of Texas at Austin scholars noted that the experiences of Chinese cities with essentially unregulated dockless bike-share services forewarned of the problems with e-scooters operated by firms like Bird and Lime. Between 2015 and 2019, the study pointed out, the use of upstart Chinese bike-share services exploded, creating widespread problems

---

11. In carbon-conscious cities like Vancouver, planning rules now specify that the developers of new multi-unit residential buildings must provide EV charging connections for every apartment's parking space.

with illegal parking and abandoned, broken bikes strewn around public spaces. 'Nevertheless,' wrote Shunhua Bai, a PhD candidate, and Junfeng Jiao, an associate professor in the U of T Austin school of architecture, 'the success of shared micro-mobility at an early stage has generated a transportation revolution in short travels.'

When Bai and Jiao looked at Austin, they observed similar dilemmas with the city's dockless e-scooter services, especially in the downtown and around the university campus. The sight of e-scooters that had been left lying on paths or along sidewalks prompted many angry calls and texts to the city's 311 service, made worse by a lack of follow-through on the part of city crews.

Considering the prospects for these services, Bai and Jiao waxed poetic: 'In a Shakespearian tragedy, we always see a tragic hero born with a fatal flaw, struggling between good and evil,' they wrote. '"To be or not to be dockless" is a Shakespearian question for shared micro-mobility. The dockless system is the tragic hero currently struggling between the virtue of flexible, car-free travel experience and the disvalue of overcrowded vehicles engulfing the public space in our cities. The overgrowth of dockless transportation systems in many Chinese cases has alerted us of a tragic ending if we do not strive to control the damage to our society promptly.'

While Bai and Jiao opined that there was potential to make better use of data analytics to confront the discarded scooter problem – for example, using algorithms to track and hopefully minimize response time by city crews to complaints – they also recognized the limits of the technology.

Another option, they argued, was a so-called 'shared responsibility' model that would allow both the city and the e-scooter companies to have access to crowdsourced 311 complaints data as a means of better managing the fleets. 'City staff could identify predominant issues and adjust license regulations to alleviate the impacts on society,' the authors suggested. '[T]he licensees could change their user instructions to address misbehaviors and enact restrictions or penalties on improper use according to the regulations from the city.' In other words, regulation.

The missing element in this particular story is the element that has allowed e-scooter businesses to proliferate: docking stations. Without these anchors in public space, e-scooter companies obviously can reduce their capital costs and therefore their rental charges while minimizing interactions with the municipal authorities that regulate what can and can't be installed on public spaces like sidewalks. (E-mobility firms like Bird recruit 'fleet managers' to look after and recharge the bikes or e-scooters.)

The physical tether between smart mobility devices and urban space, however, is a critical element, as important as the government's duty to regulate transportation. We might not think of the quotidian bike-docking stations that have proliferated in many cities as transportation infrastructure per se, to be added to a list that might include transit stations, buses, or traffic signals. Yet with rapidly growing public use of bike-sharing services, bike-docking stations can certainly be categorized as urban infrastructure. When complemented by an array of digital features, such as smart phone apps that map the locations of available bikes and offer online payment options, these bike-share services can be properly described as sustainable smart city technologies that improve urban life instead of merely cluttering up public spaces with more gadgets.

There is one more layer to the story about the use of bike-share systems to augment existing transportation networks. In many cities, municipalities or their technology partners operators have deployed bike-share infrastructure in neighbourhoods that tend to be more economically affluent and less diverse, thus exacerbating social 'stratification,' according to a 2021 study co-authored by smart city expert Rob Kitchin and National University of Ireland, Maynooth geographer Robert Bradshaw. The pair, however, cite the rollout of Hamilton's SoBi bike-share platform as an example of how planners went out of their way to consult local communities in order to situate docking stations in lower-income areas that aren't well-served by transit. They concluded that when residents were actively involved in co-creating bike-share systems, the result was a more equitable service. Kitchin and Bradshaw point out that Hamilton's approach has been taken up in places like Boston and Washington, which have sought to reconfigure their own legacy bike-share programs to be more inclusive in their coverage (Bradshaw & Kitchin 2021).

Besides relative newcomers like Lime and Bird or specialized e-bike manufacturers, global tech giants are also hustling to exploit the commercial potential in ordinary and even unsexy forms of civic infrastructure, including parking spots and sidewalks.

Since the late 2010s a Google subsidiary called Coord has been busy mapping the *curbs* of big cities. 'Curb analytics,' as the company describes this venture, involves building digital maps packed with geographical data on the locations and dimensions of 'assets' like parking spaces, loading zones, use regulations, taxi stops, wheelchair-accessible curb ramps, fire hydrants, and so on.

'A new way to see your city's curbs,' announced a Coord blog post, which itemizes commercial applications for this kind of data – visualizations for municipal planners to assist in figuring out the allocation of curb space, for loading, bike lanes, or pick-up/drop-off zones and parking spaces. In a related venture that Sidewalk Labs had planned to test in Toronto, the company would install sensors along the edges of streets to detect if a parking spot is vacant at any given moment. Such devices come with a cost, which suggests a business model and a strategy for generating revenue from them.

The company also envisioned the development of its own traffic management system, Flow, that used Google Maps, Street View, and other data sources to generate predictions about 'where people are coming or going,' according to Harvard business professor Shoshana Zuboff. One potential product dovetails with Coord's mapping: services like 'dynamic parking' and 'a shared mobility marketplace.' As she wrote, 'Sidewalk's data flows combine public and private assets for sale in dynamic, real-time virtual markets that extract maximum fees from citizens and leave municipal governments dependent upon Sidewalk's proprietary information' (Zuboff 2019, 229).

Meanwhile, up on the sidewalk, Amazon is testing delivery 'robots' – they resemble tall, enclosed children's wagons and are decked out with the company's smile logo. These vehicles are designed to make use of sidewalk space as they drop off parcels in neighbourhoods. The trials, reports *Mashable*, are taking place in Georgia and Tennessee. No doubt the trials of these compact autonomous vehicles are being closely watched, given the dramatic surge in e-commerce that occurred after the beginning of the pandemic.

Veteran Toronto mobility consultant Bern Grush has been working on developing international standards, to be adopted by the International Organization for Standardization, that would lay out rules for how such robots must function on these strips of concrete that have long been the exclusive preserve of pedestrians.

This fast-growing family of smart mobility technologies is transforming the unhurried world of curbs and sidewalks into contested, and possibly financially valuable, spaces that are of intense interest to e-commerce, delivery, and tech giants, and, perhaps eventually, fleets of shared AVs, which will have wireless access to curb maps that identify parking spots where they can stop until the next ride. 'We've never managed the sidewalk before with that complexity,' Grush says. 'They all compete for space.'

This standards development exercise, Grush observes, has raised some complex philosophical questions. 'The rules apply to the machines,' he says. 'I'm not contemplating anything in the standard to regulate human behaviour.' The prospect of AVs navigating sidewalks means they will interact with humans, dogs, people pushing strollers, and motorized wheelchairs, not to mention recycling bins, sidewalk detritus, snow, even dog poop. 'What I am saying is that if we're going to allow a robot on the sidewalk,' says Grush, 'that robot has to grant the right-of-way, it has to stick to one side. But will the robots change our sidewalk behaviour?'

It's a provocative question. Of course, private enterprises use – and make money from – public spaces in cities all the time, from restaurant sidewalk patios to street vendors, billboards, and food trucks. Their presence alters the way city dwellers use public space – where we go, what we do, whom we meet, and so on.

Yet the combination of powerful digital mapping tools and emerging types of autonomous vehicles raises the prospect of the financialization of public spaces in order to serve the interests of large corporations. After all, if Uber or Lyft someday operates a fleet of AVs that will need places to park between rides, access to real-time data about the location and availability of nearby parking spaces suddenly becomes a desirable commodity. Likewise, if parcel delivery companies become reliant on the use of sidewalks, it's not difficult to imagine that they'll eventually demand that municipalities provide more and better access, perhaps even citing data collected from those routes where they encounter obstacles, like a group of preteens ambling home from school and blocking the sidewalk, as kids do.

In a world where urban mobility becomes ever more digitally determined and eventually autonomous, the role of local and regional governments as regulators of public space seems destined to become increasingly complicated – an exercise in weighing interests that could easily rank the desires of residents well below the demands of big tech.

7
Function Creep and Surveillance

In 2016, San Diego City Council voted to approve a $30 million investment in a new smart city street-lighting system that promised to not only reduce electricity consumption but also assist municipal officials in planning and managing street parking and new bike lanes using sophisticated digital sensors.

The deal, consummated the following year, involved the purchase of 4,200 of General Electric's remote-controlled LED 'nodes' as the first phase in the replacement of 14,000 of San Diego's 60,000 street lights, all of which used inefficient sodium bulbs.

The giant conglomerate, of course, had been in the lighting business for well over a century. In recent years, its 'intelligent environment' group began thinking about how street lighting, one of the most rudimentary forms of urban infrastructure, was an 'under-utilized asset' with vast potential. GE Current (now spun off) wanted to go further than just providing illumination by reinventing the street light altogether.

To that end, the company's engineers designed CityIQ, which is essentially a weatherproof plastic box that sits at the top of a hydro pole next to the LED lamp fixture. This innocuous container houses all sorts of digital sensors, on-board computing power, and wifi connections to a city's operations centre. As for the business model, GE Current told potential customers the CityIQ nodes could be financed using energy savings from the LED lights, so it's essentially a wash for taxpayers. 'It allows the city to do lots of things,' said Jim Benson, a senior marketing executive for GE Current.

The devices come with air quality monitors, fish-eye lens cameras that can monitor bike or vehicle volumes on side streets, unsafe driving, and parking infractions. There's even an audio device linked to a third-party software system called 'ShotSpotter,' which detects gunfire, estimates the location, and notifies 911. According to procurement reports cited in a San Diego Police Department document obtained by a local newspaper, the installation of the first 4,000 nodes would allow the city to transform the equipment 'into a connected digital network to optimize parking and traffic, enhance public safety and track air quality.' (Other manufacturers include features like parking-space occupancy detectors and automatic brightness adjustments.)

At the time the purchase was being considered, municipal officials had a lot to say in public about what these devices *would* do: reduce energy consumption and identify areas with lots of cyclists in order to expand the bike lane network. What they didn't explain, however, is what they *could* do, especially in regards to public safety. As it turned out, these devices, perched inconspicuously at the tops of utility poles, were packed with surveillance technology – an unblinking eye, surveying the street below.

GE Current had sold its smart lighting systems in Portland, Atlanta, and San Diego; indeed, the market for these devices is growing rapidly. Benson insisted the sensors had been fitted out with a range of data privacy protections – the gunshot detector, for example, couldn't make out voices. But, Benson admitted, not all customers wanted the video capabilities. 'There's a lot of sensitivity around this.'

That would be putting it mildly. Revelations about the use of the video cameras by police set off a raucous local fight, pitting former mayor Kevin Faulconer and the police chief against racialized communities and civil liberties activists. San Diego council scrambled to contain the fallout. 'The city has been trying to cover up what they knew about the technology,' charged Geneviéve Jones-Wright, a San Diego lawyer who speaks for TRUST SD Coalition, a coalition of groups that banded together to fight the use of cameras.

❖

The San Diego street-lighting debacle illuminates two of the most contentious aspects of smart city technology: the potential for even more widespread surveillance and the related risk of so-called 'function creep,' particularly with complex digital systems purchased by local governments using public monies.

The world of the modern city is already intensely surveilled. CCTVs have become ubiquitous in public, commercial, office, and industrial spaces. China has layered facial recognition software onto its CCTV networks, creating the world's most extensive public surveillance system. Using a range of technologies and biometric devices, employers can monitor workers' emails, the amount of time they spend on external websites, their movements within an office, or the duration of their bathroom breaks.

Most of us consciously post all sorts of personal information to a range of social media sites – data that can become fodder for investigators, reporters, competitors, prospective employers, neighbours, criminals, and so on. Palantir, a surveillance software powerhouse created by Paypal founder Peter Thiel, has generated billions in revenues gathering, combining, and analyzing this kind of information for law enforcement, intelligence and immigration agencies, the military, and private investigators. It has been condemned by Amnesty International for failing to safeguard the human rights of people who are caught up in its surveillance web.

A great deal more digital watching takes place in the service of commerce. Websites set up cookies in your browser for digital ads. E-commerce sites track previous purchases and serve up suggestions for future ones. Google tracks and sells search information to advertisers. Social media sites use monetization strategies that rely on monitoring user behaviour and transforming those patterns into a saleable product. Smart phones and apps are designed to track an individual's movement patterns, purchase habits, and other data that can be packaged up and marketed.

Smart phones, in turn, leave trails of digital bread crumbs that can be aggregated across millions of users' accounts and put to work driving navigation apps like Waze. Those apps and the companies behind them are interested in extracting huge amounts of data from the smart phones moving around a city at all times. Each device produces a signal plume, and these are aggregated by services like Google Maps to inform users about traffic delays, optimal routes, and all sorts of other embedded location information derived from Street-view 360 images, municipal databases, satellite photos, and so on. It is a highly useful form of mass surveillance.

As Harvard's Shoshana Zuboff put it in her 2019 treatise, surveillance capitalism is 'a new economic order that claims human experience as free raw material for hidden commercial practices of extraction, prediction, and sales.' She characterized this ever-expanding sphere as not only a threat to human rights, but a 'rogue mutation of capitalism' that has produced unprecedented wealth, knowledge, and power. It is, she stated in a message that resonated with the critics of smart city ventures like Sidewalk Labs, 'best understood as a coup from above.'

Concerns about smart city technologies, in fact, have zeroed in on the risk of creating heavily surveilled cities in the name of urban quality-of-life benefits such as improved mobility, reduced emissions, or more efficient use of local services. 'This futuristic wired urban world has a dark side,' warned Robert Muggah, a principal at Ottawa-based SecDev Group, in a 2021 essay in *Foreign Policy* entitled '"Smart" Cities Are Surveilled Cities' he wrote with Greg Walton. 'Part of what supposedly makes cities smarter,' they continued, 'is the deployment and integration of surveillance technologies such as sensors and biometric data collection systems. Electronic, infrared, thermal, and lidar sensors form the basis of the smart grid, and they do everything from operating streetlights to optimizing parking and traffic flow to detecting crime' (Muggah & Walton 2021).

The second but related source of controversy around San Diego's smart lighting system was directly tied to the essential nature of digital devices, which is that they can do many things. In fact, the questions that fuelled the political fight over these devices had to do with intention: did the city set out to buy devices that could covertly assist the police in investigating street crime or was that capability essentially latent, something that was discovered once the devices were installed? Was it a case of 'function creep'?

Initially, city officials insisted the video cameras embedded in the GE smart lighting nodes were never meant to be used as surveillance devices. They were even fitted out with software that obscures details like faces and licence plates. 'It really started as an energy project,' said the city's deputy chief operating officer, Erik Caldwell.

At some point in 2018, however, San Diego police officials realized they could use the video footage, which is stored for five days, in crime scene investigations and began asking the city to release it. At the time, city council wasn't informed about the SDPD's interest in the tapes. 'In our conversations with GE and council, we made it clear we didn't want to use the system for law enforcement,' Caldwell insisted. 'That was not our intention.' Still, he added, the city had 'a legal and moral' obligation to hand over video footage when the police asked for it.

Jones-Wright offered a far more skeptical account of the city's conduct. She said officials and the mayor's office made little effort to explain the system's capabilities to constituents early on, and mostly played up the environmental benefits. 'There was never even a public discussion,' she said. 'The city has been trying to cover up what they knew about the technology. No one had a chance to weigh in on this.'

As revelations about the police use of the nodes surfaced via documents obtained through access-to-information requests made by local investigative reporters, the SDPD responded by noting how the cameras had not only assisted with investigations but disproved assault charges that had been laid against a bystander in one incident.

SDPD officials themselves have subsequently confirmed how useful the footage is. 'We had no idea what the quality of video would be, or what it would capture,' Jeffrey Jordon, who leads special projects and legislative affairs for the San Diego Police Department, told *Bloomberg CityLab*. 'The first time we saw it we were like, "Holy cow, that's really good video."'

It soon became obvious that the city was operating in a policy vacuum. There were unanswered questions about the ownership of the data and metadata generated by the nodes and whether the information could be mined or sold. There were no rules around how the police would access the video, and under what circumstances. Last, the city had done nothing in the way of community consultation around privacy issues. 'They're collecting data about how I move [around] in the city without acknowledging that we should have a say in that,' said Jones-Wright.

In 2019, the SDPD issued a procedure document outlining the use of video from the smart street lights, but critics pointed out that such policies were designed by and for law enforcement. Jones-Wright and the TRUST SD coalition called for a complete moratorium on further deployment until San Diego council had produced a legally enforceable privacy policy with public oversight.

After a year of bitter fighting, San Diego council in July 2020 cut off funding for the street lights and in mid-November 2020 approved an ordinance calling for stricter controls and better governance, including the establishment of a privacy advisory board that reports to council.

'Let us never underestimate the power of concerned community members coming together and making change,' Jones-Wright said after the ordinance passed. 'The work started because our government and public officials failed us.'

A growing number of cities are buying or considering smart lighting systems, and some, like Oakland, have opted to disable video to head off concerns about civil liberties. Erik Caldwell, for his part, pointed to the broader issue of unintended consequences. 'It's a kind of lesson for cities thinking about smart city technology.'

When municipalities buy buses, playground equipment, or traffic signals, it's generally obvious how these assets will be used, which is to say, as intended. By contrast, data-generating digital technologies like laptops are packed with features: they can do many things, not all of which are known ahead of time. The smart phone is a perfect example. Did Apple's Steve Jobs envision that someday Bluetooth-enabled electric toothbrushes would have digital features that deliver brushing-effectiveness metrics to an app on a smart phone? Probably not. Yet he certainly did recognize that the iPhone could serve as a platform from which third-party apps would operate.

The iPhone represents one link in a long chain of innovation that includes predecessor devices like the Blackberry and the pager, as well as iPods and, before those, MP3 players, cellphones, and radio transmitters. Innovation is an intrinsically iterative process, and doubly so when it involves technology.[12] An invention is launched into the world, and people begin to find various ways of using it, some envisioned and others discovered through experimentation, imagination, or accident. In the meantime, the inventors or their successors develop iterations of the original, incorporating new features that respond to evolving uses and also finding ways of improving efficiency or reducing cost. All of these intertwined processes – involving myriad end users, as well as engineers, designers, and marketers – generate feedback loops, which yield improvements, inspire competing products, and seed new industries and inventions.

Was the discovery that GE's smart lighting node could be used for police investigations an innovation or something else? Critics of smart city technology have argued that the San Diego smart lighting story, and others like it, represent examples of 'function creep' (a.k.a. 'mission creep'), not innovation.

In a 2021 paper in *Law, Innovation and Technology* journal, Bert-Jaap Koops formally defined 'function creep' 'as an imperceptibly transformative and therewith contestable change in a data-processing system's proper activity.' Koops, a professor of regulation and technology at Tilburg Institute for Law, Technology, and Society in the Netherlands, explained that the term can be applied when some kind of system shifts subtly, but not necessarily organically, with a

---

12. It is also possible to innovate processes, such as the production of a magazine or the approval of a building permit.

non-trivial alteration to the original function (e.g., from an energy-reducing street light system with a few additional features to an investigative tool). What's more, he distinguishes function creep from conventional innovation processes, as well as 'transformative' changes – such as the evolution of phones from analogue land lines to digital cellulars.

As he points out, the functions of data-processing systems frequently expand, and it is neither possible nor indeed desirable to regulate that process. For example, Excel spreadsheets were originally designed as accounting software, but they are now used for almost countless non-financial purposes.

Digital systems, however, are vulnerable to function creep, and the examples of this phenomenon, both in the smart city world and elsewhere, have piled up with the exponential growth in both big data and computing power.

In July 2019, for example, the *Washington Post* revealed that agents with the FBI and Immigration and Customs Enforcement (ICE) were using facial recognition software to scan digital databases of state-level driver's licence records, which always include photos. The goal: identify illegal immigrants and suspects in criminal cases.

Freedom-of-information requests made by the Georgetown Law Center on Privacy and Technology produced thousands of documents showing how the databases had been transformed into an unprecedented surveillance infrastructure.' Law enforcement officials, moreover, were accessing the images without obtaining consent from the licencees. The *Post* also found that neither the U.S. Congress nor state legislatures authorized such uses of state driver's licence images. The episode revealed how those databases, originally intended for one specific purpose, had been covertly used for something different and nefarious.

As the San Diego street light fight illustrated, function creep poses a particular concern with technology that collects large amounts of data in public spaces. 'These technologies can have different features turned on,' says Gilad Rosner, the IoT Privacy researcher. He advocates for the use of the 'precautionary principle' in the deployment of new technology.

Similar concerns came up when Sidewalk Labs was promoting its Quayside smart city project in Toronto. At one 2018 session of a digital strategy advisory panel established by Waterfront Toronto, the agency that invited Sidewalk to bid on the project, U of T privacy expert Andrew Clement warned that the proposed surveillance infrastructure in the company's plans, combined with the sheer volume of data-sharing envisioned by Sidewalk Labs, posed clear privacy risks. 'Function creep is a concern that may develop over time,' he said ('Minutes' 2018).

Other privacy law scholars offered even more ominous warnings. Noting the risk of what she described as 'surveillance creep,' Ellen P. Goodman, the information policy scholar at Rutgers Law School, pointed out that Google, Sidewalk's parent, had demonstrated a willingness to slip surveillance features into products like Nest, its front-door security system. Unbeknownst to consumers, the device came with an onboard microphone, as Google later admitted.

With Sidewalk's plan, 'a vendor-led project planning for a thick weave of special-purpose sensors may deploy that surveillance capability in new ways, without authorization,' Goodman wrote in a thirty-eight-page affidavit filed as part of a 2019 Canadian Civil Liberties Association lawsuit against Waterfront Toronto. 'This tendency for devices to expand their capabilities in the future is common in smart-city technologies' ('Affidavit of Ellen P. Goodman' 2020).

In San Diego, as in Toronto with Sidewalk Labs, grassroots politics spelled the end of a smart city venture gone wrong. The smart street light controversy tapped into broader political undercurrents – about class, police power, and a mayor perceived to be indifferent to race issues. After reports that the videos on the smart nodes had been used by police to monitor the protests over the George Floyd murder in Minneapolis, the city scrambled to contain the fallout.

'Mayor Kevin Faulconer's decision to turn off the city's Smart Streetlight surveillance devices until an oversight plan has been crafted and adopted makes sense,' the *San Diego Union-Tribune* opined in an editorial that characterized the origins of the program as 'bizarre' but acknowledged the potential value of 'tech tools' in solving crime. 'A city policy that clearly lays out how, when, where and if data gathered by Smart Streetlights can be used is critical' (*San Diego Union-Tribune* Editorial Board 2020).

In Toronto, public response to Sidewalk's plans was less explicitly reactive, in the sense that the backlash – from civil liberties activists, tech-skeptics, and some city officials – coalesced well before the company was able to build anything. What's more, the public and media scrutiny of Sidewalk's far-reaching proposal set in motion – at least temporarily – a broad-ranging discussion about the governance of smart city systems and the potential for function creep, as well as concerns about privacy and the monetization of data gathered from people moving through urban spaces. Those fears seemed to be confirmed when Sidewalk's privacy advisor, Ann Cavoukian, a former Ontario information and privacy commissioner, quit because she felt Sidewalk's Quayside plan lacked adequate safeguards.

Waterfront Toronto established an oversight committee to advise on digital policy matters as they pertained to a smart city project like Quayside. The city in turn set up a smart city policy consultation process. In the media, academic journals, and university classrooms, Sidewalk's highly publicized pitch set in motion a remarkable outpouring of debate about the regulation and oversight of a family of technologies whose true capabilities were not especially well understood.

Beyond the blunt-force instrument that is politics, the question hanging over both San Diego and Toronto's fraught experiences with smart city development is whether there are or could be more proactive approaches, either to regulation or to the design of these technologies themselves.

As tech critics in both cities pointed out, existing privacy laws, at least in Canada and the United States, weren't equal to the task of regulating such devices. In 2019, for example, Ontario's Information and Privacy Commissioner Brian Beamish cautioned Waterfront Toronto that Sidewalk's plans, which envisioned brand-new governance structures and dubious legal definitions of the data it gathered within the Quayside development, didn't conform to Ontario privacy rules. More generally, Beamish stated, 'The provincial government must modernize our laws to ensure that privacy protective, transparent, accountable and ethical data practices are at the forefront of all smart city projects' (Information and Privacy Commissioner of Ontario 2019).

Yet legislative action, while crucial, is only part of the picture. Some municipalities have sought to adopt a more intentional approach to procuring smart city systems specifically to head off the types of PR disasters that befell San Diego.

Barbara Swartzentruber, executive director of Guelph's smart city office, observes that the difficulty for cities is that these technologies have become intensely polarizing: 'Either you're for innovation and risk, or you're a Luddite.' Guelph's solution has been to set up processes designed to anticipate problems instead of reacting to crises as they're happening. 'It has to be an eyes-wide-open conversation,' she says, adding that Guelph officials constantly get overtures from smart city tech firms promoting the latest solutions.

The challenge for municipalities is to not get taken in by a sales pitch and end up locking in to a complex contract that effectively gives the supplier all sorts of advantages, such as unanticipated data ownership rights. At the same time, municipal managers like Swartzentruder want to find ways of taking advantage of new technologies that potentially improve services.

In Guelph's case, transportation officials wanted to figure out how they could use digital cameras affixed to city vehicles to capture images and locations of potholes, cracks, and other signs of wear on the 581 kilometres of roadway within city limits. These images would assist the city in prioritizing 311 calls and making capital plans.

Guelph officials realized early on that they would have to use technology that blurs identifying details, like licence plates or faces, to ensure privacy. The municipality also asked Guelph Lab, a small civic accelerator run jointly by the city and the University of Guelph, to research the proposal. Sam Laban, the Lab's facilitator, served up some important insights: U.S. research, he found, has shown that municipal works departments that rely on digital feedback to drive maintenance decisions don't treat all neighbourhoods equally. The law of unintended consequences seemed to be a factor.

Some studies showed, for example, that predominantly Black communities log plenty of requests for service but tend to be underserved. Meanwhile, neighbourhoods with many newcomers generate fewer complaints and may get even less attention. 'Equity isn't implicit in these technologies,' Laban says. As they scoped out the project, city officials knew they'd have to look at equity issues when vetting potential vendors in order to avoid investing in technology that serves to amplify, rather than reduce, underlying social problems. As Swartzentruber says, 'We have to go a bit faster and the tech people have to go a bit slower, and we'l meet in the middle.'

Other jurisdictions have engineered protections against function creep directly into their technology systems. Estonia is one of the best-known examples of widespread adoption of e-government technologies that don't fall prey to these kinds of headaches. In 2001, the tiny Baltic state (1.3 million residents) began building what came to be known as X-Road, a national software network that knit together the information systems and databases of dozens of public agencies, state banks, and utilities.

Residents can access the entire network – from tax filings to medical records – with a single password. Changes input by citizens or public servants are automatically updated in the appropriate databases. But security and access safeguards prevent data breaches and unauthorized or unspecified uses, such as police surveillance of drivers' licences. 'Critically,' observed public sector IT analysts David Eaves and Ben McGuire in *Policy Options* in 2019, 'there is a mechanism for citizens to see who has accessed their data to ensure no one is doing so without proper authority.'

Some places have turned to technological solutions to fix the headaches created by some forms of smart city tech. One example is Numina, a Brooklyn-based start-up that makes 'computer vision sensors' that look like tall-boy beer cans strapped to utility poles. The devices can map pedestrian activity without capturing human images – an approach Numina describes as 'intelligence without surveillance.'

The firm, which has partnered with Sidewalk Labs, says it runs the data through its analytics software to provide cities with insights about how residents are using public space – for example, recreational facilities like soccer fields in public parks or bike paths.

Numina's technology is an example of 'edge computing.' The term is used to describe highly decentralized computer networks where the heavy computational lifting takes place at the edges rather than in a mainframe processor. In the case of Numina, the beer can–shaped sensors have enough onboard computing power to be able to take a measure of the activity on a given sports field, for example, and they're also set up to obscure details that might identify individuals. All the readings are fed into a central system so Numina's clients, such as the managers of municipal parks, can get a bigger picture of what's going on – as with charts that track the changing volume of bikes on a bike path during the course of a week. The company says its technology is intended to help municipalities plan and operate these amenities based on actual traffic counts that can be generated without compromising any individual's privacy.

This approach, known as 'security by obscurity,' might head off the kind of controversy that engulfed San Diego's smart lighting project. Yet issues of privacy, surveillance, and the financialization of data collected intentionally or incidentally from people moving through public spaces are ultimately not technical questions to be solved with better technology. Nor are they simply legal questions.

The promise of so much smart city technology rests on its claim to take a close measure of urban spaces and systems, and then use those readings – in whatever form they may be – as a means of tackling urban problems. But as quantum physicists postulated well over a century ago, the act of observation is neither neutral nor passive. Rather, observation itself can alter that which is being observed, as those innocuous plastic nodes perched at the top of San Diego light standards proved.

8

The Special Case of AI and Big Data–Based Policing

In mid-2019, an investigative journalism/tech non-profit called Muck-Rock, and Open the Government (OTG), a non-partisan advocacy group, began submitting freedom of information requests to law enforcement agencies across the United States. The goal: to smoke out details about the use of an app rumoured to offer unprecedented facial recognition capabilities to anyone with a smart phone.

Co-founded by Michael Morisy, a former *Boston Globe* editor, Muck-Rock specializes in freedom of information (FOIS) requests, and its site has grown into a publicly accessible repository of government documents obtained under access-to-information laws.

As responses trickled in, it became clear that the MuckRock/OTG team had made a discovery about a tech company called Clearview AI. Based on documents obtained from Atlanta, OTG researcher Freddy Martinez began filing more requests and discovered that as many as two hundred police departments across the U.S. were using Clearview's app, which compares images taken by smart phone cameras to a sprawling database of 3 billion open-source photographs of faces linked to various forms of personal information (e.g., Facebook profiles). It was, in effect, a point-click-and-identify system that radically transformed the work of police officers.

The documents soon found their way to a *New York Times* reporter named Kashmir Hill, who, in January 2020, published a deeply investigated feature about Clearview, a tiny and secretive start-up with backing from Peter Thiel, the Silicon Valley billionaire behind Paypal and Palantir Technologies. Among the story's revelations, Hill disclosed that tech giants like Google and Apple were well aware that such an app could be developed using artificial intelligence algorithms feeding off the vast storehouse of facial images uploaded to social media platforms and other publicly accessible databases. But they had opted against designing such a disruptive and easily disseminated surveillance tool.

The *Times* story set off what could best be described as an international chain reaction, with widespread media coverage about the use of Clearview's app, followed by a wave of announcements from various governments and police agencies about how Clearview's app would be banned. The reaction played out against a backdrop of news reports about China's nearly ubiquitous facial recognition–based surveillance networks.

Canada was not exempt. *To Surveil and Predict*, a detailed examination of 'algorithmic policing' published in fall 2020 by the University of Toronto's Citizen Lab, noted that officers with law enforcement agencies in Calgary, Edmonton, and across Greater Toronto had tested Clearview's app, sometimes without the knowledge of their superiors. Investigative reporting by the *Toronto Star* and *Buzzfeed News* found numerous examples of municipal law enforcement agencies, including the Toronto Police Service, using the app in crime investigations. The RCMP denied using Clearview even after it had entered into a contract with the company – a detail exposed by Vancouver's *The Tyee*.

With federal and provincial privacy commissioners ordering investigations, Clearview and the RCMP subsequently severed ties, although Citizen Lab noted that many other tech companies still sell facial recognition systems in Canada. 'I think it is very questionable whether [Clearview] would conform with Canadian law,' Michael McEvoy, British Columbia's privacy commissioner, told the *Star* in February 2020.

There was more fallout elsewhere. Four U.S. cities banned police use of facial recognition outright, the Citizen Lab report noted. The

European Union in February proposed a ban on facial recognition in public spaces but later hedged. A U.K. court in April ruled that police facial recognition systems were 'unlawful,' marking a significant reversal in surveillance-minded Britain. And the European Data Protection Board, an EU agency, informed commission members in June 2020 that Clearview's technology violates pan-European law enforcement policies. As Rutgers University's Ellen Goodman comments, the use of data-intensive policing technologies has generated 'huge blowback.'

There's nothing new about surveillance or police investigative practices that draw on highly diverse forms of electronic information, from wiretaps to bank records and images captured by private security cameras. As early as the 1960s, a U.S. consulting firm, Simulmatics Corp., built computer simulations that purported to have the capacity to predict race riots based mash-ups of crime, demographic, and socio-economic data sets (Lepore 2020, 262). Yet during the 2010s, dramatic advances in big data analytics, biometrics, and AI, stoked by venture capital and law enforcement agencies eager to invest in new technology, have spurred on a fast-growing, well-capitalized industry that amasses huge collections of data, much of it open-source, to create powerful new tools for law enforcement agencies. As the Clearview story showed, regulation and democratic oversight have lagged far behind the technology.

U.S. start-ups like PredPol and HunchLab, now owned by Shot-Spotter, a publicly traded company, have designed so-called 'predictive policing' algorithms that use law enforcement records and other geographical data (e.g.. locations of schools) to make statistical guesses about the times and locations of future property or violent crimes. Palantir's law-enforcement service aggregates and then mines huge data sets consisting of emails, court documents, evidence repositories, gang member databases, automated licence plate readers, social media, etc., to find hidden correlations or patterns that police can use to investigate suspects.

Sarah Brayne, a B.C.-born University of Texas at Austin sociologist and author of a 2021 book entitled *Predict and Surveil: Data, Discretion, and the Future of Policing*, observes that big data's 'appeal stems from its aura of objectivity.' Echoing the safety promises advanced by autonomous vehicle advocates, Brayne observes that proponents of big data policing say the use of automated systems and huge sets of data removes the kind of bias and human error that leads to problematic policing practices, such as over-enforcement in low-income neighbourhoods. It is, in other words, the exemplar of evidence-based decision-making.

Yet as the Clearview fallout indicates, these systems are rife with technical, ethical, and political landmines. As Andrew G. Ferguson, a University of the District of Columbia law professor and authority on the subject, explained in his 2017 book, *The Rise of Big Data Policing: Surveillance, Race, and the Future of Law Enforcement*, analysts have identified an impressive list: biased, incomplete, or inaccurate data, opaque technology, erroneous predictions, lack of governance, public suspicions about surveillance and overpolicing, conflicts over access to proprietary algorithms, unauthorized use of data, and the muddied incentives of private firms selling law enforcement software. Further, as Brayne added in her study, human discretion and bias is baked into these technologies via programming, data entry, and the weighting assigned to different kinds of results (Brayne 2020, 100). The fingerprints of their creators have not been scrubbed away.

Brayne's research revealed that police officers were highly skeptical of policing algorithms.[13] Other critics point out that by deploying smart city sensors or other data-enabled systems, like transit smart cards, local governments may be inadvertently providing the police with new intelligence nodes. Metrolinx, the transit agency for the Greater Toronto and Hamilton Area, has released Presto

---

13. One contributing factor to that skepticism, Brayne explains, is that LAPD officials had developed 'policing-the-police' technologies – algorithms and monitoring devices designed to predict which officers were most likely to engage in violent conduct, then track the location of their vehicles.

card user information to police on a number of occasions, while London's Metropolitan Police has made thousands of requests for Oyster card data to track criminals. 'Any time you have a microphone, camera or a live-feed, these [become] surveillance devices with the simple addition of a court order,' adds New York civil rights lawyer Albert Cahn, executive director of the Surveillance Technology Oversight Project.

The authors of the Citizen Lab study, lawyers Kate Robertson, Cynthia Khoo, and Yolanda Song, argue that Canadian governments need to impose a moratorium on the deployment of algorithmic policing technology until the public policy and legal frameworks can catch up.

Data policing was born in New York City in the early 1990s when then-police commissioner William Bratton launched CompStat, a computer system that compiled up-to-date crime information – incidents, times, locations, etc. – then visualized the findings in 'heat maps.' These allowed unit commanders to deploy officers to neighbourhoods most likely to be experiencing crime problems.

Originally conceived as a management tool that would push a demoralized police force to make better use of limited resources, CompStat is credited by some as contributing to the marked reduction in crime rates in the Big Apple, although many other big cities experienced similar drops through the 1990s and early 2000s.

The 9/11 terrorist attacks sparked enormous investments in security technology. The past two decades have seen the emergence of a multi-billion-dollar industry dedicated to civilian security technology – everything from large-scale deployments of CCTVs and cyber-security to the development of highly sensitive biometric devices – fingerprint readers, iris scanners, etc. – designed to bulk up the security around factories, infrastructure, and government buildings.

Predictive policing and facial recognition technologies evolved on parallel tracks, both relying on increasingly sophisticated analytics techniques, artificial intelligence algorithms, and ever deeper pools of digital data.

The core idea is that the algorithms – essentially formulas, such as decision trees, that generate predictions – are 'trained' on large tranches of data so they become increasingly accurate – for example at anticipating the likely locations of future property crimes or matching a face captured in a digital image from a CCTV to one in a large database of headshots. Some algorithms are designed to use a set of rules with variables (akin to following a recipe). Others, known as machine learning systems, are programmed to learn on their own (trial and error).

The risk lies in the quality of the data used to train the algorithms – what was dubbed the 'garbage-in-garbage-out' problem in a study by the Center on Privacy and Technology at Georgetown Law. If there are hidden biases in the training data – e.g., it contains mostly Caucasian faces – the algorithm may misread Asian or Black faces and generate 'false positives,' a well-documented shortcoming if the application involves identifying a suspect in a crime.

Similarly, if a poor or racialized area is subject to overpolicing, there will likely be more crime reports, meaning the data from that neighbourhood is likely to reveal higher-than-average rates of certain types of criminal activity, a data point that would justify *more* overpolicing and racial profiling. Some crimes, in turn, are underreported, and so don't influence these algorithms or amplify feedback loops. Brayne, however, points out that big data analytics can 'retrospectively' diagnose problematic policing tactics, such as carding, through statistical analysis that can show proof of overpolicing in racialized neighbourhoods (Brayne 2020, 104).

Other predictive- and AI-based law enforcement technologies, including 'social network analysis' (SNA) – the notion that an individual's web of personal relationships, gleaned, for example, from open sources such as social media platforms or the cross-referencing of lists of gang members – promised to generate predictions that individuals already known to police were at risk of becoming embroiled in shootings and other violent crimes. Yet, as Brayne points out, when police rely on big data analytics to generate leads, there's a built-in incentive to feed the maw. As she related, during the years when she was embedded with the LAPD, she constantly found herself watching police officers aiming to ensure that seemingly innocuous details about individuals they stopped on the street would get 'into the system,' in the expectation that all the little shards of information may eventually form a pattern that powerful analytics technologies, such as those used by Palantir, will detect.

This type of sleuthing certainly seemed to hold out some promise. In one study, criminologists at Cardiff University found that 'disorder-related' posts on Twitter reflected actual crime incidents in metropolitan London – a finding that suggests how big data can help map and anticipate criminal activity. In practice, however, such surveillance tactics can prove to be explosive, as happened in 2016, when U.S. civil liberties groups revealed FOI documents showing that Geofeedia, a location-based data company, had signed contracts with numerous police departments to provide analytics based on social media posts to Twitter, Facebook, Instagram, etc. Among the individuals targeted by Geofeedia's data: protesters and activists. Chastened, the social media firms rapidly blocked Geofeedia's access.

The Chicago Police Department in 2013 began experimenting with predictive models that assigned risk scores for individuals based on criminal records or their connections to people involved in violent crime. By 2019, the CPD had assigned risk scores to almost 400,000 people and claimed to be using the information to surveil and target 'at-risk' individuals (including potential victims) or connect them to social services, according to a January 2020 report by Chicago's inspector general.

These tools can draw mistaken or biased inferences in the same way that over-reliance on police checks in racialized neighbourhoods merely results in what could be described as guilt by address. The Citizen Lab study noted that the Ontario Human Rights Commission identified social network analyses as a potential cause of racial profiling. In the case of the CPD's predictive risk model, the system was discontinued in 2020 after media reports and internal investigations showed that the police were adding people to their list based solely on arrest records, meaning they may not even have been charged, much less convicted of a crime (Foody 2020).

Early applications of facial recognition software included passport security systems or searches of mug-shot databases. But in 2011, the Insurance Corporation of B.C. offered Vancouver police the use of facial recognition software to match photos of Stanley Cup rioters with driver's licence images – a move that prompted a stern warning from the province's privacy commissioner. In 2019, the *Washington Post* revealed that the FBI and ICE investigators regarded state databases of digitized driver's licences, which had been scanned without consent, as a 'gold mine for facial recognition photos.'

In 2013, Canada's federal privacy commissioner released a report on police use of facial recognition that anticipated the issues raised by Clearview app earlier this year: '[S]trict controls and increased transparency are needed to ensure that the use of facial recognition conforms with our privacy laws and our common sense of what is socially acceptable.' (Canada's data privacy laws are only now being updated.)

The technology, meanwhile, continues to gallop ahead. New York civil rights lawyer Albert Cahn points to the emergence of 'gait recognition' systems, which use similar visual analysis techniques to identify individuals by their walk; these systems are reportedly in use in China. 'You're trying to teach machines how to identify people who walk with the same gait,' he says. 'Of course, a lot of this is completely untested.'

The predictive policing story has evolved somewhat differently. The methodology grew out of analysis commissioned by the Los Angeles Police Department in the early 2010s. Two data scientists, P. Jeffrey Brantingham and George Mohler, used mathematical modelling to forecast copycat crimes based on data about the location and frequency of previous burglaries in three L.A. neighbourhoods. They published their results and soon set up PredPol to commercialize the technology. Media attention soon followed, as news stories played up the seemingly miraculous power of a *Minority Report*–like system that could do a decent job anticipating incidents of property crime.

Operationally, police forces used PredPol's system by dividing up precincts in 150 square-metre 'cells' that police officers were instructed to patrol more intensively during periods when PredPol's algorithm forecast criminal activity. In the post-2009 credit crisis period, the technology seemed to promise that cash-strapped American municipalities would get more bang for their policing buck.

Other firms, from start-ups to multinationals like IBM, entered the market with innovations, incorporating other types of data, such as socio-economic data or geographical features, from parks and picnic tables to schools and bars, that may be correlated to elevated incidents of certain types of crime. The reported crime data is routinely updated so the algorithm remains current. (A short-lived smart phone app, initially called Ghetto Tracker and later re-dubbed Good Part of Town, used a Microsoft routing algorithm, plus user feedback on their personal sense of safety in a given location, to create 'safe' pedestrian 'travel tools.' It no longer exists [Tiku 2013].)

Police departments across the U.S. and Europe have invested in various predictive policing tools, as have several in Canada, including in Vancouver, Edmonton, and Saskatoon. Whether they have made a difference is an open question. As with several other studies, a 2017 review by analysts with the Institute for International Research on Criminal Policy, at Ghent University in Belgium, found inconclusive results: some places showed improved results compared to more conventional policing, while in other cities, the use of predictive algorithms led to reduced policing costs but little measurable difference in outcomes.

Revealingly, the city where predictive policing really took hold, Los Angeles, has rolled back police use on these techniques. In the spring of 2020, the LAPD tore up its contract with PredPol in the wake of mounting community and legal pressure from the Stop LAPD Spying Coalition, which had found that individuals who posed no real threat, mostly Black or Latino, were ending up on police watch lists because of flaws in the way the system assigned risk scores.

'Algorithms have no place in policing,' coalition founder Hamid Khan said in an interview in 2020 with MIT *Technology Review*. 'I think it's crucial that we understand that there are lives at stake. This language of location-based policing is by itself a proxy for racism.

They're not there to police potholes and trees. They are there to police people in the location. So location gets criminalized, people get criminalized, and it's only a few seconds away before the gun comes out and somebody gets shot and killed.' (Similar advocacy campaigns, including proposed legislation governing surveillance technology and gang databases, have been proposed for New York City.)

There has been one other interesting consequence: police resistance. Sarah Brayne spent two and a half years deeply embedded with the LAPD, exploring the reaction of law enforcement officials to algorithmic policing techniques by conducting ride-alongs as well as interviews with dozens of veteran cops and data analysts. In results published in 2021, Brayne and collaborator Angèle Christin observed 'strong processes of resistance fueled by fear of professional devaluation and threats of performance tracking.'

Before shifts, officers were told which squares to drive through, when and how frequently, and the location of their vehicles was tracked by an onboard GPS device to ensure compliance. But Brayne found that some would game the system by turning off the tracking device, which they regarded with suspicion. Others just didn't buy what the technology was selling. 'Patrol officers frequently asserted that they did not need an algorithm to tell them where crime occurs,' she noted.

Brayne says that police departments increasingly see predictive technology as part of the tool kit, despite questions about effectiveness or other concerns, like racial profiling. 'Once a particular technology is created,' she observed,' there's a tendency to use it.' Brayne, however, added one other prediction, which has to do with the future of algorithmic policing in the post–George Floyd era – 'an intersection,' as she says, 'between squeezed budgets and this movement around defunding the police.'

In July 2018, Toronto city council voted to ask the federal and provincial governments for $44 million for a long list of outlays meant to confront sharp increases in gun violence across the city. The funding was to go toward youth recreation and employment initiatives, various intervention efforts involving the police, and funding for children's mental health services.

But council, after a divisive debate, also supported a request from the police for an extra $4 million for a lot more CCTVs, as well as the deployment of the gunshot detection technology ShotSpotter, which uses specialized microphones and sophisticated software to identify and locate the source of outdoor gunfire, then automatically alerts 911 (Toronto Police Services Board 2018). Among the most outspoken proponents: Mayor John Tory, who said he 'strongly supported' the ask.

Less than half a year later, however, Toronto Police abruptly backed out of the ShotSpotter deal, citing potential legal concerns. 'They are not proceeding for the same reason many of us voted against it in the first place ... an invasion of privacy, that there were severe risks around data collection and use.' former city councillor Joe Cressy told the *Globe and Mail* at the time. 'Frankly, it was a shiny object in a Robo-Cop-style of enforcement model that was intended in the midst of the summer of the gun to make us all feel better' (Gray 2019).

Founded in the mid-1990s by three engineers, ShotSpotter has developed a technology that claims to distinguish between gunshots and other explosive sounds, like firecrackers or backfiring mufflers. When its hidden microphones pick up a sound, it is electronically analyzed, not just for its characteristics – pitch, reverberation, etc. – but also potential location.

The latter estimates are generated by triangulating sounds picked up by several of ShotSpotter's acoustic sensors (each one is programmed to estimate the distance between the sensor and the gunshot based on the time it takes for the sound to reach the micro-phone). The company says the audio fingerprint from detected gunshots is immediately relayed to a high-tech data processing centre, where analysts check them out and notify police if they fit the acoustical profile of a weapon being discharged. The notifications to police come with data such as the calculated location of the sound and a time stamp.

The California-based company – which went public on NASDAQ in 2017 and had a market capitalization of US$340 million as of late 2021 – promotes its technology to municipalities, universities, and other campus-based institutions by asserting that most gunshots are either not reported or cannot be accurately located. The company's website is packed with statistics about the impact of its technology in different cities, as well as other claimed benefits, such as reduced homicides, improved police response times, and decreased mortality of gunshot victims. The firm generates revenue through annual fees based on the size of the area to be covered.

In the mid-2010s, the company's claims began to receive more focused attention from reporters and criminologists. A 2021 peer-reviewed study published in the *Journal of Urban Health* and led by a researcher from the Center for Gun Violence Prevention and Policy at Johns Hopkins Bloomberg School of Public Health looked at crime data from sixty-eight big cities gathered between 1999 and 2016, where ShotSpotter was used.

The study concluded that the presence of ShotSpotter had 'no significant impact on firearm-related homicides or arrest outcomes' and further pointed out that a much more determinative cause of gun-related deaths had to do with state-level firearms policies, such as right-to-carry laws or more demanding permit-based systems. The authors also pointed out that the stats cited by ShotSpotter in support of its claims had not been peer-reviewed or exposed to more 'robust' research evaluations (Doucette et al. 2021).

Other skeptical reviews also rolled in, including a 2021 evaluation by the City of Chicago's inspector general of the Chicago Police Department's use of ShotSpotter, at a cost of US$33 million per year. 'Of the 41,830 ShotSpotter alerts that logged a police response, only 4,556 – 9.1% – resulted in viable evidence that a gun-related criminal offense had occurred,' a summary of the IG's report noted. The problem, the analysis found, was that police weren't necessarily acting on those ShotSpotter leads, or at least bringing in potential perpetrators. As an editorial in the *Chicago Tribune* stated, 'It's abundantly clear that the city needs to take a hard look at the merit of ShotSpotter' (Editorial Board 2021).

At around the same time, investigative reporting by *Vice* Motherboard and the Associated Press offered stories of police in various cities requesting ShotSpotter analysts to modify their reports, in some instances in relation to incidents when police officers discharged their guns, with those shots detected by the company's monitors. Court documents obtained by *Vice*/AP 'suggest that the company's analysts frequently modify alerts at the request of police departments – some of which appear to be grasping for evidence that supports their narrative of events' (Feathers 2021).

That wasn't the only uncomfortable finding. The reporting pointed out that ShotSpotter hasn't allowed independent verification of its accuracy claims, which have risen steadily over time. It also cited a case of a man wrongfully accused and then found guilty of murder based on ShotSpotter evidence; the conviction was eventually overturned when a court found that the prosecutors hadn't produced enough evidence.

In its own case against ShotSpotter, the American Civil Liberties Union also claimed the company's acoustic sensors tended to be disproportionately located in racialized low-income communities – a practice that 'can distort gunfire statistics and create a circular statistical justification for over-policing in communities of [colour].'

ShotSpotter, however, pushed back against what it described as 'false claims' with libel suits and extensive rebuttals posted prominently on its website. CEO Ralph Clark strongly denied that the company's technology relies on artificial intelligence algorithms to evaluate whether a sound picked up by its sensors comes from a gun or another source. Those judgments, he insisted, are made by human beings.

'The technology is a focused tool – highly accurate and unbiased in delivering evidence of a gunshot incident, including recorded sound of gunfire and the time and location of a shooting,' he wrote in an op-ed. 'This highly objective and factual evidence is commonly used by courts and can be examined and tested by both the prosecution and defense. ShotSpotter evidence on its own has never been nor could never be responsible for the charging, arrest or conviction of anyone accused of a crime.'

While the company continues to generate millions in revenues and to add customers, its stock and its earnings slid throughout 2021 – an indication that skepticism about its brand of high-tech policing had penetrated financial markets.

One of the unanticipated by-products of Sidewalk Labs' attempt to build a wired community on Toronto's waterfront is that it seemed to prompt heightened scrutiny of the use of digital technology by the city's police service, including facial recognition systems and predictive policing techniques. A *Toronto Star* poll conducted not long after the city abandoned its ShotSpotter deal found four in ten respondents mistrusted police use of facial recognition, but almost as many thought the technology would help fight crime. In early 2020, Toronto's police chief halted the use of Clearview's technology, and the civil oversight body moved to seek public input on policy and rules to guide the use of any future AI-based policing technology.

At the core of the debate is a basic public policy principle: transparency. Do individuals have the tools to understand and debate the workings of a suite of technologies that can have tremendous influence over their lives and freedoms, and potentially violate their civil rights?

It's what Andrew Ferguson and others refer to as the 'black box' problem. The algorithms, designed by software engineers, rely on certain assumptions, methodologies, and variables, none of which are visible, much less legible, to anyone without advanced technical know-how. Many, moreover, are proprietary because they are sold to local governments by private companies. The upshot is that AI algorithms have not been regulated by governments or oversight bodies, despite their use by public agencies.

New York City Council tried to tackle this question in May 2018 by establishing an 'automated decision systems' (ADS) task force to examine how municipal agencies and departments use AI and machine learning algorithms. The task force was to devise procedures for identifying hidden biases and to disclose how the algorithms generate choices so the public can assess their impact. The group included officials from the administration of Mayor Bill de Blasio, tech experts, and civil liberties advocates. It held public meetings throughout 2019 and released a report in 2019. NYC was, by most accounts, the first city to have tackled this question, and the initiative was, initially, well-received.

Going in, Albert Cahn saw the task force as 'a unique opportunity to examine how AI was operating in city government.' But he describes the outcome as 'disheartening.' 'There was an unwillingness to challenge the NYPD on its use of ADS.' Some other participants agreed, describing the effort as 'a waste.'

If institutional obstacles thwarted an effort in a government the size of the City of New York, what does better and more effective oversight look like? A couple of answers have emerged.

In his book on big data policing, Andrew Ferguson writes that local governments should start at first principles, and urges police forces and civilian oversight bodies to address five fundamental questions, ideally in a public forum:

- Can you identify the risks that your big data technology is trying to address?
- Can you defend the inputs into the system (accuracy of data, soundness of methodology)?
- Can you defend the outputs of the system (how they will impact policing practice and community relationships)?
- Can you test the technology (offering accountability and some measure of transparency)?
- Is police use of the technology respectful of the autonomy of the people it will impact?

These 'foundational' questions, he writes, 'must be satisfactorily answered before green-lighting any purchase or adopting a big data policing strategy' (Ferguson, 88).

In addition to calling for a moratorium and a judicial inquiry into the uses of predictive policing and facial recognition systems, the authors of the Citizen Lab report made several other recommendations, including the need for full transparency; provincial policies governing the procurement of such systems; limits on the use of ADS in public spaces; and the establishment of oversight bodies that include members of historically marginalized or victimized groups.

Other watchdog groups raised related concerns. The Women's Legal Education and Action Fund has pointed out that AI algorithms are, by their nature, inequitable because they are trained on data sets that invariably contain distortions. As a result, these flaws can't be managed away simply by better policy or technological tweaks. Moreover, when AI algorithms are developed by private companies subject only to market forces, the predictions they generate can be more vulnerable to legal challenges. 'Having more accurate AI systems does not mitigate inequality,' the group wrote in a 2021 legal brief submitted to the Toronto Police Services Board (Thomasen et al. 2021).

Sarah Brayne adds that the proliferation of digital sensors in public space (e.g., ShotSpotter mics, CCTVs, or automated licence-plate readers) and the growth of very large sets of accessible data have boosted the capability of police to steadily widen their surveillance activities. One question, she points out, is whether the mere presence of someone's information in databases accessed by law enforcement agencies raises the prospect of unlawful searches, in the form of repeated police queries of large data sets.

Despite such warnings, the Canadian government has sought to develop a more intentional and transparent approach, which University of Ottawa law professor and privacy expert Teresa Scassa describes as highly promising.

The Treasury Board Secretariat's 'Directive on Automated Decision-Making,' which came into effect in April 2019, requires federal departments and agencies, except those involved in national security, to conduct 'algorithmic impact assessments' (AIA) to evaluate unintended bias before procuring or approving the use of technologies that rely on AI or machine learning. The policy directs the federal government to publish AIAS, release software codes developed internally, and continually monitor the performance of these systems. In the case of proprietary algorithms developed by private suppliers, federal officials have extensive rights to access and test the software.

Scassa points out that the policy includes due-process rules and looks for evidence of whether systemic bias has become embedded in these technologies, which can happen if the algorithms are trained on skewed data. She also observes that not all algorithm-driven systems generate life-altering decisions, e.g., chatbots that are now commonly used in online application processes. But where they are deployed in 'high impact' contexts such as policing – e.g., with algorithms that aim to identify individuals caught on surveillance videos – the policy requires 'a human in the loop.'

The directive, says Scassa, is getting interest elsewhere. Ellen Goodman, at Rutgers, is hopeful this approach will also gain traction in the U.S., where municipal police departments were far more aggressive in their acquisition of these kinds of technology tools. The upshot is that Ottawa's low-key but thorough approach could point to a way for citizens to shine some light into the black box that is big data policing.

9
The Utopianism of Smart City Megaprojects

A languishing brownfield site. A developer's visions of castles in the sky. Corporate partnerships to build cutting-edge smart city infrastructure. And the promise of luring tech giants prepared to invest billions.

The hype could have easily described Sidewalk Labs' now-aborted Toronto venture, but this story actually played out near Boston, on a decommissioned air base in Weymouth, about half an hour southwest of a city known for its Ivy League colleges and the booming tech industry spawned by MIT.

When LStar Ventures, a North Carolina developer, began building Union Point in the mid-2010s on that base, it looked a lot like many generic master-planned edge-city projects. But a partnership LStar established with General Electric in 2017 promised much more: not just a fully wired community, but intelligent lighting, autonomous vehicles, green energy 'micro-grids,' and streets fitted out with sensors that would gauge traffic, locate parking spots, and even alert police if gunshots are detected.

As the *New York Times* noted in a 2018 profile of the project, 'General Electric will use Union Point as a laboratory for testing new products and as a showroom for working systems.' It could have been describing Sidewalk.

LStar and Weymouth officials were so bullish they felt Union Point was a shoo-in to be chosen as Amazon's second headquarters, a strange urban beauty contest that drew bids from cities across North America, including Toronto. As Kyle Corkum, LStar's managing partner, told the *Boston Business Journal*, 'I feel sorry for the rest of the competition in the United States, because, honest to God, I have a hard time imagining another site that can score the way we're going to score.'

Amazon, of course, ended up choosing New York (which promptly changed its mind), and the rest of LStar's Union Point vision soon collapsed in a cloud of recriminations, lawsuits, and complaints from residents who couldn't even buy a cup of coffee in their cutting-edge smart city because there were no cafés. Weymouth authorities took desperate measures to push out LStar, even blocking sewer hookups. In January 2021, Toronto office developer Brookfield was chosen to take over the languishing project.

As a critical McGill University study published in the journal *Cities* concluded, 'Union Point represents an example of how smart city rhetoric seduced local officials who were dazzled by the possibility of having an instantly lucrative, tech-focused "smart" city, with little awareness of the underwhelming antecedents and the many potential costs to their constituents.'

While much of the public and media attention focused on smart city technology tends to involve data, privacy, and space-age applications, the Union Point saga hints at a larger story, about the proliferation of tabula rasa, master-planned smart city development projects. These are typically promoted by national or regional governments in partnership with tech multinationals like Cisco and IBM, as well as global consultants, such as McKinsey, Accenture, and the Big Four accounting giants.

Sidewalk Labs, Union Point, and a Bill Gates–backed venture in Arizona known as Belmont are among the handful of North American examples. Many more have sprung up or are being proposed in the Global South, where national governments, besotted with the prospect of foreign direct investment and public-private partnership, have promoted explicitly utopian smart city strategies intended, in some cases, to end-run the messy and often anarchic world of the developing world's teeming megacities. China, for instance, is planning to build five hundred smart cities in coming years (Das 2020). According to Ayona Datta, a University College of London geographer who has researched India's one hundred smart cities 'mission,' '[s]mart cities are part of the dreams and aspirations of "success" of a young urban population who are ... "[p]roducts and promoters of globalization."'

Sarah Moser, an associate professor of geography at McGill, is one of the leading experts in the emergence of these new cities, which have also cropped up in places like Ecuador, Nigeria, the United Arab Emirates, and Saudi Arabia. Many share key traits: state-of-the-art security, management contracts with private firms, and intensive sales efforts meant to woo property investors and tech firms. At least one – King Abdullah Economic City, in Saudi Arabia – is a publicly traded company. International consulting firms like McKinsey and Deloitte are involved in the promotion and planning of these places. Some tabula rasa smart cities in Africa are part of China's 'new silk road' strategy. 'We're seeing it all over the global south,' says Moser, noting that government officials often fall for the glitzy sales presentations because their digital literacy is 'shockingly low.' 'These are private cities being developed for a million people.'

The master-planned smart city industry is being driven by a number of factors, including investors' search for profits and the tech sector's drive to secure new markets. 'Like other trending labels used to promote urban developments such as "green" or "eco," the "smart" city tag is fluid, ambiguous, and intimately tied to the rise of entrepreneurial urbanization,' Moser has observed (Rebentisch et al. 2020). But as she and other researchers have found, many fall well short of the utopian hype, take far longer to build than anticipated, and sometimes need to be scaled back or simply fail. Still, she adds, the emergence of this development-plus-technology-plus-data model has raised tough questions about the emergence of heavily monitored and quasi-privatized new cities in the twenty-first century.

❖

Scholars of urban utopianism often point to a pair of places that exemplify the modernist – and post-colonial – impulse to build cities from scratch.

One is Brasilia, the national capital of Brazil, a master-planned city that was carved out of the western highlands and completed in 1960. Its modernist institutional architecture, much of it the work of Brazilian architect Oscar Niemeyer, as well as its meticulously geometric urban plan and slab apartments inspired by Le Corbusier's Radiant City, were intended to reflect the country's forward-looking political aspirations.

The other is an earlier Le Corbusier project – the City of Chandigarh, the capital of Punjab, planned and built out in the years immediately following India's independence. 'Jawaharlal Nehru, the first Prime Minister of India, was determined that this new city should project an image of modernity and progress,' according to a history of the project published by *Arch Daily* (Fiederer 2018). After the two presiding architects quit, Le Corbusier was brought in, and he put his signature style on both the grid-oriented urban plan, with its wide boulevards, and the city's bold, modernist architecture.

Diganta Das, an associate professor of geography with Singapore's Nanyang Technological University, points out that post-independence India staked its social and economic future on urbanization. But in the neo-liberal climate of the 1990s, the national government rebranded its goal as 'entrepreneurial urbanism, 'which meant a much stronger emphasis on technology, modern infrastructure, and private investment.

In the early 2010s, when India emerged as an economic powerhouse in the Global South, a highly controversial regional politician moved to double down on these developments by pledging to create a smart city in Dholera, a village in a low-lying and predominantly agricultural region between Mumbai and Delhi in the state of Gujarat, in western India. Narendra Modi, then the chief minister for Gujarat, came up with a plan to build a state-of-the-art metropolis fitted out with a new airport, all the necessary information and communications technology, and newly constructed municipal services. The goal, according to the developer's website, is to build 'the most ambitious infrastructure development project which aims to make Dholera a global manufacturing hub.' Datta says the government's master plan for the region, which would be connected to both Mumbai and Delhi with modern transportation infrastructure, position it as a kind of 'all-encompassing utopia of a future city.'

Despite his claims to be a modernizer, Modi had a deeply troubled political past. In early 2002, anti-Muslim rioting broke out in Gujarat after a train filled with Hindu pilgrims was set on fire, killing dozens. Thousands of people died in sectarian rioting, the vast majority of them Muslims, many killed in horrific ways by Hindu extremists. Modi, who rose to power as a Hindu nationalist and promoted privatization in office, 'offered no consolation to the state's Muslims and expressed satisfaction with his government's performance,' according to a *New York Times* report, which cited sources who described the rioting as a 'state-sponsored pogrom' (Dugger 2002).

While Western governments condemned Modi and many (including Canada) cut ties, he was never indicted by a court and went on to be elected prime minister in 2014. Soon after taking office, Modi extended his smart cities strategy beyond Gujarat to the entire country: he established a plan for India to build 100 such places, ostensibly to improve living standards, attract employers, and boost the economy.[14] Some observers saw these moves as Modi's bid to refashion himself as a visionary builder willing to act decisively, notes Datta. The decades-long program was estimated to cost $150 billion.

Needless to say, Modi did not dream up the smart cities program on his own. Global firms like McKinsey, IBM, and Cisco, the networking giant, were actively promoting smart city/big data technologies for transportation, security, and infrastructure to Indian officials. Their pitch was slick and compelling. 'Through these corporate

---

14. Interestingly, the worldwide peak for Google searches of the phrase 'smart city' occurred not long after India announced its one hundred cities plan.

connections, advertisements, glossy images, and websites with captivating presentations and templates, governments and agencies could be seduced by neoliberal ways of looking for urban solutions through "best practices,'" observes Das. 'With "smart cities" being the jargon for an all-encompassing solution for the urban world and its increasing popularity in the Global South, developing 100 smart cities therefore became the ultimate panacea for India's multi-pronged urban challenges.'

Cisco, in particular, had made a big bet on promoting smart city systems – which of course depended on the company's fibre-optic networks and routers – elsewhere in the region: South Korea. In fact, the oft-cited prototype of the master-planned smart city has been rising from a former tidal flat just off the Yellow Sea port of Incheon, South Korea, since the mid-2000s. Known as Songdo, this corporate metropolis, now home to over 90,000 people and hundreds of businesses, is a multi-billion-dollar joint venture between a South Korean economic development region, the Boston-based developer Gale International, and Cisco. The Silicon Valley firm had begun promoting itself as a builder of 'smart and connected communities' in 2009, according to a detailed 2013 study on 'test-bed urbanism' published in *Public Culture*. (The four authors, Orit Halpern, Jesse LeCavalier, Nerea Calvillo, and Wolfgang Pietsch, study AI, management, architecture, and innovation history, respectively at universities in Canada, Spain, and Germany.)

From the beginning, Songdo was envisioned as a state-of-the-art city that would be fitted out with high-speed digital networks and a range of sustainability features, including LEED-certified green buildings, bike paths, rapid transit access, and a pneumatic waste-disposal system linked to a high-tech incinerator and recycling facility that eliminates the need for garbage trucks. As the developer boasted, it's an approach to 'future proofing Asian cities the smart way.'

Today, satellite campuses of four international universities are located in Songdo. But the streets have a generic corporate feel one finds in many rapidly developing high-rise districts, among them Mississauga City Centre and Toronto's South Core. The early buzz around Songdo has abated, as media reports have surfaced in recent years quoting residents complaining about the area's seeming emptiness. 'More than a decade on from its inception and the city is less than a quarter full,' observed a 2018 report in *This Week in Asia*.

Aesthetics and investment aside, perhaps the most notable element of the Songdo experiment involves its governance. As the *Public Culture* authors noted, the area's services are managed through a public-private partnership that includes Cisco, various Korean municipal agencies, and other firms, with residents and businesses purchasing services on a pay-as-you-go model. 'Cisco hopes that this will make for both a more profitable and a more effective way of developing new technology around its smart and connected communities projects.' The municipality, they add, sees this business model as a way of financing services.

Sarah Moser, at McGill, also explains that the Korean government has positioned Songdo as a kind of integrated export product for other regions thinking about building smart cities from scratch. Government officials from the Middle East, Africa, and Latin America regularly come to Songdo for 'policy tours,' she says. 'Korea is selling their model of smart cities to places that can't do it on their own.'

Some 4,500 kilometres to the south, Forest City, a strikingly similar master-planned enclave, is rising on four man-made islands just off the coast of Singapore, which has also branded itself as 'a smart nation.' (The island city state ranks first in the world in a Smart City ranking published by a consortium of universities.) The venture, launched in 2006 and described in its sales materials as a 'smart and green futuristic city,' is backed by the Chinese government and Chinese developers. It is meant to someday become home to 700,000 people. Moser describes Forest City as something of a high-tech gated community – a 'neocolonial outpost' situated on a strategically critical shipping route linked to China's 'Belt and Road initiative' ('Forest City Overview' n.d.).

Though Forest City is nominally part of Malaysia, Moser says the national government has 'granted extraordinary and unprecedented concessions of sovereignty' to the co-developer, Country Garden

Group, a Chinese mega-builder that generated sales of US$67 billion in 2021. '[It] is a completely private city with no publicly provided services,' she concluded in a 2018 paper. 'Education, health care, securities, utilities, management, and so on are all privatized and cater to Chinese nationals.'

Songdo and Forest City are long-term development plays, with a build-out horizon measured in decades. But despite aggressive marketing to potential investors, both have suffered from sluggish sales, a trend exacerbated by the pandemic (Liu 2021). What's more, Forest City, characterized by one recent academic study as 'speculative green urbanism,' has become a kind of lightning rod, as some accounts laud the developers for getting off to a quick start and others dismiss it as a 'useless megaproject.' (Recent photos and Google Street View images depict dense clusters of high-rise buildings and luxury resorts, but very few people (Koh et al. 2021).)

However, the delays facing Songdo and Forest City pale in comparison to the problems that have dragged down India's smart city plan. Early on, in Gujarat, the Dholera smart city venture – estimated to cost US$9–$10 billion, with contributions from the government and several large Japanese corporations – became tangled in India's archaic land laws. Even though the government passed new legislation intended to exempt Dholera's smart city and reclassify it as a 'special investment region,' lower-caste rural farmers, worried they'd be muscled off their land without compensation, successfully challenged the project in the courts (Das 2020, 70).

Datta points out that Modi's grand plan for building a globally connected Gujarat turned on simply circumnavigating the region's congested urban areas, with all their entrenched social pressures and inadequate infrastructure. She also notes that the tactic of dispossessing poor rural residents can be traced back to the colonial era and British land-acquisition laws. Other experts who have scrutinized India's smart city ambitions have noticed similar ironies, but note that the new colonialists are tech corporations and giant developers whose boosters in state and national governments are more than happy to preside over the creation of quasi-privatized new cities where traditional municipal authorities have been shunted to the sidelines.[15]

'India's [smart city mission] intends to move forward with its trusted corporate partners at the city level, while adopting technology to solve city crises,' concludes Das. 'However, not much deliberate effort has been made in citizen engagement at various levels and tackling the existing range of inequalities; instead, efforts are redirected towards making smarter citizens' (Das 2020, 74).

In the urban regions of the Global North, the smart city industry has tended to focus on more surgical interventions, with large tech firms and start-ups alike aiming to sell systems and hardware that can replace older gear, such as traffic control centres, with digital, wireless solutions. However, the speculative megaprojects involving land reclamation or sprawling greenfield tech hubs situated well away from existing cities are much less common.

Perhaps the most notable can be found on the west side of midtown Manhattan, the gleaming cluster of glass high-rises known as Hudson Yards. Constructed during the 2010s on top of an 11.3-hectare rail yard in a long-neglected industrial zone, the US$25 billion megaproject has been characterized as America's first fully 'quantified community,' a collection of ultramodern structures that are fully wired, fitted out with extensive networks of digital sensors, and operated by hidden infrastructure systems, including pneumatic waste chutes and an on-site co-generation plant. All of it is intended to produce torrents of data that can be analyzed in order to do everything

---

15. Many parts of Africa have witnessed similar speculative real estate activity in recent years as state and national governments have sought to attract investment to modern satellite cities, some of which are branded as innovation hubs, such as Kenya's Konza Technopolis, a greenfield project southeast of Nairobi that markets itself with sales claims and visuals that are indistinguishable from large-scale development plays at the edges of any North American city. Chinese state and private investors are also very active in these ventures.

from improving the energy efficiency of buildings to developing apps for people who live and work in the area.

Architectural giant Kohn Pedersen Fox created the project's master plan; the firm, not coincidentally, drew up the Songdo blueprint. The complex serves as the head office for Sidewalk Labs, whose now-retired founder, Dan Doctoroff, was heavily involved in the development approvals when he served as New York deputy mayor. In many ways, Hudson Yards can be seen as the most direct inspiration for Sidewalk's plans for Quayside in Toronto – another brownfield site situated at the edge of downtown, waiting to be massively intensified.

It was initially pitched as a self-financing development project. But Hudson Yards' builders, Related Companies and Oxford Properties, benefited greatly from direct and indirect subsidies served up by New York City under former mayor Mike Bloomberg, according to a 2015 evaluation by Bridget Fisher, an economist with the New School for Social Research. The project also reaped hundreds of millions from the proceeds of a federal visa program intended to direct offshore investment to low-income areas, according to investigative reporting published by *Bloomberg CityLab*.

Smart city scholar Shannon Mattern, who has scrutinized Hudson Yards, observes that the project's 'embedded' data infrastructure meshed well with Bloomberg's outlook. '[His] belief in the power of data shaped his initiatives,' she commented in *Places Journal*, adding that the mayor's signature moves included building a science and engineering campus and establishing the Center for Urban Science and Progress, a Brooklyn-based think tank dedicated to exploring city data. Indeed, as she notes, CUSP forged a partnership with Related/Oxford that would allow its researchers to slice and dice Hudson Yard's voluminous data as a way of testing 'new physical and informatics technologies and analytics capabilities.'

The finished product, for all its size and glitz, is underwhelming as a new part of a city that embodies the idea of urban sense of place. The architecture is monumental, antiseptic, and, in the case of the giant sculptural object known as the 'Vessel' situated in the middle of the Yards, weird. Apart from a few hundred affordable rental apartments, the entire project is skewed toward the highest of the high-end – brand-name luxury shops, the offices of corporate behemoths, and luxury condos.

New York Times architecture critic Michael Kimmelman offered a scathing review of what he deemed to be little more than a very expensive suburban office park designed by global-trotting starchitects: 'With its focus on the buildings' shiny envelopes, on the monotony of reflective blue glass and the sheen of polished wood, brass, leather, marble and stone, Hudson Yards glorifies a kind of surface spectacle – as if the peak ambitions of city life were consuming luxury goods and enjoying a smooth, seductive, mindless materialism.' The entire undertaking, he concluded, 'gives physical form to a crisis of city leadership' (Kimmelman 2019).

Nor does it seem to be especially smart. As with other such mega-projects, the quality-of-life benefits from Hudson Yard's heavily hyped investment in data gathering have yet to be realized. 'We're thinking about that digital infrastructure, then data and sensors as a way to collect information about how the neighborhood functions and the environmental surroundings,' Constantine Kontokosta, the New York University planning and engineering expert leading CUSP's work with Hudson Yards, told *Metropolis Magazine*. 'There's a lot of work that needs to be done to connect the two ... The reality is, nobody has demonstrated on the ground that they've used technology in such a way that the average person has actually benefited' (Nonko 2019).

10

The Politics of Smart Cities

One morning in October 2017, I was working on my laptop in a local coffee shop when I noticed a new follower on my Twitter account: @SidewalkToronto. When I clicked through, the Sidewalk Toronto website offered breezy watercolour maps and sketches of city street scenes, plus links to information about a new waterfront project for something called Quayside.

I'm not sure why this moment sticks in my memory, but I do recall thinking that the visuals and feel of the site suggested something savvy, urban, and not at all corporate, or at least not like the hard-sell dream-state renderings served up by preening condo and office developers. Even the name – Sidewalk Labs – felt fresh, a confection of Jane Jacobs ('the ballet of the sidewalk') and the serendipitous vibe of a more innocent time in the world of tech.

Of course, I couldn't have been more wrong.

Over the next several months, Sidewalk and its coterie of Canadian lobbyists and advisors rolled out an impressively choreographed reveal, capped by a joint public appearance by Prime Minister Justin Trudeau and Google chair Eric Schmidt. The debut included 'public consultations' in large halls filled with 'volunteers' wearing blue T-shirts, stagey panel discussions, stage-managed media interviews, meticulously pre-negotiated endorsements from local luminaries, and slick multimedia presentations. As launches go, it could scarcely have been more corporate: a Silicon Valley take on street cred.

Among its other duties, Waterfront Toronto, the public agency tasked with revitalizing the city's brownfield lakefront lands, regularly selects private-sector entities that have bid on the rights to develop parcels within its planning jurisdiction. But none had ever been welcomed with this kind of song and dance. What's more, Sidewalk hadn't even been selected as the winning proponent in a request for proposals (RFP); it had merely won the right to develop a so-called 'master innovation and development plan' for Quayside, a mostly vacant 12-acre site dominated by an abandoned grain silo. Even though its board would eventually be asked to sign off on the proposal, Waterfront Toronto officials were already talking about the company with terms of endearment like 'joint venture' and partnership, as if the whole thing was a done deal.

Though it ran to well over a hundred pages, Sidewalk's preliminary proposal had two noteworthy details: first, that the company planned to fit out this new precinct with all manner of automation and sensor technology designed to cull as much data from the neighbourhood as it would yield. That information, in turn, would be made available to other software companies and start-ups intent on developing smart city applications – a process Sidewalk described as building a neighbourhood 'from the internet up.'

The concept was not unlike the principle that underwrites the smart phone: the device itself is merely a technology 'platform' for downloadable apps that are created by other entities, from retailers to governments to coders who have invented an addictive digital game. In Sidewalk's case, the platform would be a corner of the waterfront – Quayside – while the word 'Lab' was a nod to the open-ended and experimental nature of this novel approach to smart cities – a phrase, incidentally, that Sidewalk conspicuously avoided. Sidewalk's explicit goal was to invite entrepreneurs, start-ups, and established software developers to find novel uses, or apps, for all the raw data the company planned to collect within Quayside's borders.

The other noteworthy detail about Sidewalk's pitch to Waterfront Toronto is that while the plan ostensibly focused on Quayside, a relatively small space, the company's documents were filled with references to the much larger 715-acre brownfield site known as the Port Lands, a derelict and heavily contaminated corner of the water-front built by lake-filling in the 1910s. The frequent mentions of what Sidewalk described as the Eastern Waterfront suggested the company's ambitions extended well beyond Quayside – something Waterfront Toronto had encouraged the company to think about as it developed its long-term smart city plan. All told, Sidewalk's proposal represented a huge land grab. The fact that the firm offered $50 million in no-strings cash, regardless of whether Waterfront Toronto eventually gave Sidewalk's smart city plan the go-ahead, further underscored the scale of the company's ambitions. That point, raised by various critics and reporters (myself included), turned out to be an exposed nerve.

Sidewalk's gambit set off a highly polarizing political maelstrom that extended well beyond the confines of Toronto's waterfront, or even the city itself. Its launch garnered global media attention, as could be expected of a company with deep ties to both Wall Street and Silicon Valley. The coverage of Sidewalk's plans turned up in the *New York Times*, the *Wall Street Journal*, *Wired*, and *Bloomberg*, among others. Academics from around the world embarked on dozens of critical studies of the project. Anti–big tech grassroots activists from around the world sprang into action, as did deep-pocketed tech veterans like Blackberry co-founder Jim Balsillie, who, from his rural redoubt in Guelph, orchestrated a multi-front fight to jam Sidewalk's gears.

The company, in turn, lined up an impressive cheering section of local ex-politicians, planners, architects, lawyers, consultants, academics, local advocacy groups, and think tanks in an effort to ingratiate itself to the city's powerbrokers and, ultimately, the Waterfront Toronto board of directors. It held numerous town halls and 'consultation' sessions that felt more like somewhat patronizing discussions of urban issues than focused presentations on aspects of Sidewalk's plan. The company hosted open houses in a funky former warehouse space located near the Quayside site. But when Sidewalk's top officials encountered media coverage they didn't like, they pushed back hard, an elbows-out stance that had the feel of New York's pugilistic street politics.

Along the way, Waterfront Toronto, a generally well-regarded public sector agency founded in 2002, found itself in the crosshairs of Sidewalk's growing contingent of critics, who accused its senior officials of getting into bed with a tech giant well before the board and city council had had a chance to weigh in. As the controversy spread, Waterfront Toronto was forced to appoint an independent advisory panel to vet Sidewalk's evolving plans. As the months passed, a top Waterfront Toronto official was forced to resign, a Sidewalk privacy advisor quit, a damning auditor's report surfaced, and secret documents were leaked to the press. Members of Toronto council, increasingly uneasy with allegations that the city was allowing one of the world's richest companies – Alphabet at the time had cash reserves in excess of US$100 billion – to help itself to a swath of waterfront, began pushing for more oversight, as well as veto power over Sidewalk's final proposal.

It was not a coincidence that the blowback coincided with revelations about Cambridge Analytica, the political data-mining consultancy that gained access to huge tranches of Facebook user information and passed it along to Donald Trump's campaign.

By the time Sidewalk pulled the plug on its Toronto plans, in the spring of 2020, there could be little doubt that the bright aura of progressive digital innovation that clung to the so-called FAANG giants – Facebook, Amazon, Apple, Netflix, and Google – had completely vanished. The platform plays (Airbnb, Uber, etc.) had become demonstrably toxic, while the extraordinarily potent algorithmic surveillance capabilities embedded in the commercial foundations of the search and social media giants could no longer be ignored or dismissed.

Sidewalk's plans on Quayside, and the opportunity to use this one project to test-drive all sorts of emerging urban data technologies, collided head-on with this late-2010s tech-lash. The details of the company's plans, what's more, exposed critical gaps in federal and provincial privacy regulations, as well as shortcomings in Canada's intellectual property laws. Revelations about extensive National Health Service patient record breaches in the U.K. involving another Alphabet/Google subsidiary, DeepMind, provided a bracing case study of how much can go wrong when public sector agencies get into bed with the world's most voracious data-miner.

One can reasonably ask, however, why Sidewalk's scheme turned into such a lightning rod, and not just in Toronto. After all, most of us have pawned off our privacy, knowingly or not, through our use of social media platforms, e-commerce sites, streaming services, and so on. Our smart phones constantly transmit precise location information – anonymized data that is fed to navigation apps or used to push online promotions. Our computers are clogged with cookies. While search engines hoover up intimate personal data and sell it to advertisers, we've become so utterly dependent on the utility and convenience that the trade-off seems reasonable. Few people can claim that they don't leave a trail of digital bread crumbs wherever they go, either online or off.

It's possible that many Torontonians recoiled from Sidewalk's plans because their 'solutions' appeared to have surpassed some kind of digital tipping point, beyond which the intrusive nature of these technologies becomes untenable. The dystopian prospect of panoptic urbanism suggested not only the consolidation of a surveillance society, but also a future in which cities are problematically dependent on the use of sensors, data analytics, and prediction engines to automate or at least drive decisions about civic life, public space, and infrastructure.

The problem wasn't just about whether Sidewalk's many sensors would impinge on the privacy of the people who would eventually live, work, or visit Quayside. Sidewalk, to be fair, made numerous public statements about its intention to respect Canadian privacy laws and make use of anonymization technologies. Rather, the company's longer-term goal lay in aggregating the raw data gathered within Quayside's public and private spaces, and then inviting software developers to come up with novel ideas for manipulating all that information – ideas that could then be transformed into business models and scaled up globally. A lab.

With or without the adjective 'smart,' cities are innovation-saturated spaces teeming with creativity, experimentation, and serendipitous social encounters that spark new ways of thinking and being. So why did Sidewalk's notion of hiving off one small corner of Toronto and turning it into an urban technology sandbox expose a raw nerve?

Perhaps the answer has something to do with our understanding of cities as self-governing places, certainly subject to the vicissitudes of market forces, immigration, and other powerful influences, but not explicitly curated, much less administered, by private entities with opaque accountabilities.

Although Toronto's rocky ride with Sidewalk Labs, not to mention the overhyped smart city megaprojects in countries like India and South Korea, raises doubts about the political viability of large smart city schemes, there's certainly evidence that more focused and better regulated initiatives can deliver the desired city-building goals.

In Hamburg, after a Green/Social Democrat coalition won control of the state parliament in a February 2020 election, the new government moved quickly to launch an ambitious transportation strategy for the fast-growing urban region of 5 million people. 'We need to change the way mobility is organized in our city,' Dennis Heinert, a government spokesperson, told me. (The Free and Hanseatic City of Hamburg has long enjoyed state status in Germany.)

The coalition's goal was ambitious, and informed by a strong climate imperative: 80 per cent of trips within the city will be via transit, walking, cycling, or other shared modes by 2030 in order to cut private vehicle use and carbon emissions. The plan called for better transit service without fare hikes, a major expansion of the cycling network, and a strategy to load up transit hubs (known as 'switch points') with a range of mobility options, such as e-bike rentals, that cover the so-called last mile between transit stations and home or work.

A central feature of the strategy was the concept of an intelligent transportation system, using various smart city technologies to knit all the pieces together. The elements include self-piloted subway trains and autonomous minibuses, and, eventually, a mobility-as-a-service system that allows travellers to book bike or scooter rentals, carpooling trips, or ride shares from a single app.

How will city officials evaluate the components of the ITS? 'Very easy,' replied Heinert. 'Will it help our political goal of the transition of mobility?' State officials, he continued, will vet the portfolio of mobility technologies in terms of how they promote safer, greener, and more efficient movement within the region. 'There is no project within this whole ITS which is not working towards those goals.'

The oversight of Hamburg's mobility-technology game plan isn't difficult to discern: an election brought in a sustainability-minded coalition, which wants to advance a program that includes a range of technologies, as well as a bureaucratic framework for evaluating those systems. In other words, voters in coming years will be able to judge the coalition's success.

Governance is a somewhat nebulous term that orbits around the politics of smart city technology, frequently cited but rarely defined with any degree of precision. At the most abstract level, governance is or should be about accountability. How can ordinary people – and the public institutions that act on their behalf – be assured that these emergent technologies deployed in and around cities will do more good than harm? With the dramatic acceleration of pandemic-related service digitization, as well as the continued rapid growth of platform companies, that question has taken on even more saliency.

When Sidewalk Labs revealed its master innovation and development plan for Quayside in June 2019, the hefty four-volume document included a range of governance proposals for how this new smart neighbourhood would be managed. They included several specially created entities – 'Open Space Alliance,' 'Waterfront Transportation Management Association,' 'Urban Data Trust' – with real regulatory power and nebulous financing arrangements and ties to Sidewalk Labs, but unclear relationships to the municipal agencies (i.e., the public) that perform core tasks like waste or transportation management. The proposals drew sharp criticism, with the city and Waterfront Toronto swiftly shooting down any notion that Sidewalk's experimental community would be allowed to write its own rules.

So what are we talking about when we talk about smart city governance?

One way to think about this problem is to unpack the layers of governance baked into two very common categories of objects in the public realm: bridges and buildings. Like many of the data or digital devices discussed in this series, both can be seen as systems of engineered technologies, reflecting generations of innovation.

Bridges and buildings designed and constructed by architects, planners, engineers, and contractors who are professionally trained and accredited, as well as legally accountable for the projects they construct. Both are subject to a range of municipal and provincial policies and regulations, from procurement processes to development approvals, zoning bylaws, design codes, budget expenditures, and transportation plans.

These structures typically involve public consultation and political approval. The decision-making processes, in turn, are mostly transparent, thanks to routine disclosure policies and access to information laws. Provincial and federal building codes regulate the materials used and the minimum standards for their assembly. Inspectors monitor construction prior to completion, and then upkeep and structural integrity afterwards. Moreover, the fact that a building is privately controlled doesn't exempt the owner from most of these governance systems, nor their obligation to pay taxes and adhere to relevant laws and regulations.

It's also worth noting that with both bridges and buildings, the interface to the public realm isn't left to chance. Local bridges, needless to say, are never off-limits to general traffic. As for buildings, municipal regulations dictate their aesthetic and logistical relationships to the outside world, even if those connections may be limited by practical necessities such as fences, secured perimeters, and so on. Governance, in other words, is about the wider context as well as accountability.

Smart city technology, clearly, poses very different questions about the nature and form of governance. The devices, software and data, in many cases, are neither tangible nor easily understood. One system may have the potential to do many tasks, some of which have yet to be determined. Data, in turn, is amorphous, fast-moving, and malleable. It may be stored not only outside the city but beyond our national borders. Yet some common themes emerge: an expectation of technical robustness and reliability; the existence of professional standards; and the role of policy and regulation in determining how these systems function, including those that have nothing to do with local government but impact urban spaces. Finally, adequate governance entails some measure of public engagement and approval, which confer on such technologies and their creators the social licence to operate.

As Rutgers' Ellen Goodman has commented, cities face a crossroads in their 'embrace of the Internet of Things and "smart city" agendas. Will they do it in ways that give control over city functions and citizen information to private companies and impenetrable algorithms or will there be public control and accountability?'

Many experts point to Barcelona as a model for progressive smart city governance that balances the Catalonian capital's desire to attract tech investment with other goals, like citizen engagement, privacy, and sustainable development. Barcelona officials began talking about smart city tech in 2011, and the municipal council in 2016 adopted a sweeping 'Digital City Plan' designed to ensure that all public services are provided through digital channels. The strategy established a specialized smart city directorate within the municipal government, funding schemes, citizen engagement processes, and a range of technical policies aimed at procurement, data standards, and network architecture.

But Barcelona's outlook is grounded in values, according to Josep-Ramon Ferrer, the former deputy chief information officer and director of the program. Chief among these is preparing the city for rapid twenty-first-century urbanization while recognizing technology 'as a facilitator, not a goal in itself.'

Other cities, of course, have adopted these kinds of high-level governance visions, and a growing number have also signed on to even broader pan-urban efforts to ground rapid technology deployment in ethical or humanitarian principles. The Cities Coalition for Digital Rights, launched in 2018 by Barcelona, Amsterdam, and New York, includes metros around the world that have signed on to a declaration calling for improved privacy policies, more accessible internet access, and measures to ensure that residents have the ability to question artificial intelligence or automated decision-making-based systems to ensure they don't discriminate or perpetuate hidden data biases.

The City of Toronto, in fact, belongs to this coalition (as of June 2019) and began creating its own smart/digital city governance policies, largely in response to the controversy generated by Sidewalk Labs. Municipal officials developed a Digital Infrastructure Plan, which laid out five core guiding principles, including equity and inclusion; effective local government; social, economic, and environmental benefits; privacy and security; and democracy and transparency.

Other GTA municipalities have been working on their own strategies. Mississauga's smart city master plan, developed in response to a federally sponsored 'smart city challenge' competition, includes elements such as 'living labs' for showcasing new technologies, parks with free wifi, smart LED street lights, air quality sensors, and the deployment of an AI-powered chatbot on the city's 311 website. 'It's my job to make them stick,' Anthea Foyer, a sculptor and former digital curator and former lead for Mississauga's smart city program, told me.

She cited one proposed initiative that bobbed to the surface: the deployment of outdoor digital touch screens with parks-and-recreation listings or other municipal information. The devices, however, come with an additional feature: a built-in facial recognition camera that scans eye movement to determine if users appear to understand the content and how the screens function. Foyer has found herself talking to plenty of vendors. 'It feels like such a game changer for me,' she said, noting that the inner workings of such technologies are 'esoteric and hard to understand.' She insists, 'I would want to make sure residents feel comfortable with it.'

The crux of the smart city governance riddle, in fact, has to do with what happens between the lofty vision statements adopted by municipal councils like Barcelona's and the day-to-day choices made by civil servants like Anthea Foyer.

To get to the point where smart city technology is subject to the type of robust governance that applies to buildings and bridges, governments need to establish a range of policy, legal, and regulatory reforms that allow cities and metropolitan regions to make these investments safely. Such changes, moreover, should also apply to technology vendors and platform companies that provide systems or digital services that impact urban regions.

Privacy Legislation Reform

As critics of the Sidewalk Labs proposal argued, Canada's privacy laws weren't equipped to respond to many of the data-gathering and surveillance technologies that fall under the smart city rubric. The federal Liberals in late 2020 introduced legislation, dubbed the Digital Charter Act, that meant to reform national privacy laws with measures to provide individuals with more rights over personal information gathered by companies. (As of early 2022, the legislation had yet to receive royal assent.)

But information technologies such as artificial intelligence tend to advance far faster than public policy, observes Markus D. Dubber, a University of Toronto law professor and director of the Centre for Ethics. For example, even though the European Union's General Data Protection Regulation is seen as the world's most expansive privacy law, it wasn't robust enough to halt the use of facial recognition technology. In fact, even before the Clearview controversy broke, a 2019 analysis by Orla Lynskey, a London School of Economics law professor, warned that 'the protection offered by [the EU] legal framework to those impacted by predictive policing technologies is, at best, precarious.'

Regulatory Procedures

In the way that significant public sector projects, from transit lines to new gas distribution networks, are subject to detailed environmental assessments and public consultation, it seems reasonable to expect that smart city technology ventures be subjected to similar scrutiny. These could include requirements that municipalities undertake privacy impact assessments, which are evaluation procedures used in other parts of government, as well as versions of the new federal directive on automated decision-making systems (discussed in Chapter 8) if the smart city system uses AI or machine learning software.

A critical element of this kind of oversight involves testing the durability of so-called 'data anonymization' measures. Municipalities release ever-larger tranches of digital information through open data portals, and it is standard practice that any personally identifying information (PII) is stripped away.

But a study published in 2019 in *Nature Communications* itemized many examples of successful de-anonymizing efforts that cross-reference multiple data sets in order to identify individuals in databases considered to be shorn of PII. (An April 2019 *New York Times* investigation came to similar conclusions by identifying pedestrians caught on a CCTV walking through Bryant Park in Manhattan using internet searches.) The findings, the authors of the *Nature Communications* paper note, 'question whether current de-identification practices satisfy the anonymization standards of modern data protection laws' in places like the EU and California.

Data Governance, Ownership, and Standards

In June 2020, the City of Toronto published an seventy-seven-page consultant's report on 'data governance and digital infrastructure,' prepared by a Montreal-based tech policy research non-profit called Open North. A detailed and far-ranging assessment, the document offers what amounts to a 360-degree survey of the largely unresolved policy, legal, and tech management issues facing Toronto as it undertakes the kind of transformation cities like Barcelona have pursued.

It's a long list that covers everything from approaches to the ownership of data (a hot button topic while Sidewalk Lab's plans were still on the table), ethical uses, gaps in federal legislation, and technical standards. While the smart city industry has been roaring along for years, the report offers a caution: '[D]ata governance in the smart city context is still an emerging field. Therefore, tracking and measuring the outcomes of specific initiatives will require future research.'

A case in point involves a pair of arcane concepts – data interoperability and open standards – that come up constantly in debates about digital technology. The concept of open standards refers to the use of widely accepted technologies, such as electrical outlets. When you buy an appliance, you don't worry whether it can be plugged into a socket because the standards for electrical wiring and plug size are open. But when Apple abandoned standard USB ports on its Macs for a proprietary version meant to drive sales of Apple devices, millions of consumers learned a hard lesson in the importance of open standards.

For government officials, the importance of open standards in the context of smart city governance is that they prevent technology suppliers, especially very large multinationals, from making themselves indispensible (and therefore entrenched monopolies) because no other company's systems or software can be added on to existing ones.

(Sidewalk Labs attempted just that with a subtle proposal to deploy outdoor mounts dubbed 'Koalas,' into which its public space sensors could be plugged. These were ostensibly designed to make it easy to upgrade equipment, but the devices are proprietary to Sidewalk/ Google, and trademarked, instead of standard USB ports.)

Mark S. Fox, a University of Toronto professor of computer science, is leading an effort to establish common standards for 'city data' through the International Organization for Standardization. It is a work in progress that tends to be overlooked in smart city debates because the subject is seen as dauntingly technical, he told me in late 2020: 'The adoption of standards is a governance dimension that has received little or no attention in the media, yet it represents the Achilles heel on the path to smart cities.'

Institutional Capacity

Cities employ engineers, planners, architects, public health experts, and a range of other professionals who have the expertise to devise and evaluate policies, deliver services, and provide technical input on procurement.

Municipalities, like other large government and private sector organizations, also employ IT staff – programmers, systems engineers, cyber security experts, etc. Yet if local governments intend to invest in smart city technology and infrastructure, they must also be recruiting professionals from disciplines like data analytics, data science, artificial intelligence, data visualization, and digital anthropology, all with the goal of creating the kind of bench strength found in other city departments.

The City of Toronto since 2015 has had a big data innovation team, which is primarily focused on transportation applications. But smart city tech cuts across many other departments, so it will be important for municipal officials to ensure that these skills are present throughout the organization.

Communication

In the fall of 2020, Julia Stoyanovich, a New York University assistant professor of computer science, engineering, and data science, and Falaah Arif Khan, a research fellow and artist-in-residence at NYU's Center for Responsible AI, published *Mirror, Mirror*, the first of a series of 'scientific comics' entitled 'Data, Responsibly.'

Although AI might not seem like an obvious topic for a graphic novel, Khan and Stoyanovich (who sat on New York's Automated Decision-Making Systems task force) have a clear-eyed view of their project. Their aim is to use relatable metaphors to explain AI (e.g., either rule-based recipes or cooking by trial and error) in order to make the concepts accessible to people without college degrees or those who live with disabilities that exclude them from accessing technology or other facets of urban life. 'This is the population that is most likely to be hurt by AI and algorithms,' says Stoyanovich, who points to New York City's recent attempt to regulate employers' use of AI-enabled screening software in hiring practices. The idea isn't to side with either the 'techno-optimists' or the 'techno-bashers,' she adds. 'Our goal is really to create a nuanced understanding.'

At U of T, meanwhile, the Centre for Ethics hosted multidisciplinary and open-ended public sessions about the applications and implications of the use of AI. As with 'Data, Responsibly,' the goal is to yank the subject out of the hands of computer scientists. '[AI] is not a narrow technology-specific issue that should be defined and solved by technical people,' says the Centre's director Markus Dubber, a professor of law and criminology who organizes these dialogues. 'The more people who participate from different backgrounds, the more they realize there's no single answer.'

While neither of these projects explicitly targeted smart city tech, the overlaps are substantial as AI becomes increasingly integral to a wide array of digital and data-driven systems, including those used in AVs, traffic control, and policing. Both examples also serve as a prompt for municipal officials to find innovative and inclusive approaches to citizen engagement when it comes to developing smart city systems.

Consultation on matters such as planning is deeply embedded in our civic culture. But the city's long-established outreach practices can be rote, exclusionary, inconvenient, or just dauntingly bureaucratic. Yet, as Stoyanovich makes clear, the power of these technologies demands, if anything, a far higher degree of public engagement to head off unintended consequences never envisioned in the slick and upbeat presentations of technology companies.

In early 2020, I interviewed a Dutch academic, Albert Meijer, who has published extensively about smart city technology, data infrastructure, digital governance, and other related topics. Despite the Netherlands' pragmatic and upbeat outlook on smart cities, his research has turned up mixed results.

Meijer had developed a systematic way of assessing the success of such investments. He concluded that there isn't much evidence that smart city technologies generate value for money – an intriguing result, given the size of the smart city tech sector. Smaller, more focused systems can deliver results, he told me, but the more ambitious ones have a way of falling short. 'It is technology looking for a problem rather than the other way around,' he said.

In a pointed assessment published in the *Journal of Urban Technology*, Meijer and three other Utrecht University scholars turned their attention to 'smart governance,' which they describe as urban governments that had been set up to solicit citizen participation using various digital technologies – online public meetings, social media, etc. – to guide policy decisions.

Despite the proliferation of digital communications channels available to anyone with a smart phone or a wifi connection, Meijer and his colleagues found that many residents still preferred to engage in person, while those who participated remotely had a tendency to drop out or lose the plot. 'The wide net of online activities of many people breeds shallow attention ... and transitory involvement,' they observed. 'Our review demonstrates that there is certainly no reason for having blind faith in smart governance.'

Their conclusion was clear. Cutting-edge digital infrastructure can play a role, either positive or negative, in determining how twenty-first-century urban regions evolve and function. But as has been true for millennia, cities will also remain defiantly social spaces, populated by human beings messily, and often sub-optimally, going about their business.

Indeed, this singularly implacable fact of urban life became impossible to ignore during the pandemic.

Conclusion

1
Science, Technology, and Pandemic Cities

About two weeks after the World Health Organization declared a global pandemic in March 2020, Google launched a digital service ostensibly designed to help public health officials around the world respond to the COVID-19 outbreak. The project provided data and data visualization tools that could allow health officials to 'see how your community is moving around differently due to COVID-19.' As the search giant explained, 'we've heard from public health officials that the same type of aggregated, anonymized insights we use in products such as Google Maps could be helpful as they make critical decisions to combat COVID-19.'

The Community Mobility Reports 'charted movement trends over time by geography across different categories of places such as retail and recreation, groceries and pharmacies, parks, transit stations, workplaces, and residential' ('See How Your Community ...' 2022). For any geographical unit – from nations to states, provinces, counties, and cities – these reports would show how traffic in these six categories compared to a 'baseline,' established presumably before the pandemic.

The idea, apparently, was to visually depict whether people were adhering to lockdown orders, travelling less, or changing their use of public spaces, like parks. (The reports were created by aggregating location data generated by smart phones with the Google Maps app – a technique developed for the company's various mapping services.

The data is available only if the user has enabled location tracking on their device.)

Google's public relations teams pushed out news of this initiative, and media organizations from around the world eagerly offered up coverage. 'With the data, public officials can, for instance, recommend changes in the business hours of grocery stores to thin out crowds,' reported Singapore's *Straits Times*. 'Similarly, crowding at certain transportation hubs might indicate the need to run more parallel routes for social distancing.' Senior Google executives stressed that the data being used had been anonymized to protect privacy.

Noting Singapore's strict COVID-19 containment policies, the *Straits Times* in the same article also mentioned another digital technology that emerged early in the pandemic – so-called 'contact-tracing apps' that were already in wide use in China and South Korea. Once installed and activated on a smart phone, these apps would hold information about whether or not the owner had had a positive COVID-19 test, and if so, when. If an infected individual came within 2 metres of anyone else carrying a smart phone with a contact-tracing app, the two devices would acknowledge each other through a Bluetooth signal. When that happened, the app automatically notified the local public health authority, whose staff would reach out to the potentially exposed individual to determine if the exposure required a follow-up or isolation.

Google and Apple collaborated on the technology and made it available to governments scrambling to find ways of limiting the spread. In a paper published in *Science*, the prestigious academic journal, a team of Oxford University big-data experts modelled the potential of 'digital contact tracing' and concluded that 'a contact-tracing app that builds a memory of proximity contacts and immediately notifies contacts of positive cases would be sufficient to stop the epidemic if used by enough people, in particular when combined with other measures such as physical distancing and widespread testing.' In interviews, the principal investigators predicted that widespread deployment of these apps would massively reduce transmission, prevent resurgence, and help limit the social and psychological impacts of lockdowns ('Controlling Coronavirus Transmission' 2020). The research was backed by the Bill and Melinda Gates Foundation and the Wellcome Trust (Ferretti et al. 2020).

While *Science*'s contact-tracing paper was downloaded over 21,000 times and governments around the world hustled to promote these apps, the miracle of automated contact tracing did not materialize. Whether due to technical glitches or an insufficient number of users, the hype around contact-tracing apps ebbed almost as swiftly as it crested. A few assessments, in the U.K. and Switzerland, found some positive results, but the proportion of the overall population that had downloaded the apps remained relatively low, limiting the effectiveness of a technology that seemed, well, overdetermined. By the end of the pandemic's first year, few health officials were paying attention to these apps, and many people had deleted them (Lewis 2021).

Google's community mobility reports met a similar fate. After a burst of publicity, and the occasional media report showing how traffic patterns had changed, these data visualizations didn't appear to be doing much to assist public health officials. They were much more focused on collecting actionable data, such as differences in infection rates among wealthier and lower-income neighbourhoods, or the accessibility of vaccines.

One of the few academic studies to cite the mobility reports, a 2021 paper on the effectiveness of stay-at-home orders published in the *American Journal of Public Health*, used the mobility reports in its analysis but cautioned that Google's data came with significant caveats: it didn't register movement by people who'd turned off location tracking or weren't carrying their phones, and lacked sufficient granularity to provide a crisp picture of whether stay-at-home orders were affecting different neighbourhoods or socio-economic groups.

While neither of these technologies were developed as part of a smart city agenda, they had all the hallmarks: novel (and unanticipated) uses for big data and mobile devices within an urban context, pressed into action to support a public service. Though neither contact-tracing apps nor Google's community mobility reports had an explicitly urban focus, these 'solutions' were oriented toward the ways in which people move around and encounter one another in public spaces and dense city regions. They were, in short, heavily hyped smart city technologies, and both failed to deliver when the chips were down.

Technologies falter and die, or, more commonly, are upstaged by better solutions. Some never develop traction: Betamax video. 8-track tapes. Zeppelins. Sony Discmans. Gas-powered refrigerators. Landfills are filled with still-born examples. It seems likely that we can add contact-tracing apps to this list, and possibly other more complicated smart city technologies that have, or will, struggle to lift off, like fully autonomous vehicles or hyper-loops.

There's nothing wrong with this picture; innovation requires imagination and a knack for problem solving, but also an appetite for risk. Sometimes great ideas don't pan out as expected, and, as every solid scientist will agree, those failures provide crucial information and insights about the path forward in any field of discovery. In other cases, emergent technologies – holograms, for example – seem to be solutions in search of problems.

The global pandemic, however, presented the world with problems of almost unfathomable complexity, and these were not, of course, limited to cities. But the residents of city regions experienced the pandemic in very particular ways; among the many societal, economic, and public health responses to COVID-19 were an ever-widening family of technologies that sought to confront the urban experience of the crisis. Some involved digital solutions, but others drew on older civil and chemical engineering technologies, and scientific insights traceable to lethal pandemics and infectious disease outbreaks from much earlier periods. What's more, a few of the smartest solutions had nothing to do with technology at all.

One of the most compelling, and least gimmicky, involved 'wastewater surveillance,' which has nothing to do with the kinds of surveillance condemned by technology critic Shoshana Zuboff. Early in the pandemic, a handful of local public health agencies – Ottawa was an early mover – decided to begin systematically testing sewage for minute traces of the COVID-19 virus. Epidemiologists knew by that point that infected people will 'shed' fragments of the virus through their feces, and do so before they are experiencing symptoms.

Bits of COVID-19 in poop, in other words, represented a potential early-warning system. Across a population, those traces, if measured in a timely and accurate way, could let public health officials know about pre-symptomatic community transmission before people began showing up in long lines, feeling lousy and waiting to be tested. When this kind of sampling was conducted for an entire city region – i.e., the whole so-called 'sewershed' – the results could provide public health agencies with a short but valuable head start for putting in place additional precautions, e.g., ordering limits on visitors to seniors' homes. The results were also more comprehensive than testing because they captured non-symptomatic infection and infections among people who didn't bother getting tested.

This approach drew on generations – even centuries – of advances in microbiology, chemistry, and virology, as well as the generations of technical innovations that enable modern labs to not only detect, but 'read,' the tiniest bits of DNA. Yet the foundation of wastewater surveillance – the 'platform,' to use the tech world's term – is the hard infrastructure designed by civil engineers through trial and error during the eighteenth and nineteenth centuries in response to two of the most basic needs of rapidly growing cities: fresh water and sewage disposal, both provided at scale.

Wastewater infrastructure has evolved massively, of course: wood drains were replaced by brick-lined sewers, which in turn have been eclipsed by concrete. Unlike nineteenth-century London, raw sewage is treated before being dumped into water bodies. And in many newer parts of cities, drains handling wastewater (i.e., from rain and runoff) and sewage (from toilets) function as separate networks, with differing treatment requirements.

The notion of testing wastewater for evidence of infectious disease is not new, dating back, interestingly enough, to years immediately following the introduction of the polio vaccine, in the 1950s. A devastating childhood illness, polio was a highly infectious and much feared disease, and research to find a vaccine culminated with the discovery of an effective agent by Jonas Salk in 1953. As with the COVID-19 vaccines, its introduction involved some significant obstacles. At least one of the early polio vaccine brands, made by a firm called Cutter, produced alarming side-effects (paralysis) in some patients and prompted the U.S. government to set up a system of intensive regulation and oversight ('Historical Vaccine Safety Concerns' 2020).

As the polio vaccine rolled out, epidemiologists wanted to know whether it was actually reducing the incidence of the disease, and developed techniques for testing sewage samples for residual evidence of the virus. (A 2001 study found that a single toilet flush containing poliovirus could be detected at a nearby treatment plant for more than four days [Sinclair et al. 2008].)

The results confirmed that an effective vaccination campaign did produce results, measured across a city or community. Over the following several decades, however, municipal works departments took over the practice of sampling sewage, using the tests to determine treatment levels and whether an excess of raw sewage was finding its way into water bodies, rather than providing data for public health purposes.

As the opioid epidemic gained momentum, public health officials in some jurisdictions revived the practice of wastewater surveillance, testing raw sewage to determine trace levels of these drugs. They could then triangulate the sampling data with other locally sourced information – e.g., the volumes of properly prescribed opioids – to gauge how much of the drug was entering a community through illicit channels. The sewage sampling on its own also provided public health authorities with real-time information on the extent of an epidemic of addiction that reached into every corner of society. These initiatives in particular prompted health authorities to begin looking for traces of the COVID-19 virus in sewage when the pandemic began in early 2020.

Testing sewage for traces of virus is the proverbial needle-in-a-haystack challenge, and it is not especially automated – at least not yet. Samples of wastewater have to be physically removed from sewer mains or drawn from holding tanks at wastewater treatment plants, then shipped to a lab for testing. Treatment plants are fitted out with equipment that automatically draws samples, but epidemiologists who worked on this approach were also interested in collecting 'upstream' data – for example, samples taken near hospitals or long-term care homes – to gain more granular information on transmission that might be taking place in these kinds of settings. Obtaining such samples, however, meant prying open manhole covers and inserting tubes into the pipes running beneath the streets.

The epidemiologists pushing the frontiers of wastewater surveillance are also drawing on insights about human behaviour, the nature of the labour force, and the extent of sewer infrastructure. A 2021 study published in the U.S. by the National Institutes of Health pointed out that morning samples seem to produce the best results, because that's when most people use the bathroom. But, they cautioned, such tests might miss shift workers, who were among the groups more vulnerable to COVID-19 exposure due to the nature of their work, inflexible employers, or other factors. (People living in rural areas with septic tanks are also absent.)

'Prioritizing vulnerable communities could catch upticks in transmission early and prevent health care systems from being overwhelmed,' recommended the authors, all scholars at Mathematica, a 1,600-employee data analytics firm in Washington, D.C. 'As transmission begins to decelerate, sampling might prioritize key transmission nodes, such as international airports, shipping ports, travel hubs, and public gathering spaces' (Keshaviah et al. 2021).

Besides the mechanics of sampling and testing, the other complication that emerged had to do with bureaucratic silos. In Toronto, for example, works officials charged with running sewage treatment plants didn't have much involvement with public health officials. To create an effective system, the two entities would need to work together to gather, transport, and test samples, so information about changing viral loads could be pressed into service. In sum, the potential benefits of this kind of testing depended on forging new bureaucratic connections, additional funding, and more lab capacity. The promise of this approach, in other words, didn't just involve repurposing data that already existed in some giant server farm; the innovation extended to new approaches that municipalities had to adopt in order to deliver service.

The potential benefits, however, proved to be so compelling that governments in many parts of the world began investing significant sums to transform wastewater surveillance from an academic exercise into an operational reality. In the U.S., the Centers for Disease Control and Prevention announced in 2020 its plan to establish a national wastewater surveillance system involving state and local partners. As *Nature* reported in 2021, the number of such projects grew from a few dozen in 2020 to over two hundred a year later, the vast majority in affluent countries. The approaches varied widely, from the testing of sewage in commercial airliners to samples gathered near apartment buildings, correctional facilities, and campuses (Kreier 2021).

A Boston-based biotech firm, Biobot Analytics, developed 'sampling kits' for workplaces and pitched its product to employers: 'Return to the office with confidence,' its marketing pitch read. 'Analyzing your building's sewage generates powerful health data. Biobot tells you how to leverage that information to keep your employees safe and productive.' Yet the company, founded by two MIT scientists, has also conducted scientific analyses of the advantages and limitations of the various approaches. 'As it becomes an important pillar of pandemic and epidemic preparedness and response systems,' a Biobot study published in 2021 concluded, 'wastewater-based epidemiology can support public health policy as an established surveillance tool for emerging infectious diseases and biological threats' (Sharara et al. 2021).

Yet some data and privacy experts counsel caution about these technologies for reasons that will be familiar to anyone who's been paying attention to the thorny ethical questions raised by the deployment of digital sensors in public space, especially when these systems will be used to identify other trace substances in wastewater. For example, samples taken very close to specific buildings or communities could yield data that could be used to profile those areas, notes a 2022 study on the ethical, legal, and civic implications of the 'datafication of wastewater.' The authors, University of Ottawa's Teresa Scassa and Toronto Metropolitan University planning scholar Pamela Robinson, point out that because wastewater surveillance depends on municipal infrastructure, decisions around how, where, and what to sample need to be considered more broadly and inclusively than is presently the case. As they conclude 'An otherwise harmless social necessity – the disposal of human waste – has become an opportunity for increased technological surveillance' (Scassa et al. 2022).

In the conclusion of their own evaluation of wastewater surveillance, the Mathematica research team included a shout-out to a pair of health practitioners from a very different era, pioneers whose insights continue to inform public health practice.

One was Florence Nightingale, the British nurse who tended to soldiers in military hospitals during the Crimean War, in 1854. An amateur mathematician, Nightingale collected statistics from those hospitals on the causes of death of the patients and published them as novel and highly influential data visualizations. They showed that soldiers were far more likely to die from infections picked up in hospital settings than from the injuries they sustained on the battlefield.

The other reference was to Dr. John Snow, a London physician who found himself treating the victims of a cholera outbreak that had killed over five hundred people in Soho around the same time. Cholera, long considered to be spread through 'miasma,' or foul-smelling air, had been an urban scourge for generations, yet had become more pronounced with the crowding of the urbanization of the industrial era. Snow began marking the location of the homes of victims on what came to be known as 'the ghost map' – a seemingly modest form of data visualization that revolutionized epidemiology. He supplemented his findings by knocking on doors and talking to the people who lived and worked in the afflicted neighbourhood.

Gradually, two curious details emerged from his fact-finding: one, that many of the victims lived or worked near a water pump over a well on Broad Street; and two, that workers at a nearby brewery seemed less likely to fall ill or die. As Snow probed further, he realized the victims had depended on water from that Broad Street pump, which turned out to have been located close to several leaking underground privvies. As for those brewery workers, they tended to drink beer while on the job, not well water from the pump. Armed with his data, Snow recommended to local authorities that they remove the handle of the Broad Street pump. That decision, immortalized in the annals of urban public health, halted the outbreak.

'Taking lessons from those who battled pandemics in centuries past, we see the need to take a big, bold approach to adapting and advancing our infrastructure for disease surveillance now, while the crisis window is open,' the Mathematica team wrote. 'If we do so strategically, with a view toward the next epidemic, we may revolutionize public health once more.'

The public health narrative that connects these breakthroughs from the middle of the nineteenth century to the early twenty-first century and the pandemic tells a story about how a handful of scientific and technological advances made urban life safer and more livable, and thus set the stage for the mass urbanization that occurred after World War II.

Some of those discoveries had nothing to do with cities at all. One of the most consequential occurred in Vienna during the late 1840s. Ignaz Semmelweis, a Hungarian obstetrician working in a Viennese hospital, observed unusually high rates of mortality among the women in one particular ward. When he began to probe further, he observed that physicians and medical students who were treating those patients had often come from the morgue, where they had been performing autopsies. By contrast, women in the wards staffed by midwives had very low mortality rates. Though the scientific understanding of bacteria was still in its infancy, Semmelweis reasoned that the physicians had something on their hands that they transmitted to their patients. 'Wash your hands,' he told them, and that simple, non-technological requirement profoundly altered the spread of infectious diseases (Flynn 2020).

Then, in the early 1860s, two scientists, Louis Pasteur, from France, and Robert Koch, from Germany, confirmed that microbes transmitted some food or water-borne diseases – the so-called 'germ theory.' Pasteur, who also invented some early vaccines, including the rabies vaccine, developed a method for killing harmful bacteria in wine and beer. Known as pasteurization, the technique involved rapidly heating and then cooling the liquids to prevent them from spoiling. A few years later, a German scientist figured out how to pasteurize milk, a process soon commercialized in Germany. A chemist, in turn, invented equipment for treating bottled milk. Though it met with some resistance, including from some scientists, the practice of milk pasteurization rapidly spread through the dairy industry in northern Europe and Scandinavia, and eventually reached North America, where activists urged dairies and local authorities to adopt the technique (Currier & Widness 2018).

In some cities, including Toronto, some public health leaders zealously advocated pasteurization to rein in local dairies that diluted their milk with contaminated water – a practice that contributed to high infant mortality rates. Dr. Charles Hastings, the city's crusading medical officer of health from 1909 to 1929, 'engaged in friendly persuasion, modern publicity methods (such as publishing lists of "first-class dairies" in the monthly *Health Bulletin*), and hard-nosed negotiating,' according to public health historian Heather MacDougall. 'His efforts ensured that by October 1915 … the city's well-inspected and bacteriologically tested supply had become a model for other urban centres. The proof of the effectiveness of these changes was a sharp decline in outbreaks of milk-borne disease and a drop of roughly one third in the number of infant deaths' (MacDougall 2018).

A parallel development, and one that had a more direct relationship with municipal infrastructure, involved chlorination for disinfecting the water supply. Though chlorine was isolated as a chemical in 1810, chemists and municipal engineers only began experimenting with the compound as a potential disinfectant around the turn of the century, first, experimentally, in Louisville, Kentucky, and then in Belgium and municipalities like Jersey City, which became the first place in the U.S. to begin continuously adding chlorine to water stored in the 700-acre Boonton Reservoir, located about 40 kilometres northwest of New York City (American Water Works Association 2006).

The introduction of chlorine led to dramatic declines in the prevalence of water-borne illnesses such as typhoid, dysentery, and cholera by the 1920s. Typhoid mortality in the U.S. fell from thirty deaths per 100,000 in 1900 to virtually zero by 1940. Yet the use of the chemical had unanticipated consequences. Chlorine interacted with some organic compounds in water to produce traces of a by-product chemical identified early on as a potential carcinogen. By the 1970s, federal laws in the U.S. and elsewhere required local water authorities to ensure not only a disinfected water supply, but also one free of harmful secondary substances. As the Centers for Disease Control and Prevention put it, the advent of chlorination marked 'one of the ten greatest public health achievements of the twentieth century' ('History of Drinking Water Treatment' 2012).

With the mounting public concern about the environment that welled up during the 1960s following the publication of Rachel Carson's 1962 bestseller, *Silent Spring*, governments began to pass parallel laws regulating air pollution, lead additives in gasoline and paint, smokestack emissions, hazardous waste disposal, and, in places like England, the use of coal for home heating. These laws were typically national in scope, but their public health impacts tended to be urban – e.g., focused on reducing smog in big cities or countering respiratory illnesses afflicting children living near highways or downwind from factories.

Not coincidentally, the regulatory changes spurred investment in a wide array of engineering-driven technologies, from more fuel-efficient engines to scrubbers, high-efficiency gas furnaces, recycling facilities as alternatives to municipal incinerators, and remediation techniques for heavily contaminated brownfields. None of these innovations were driven by information and communications technology or anything that might now be described as smart city systems, yet they all contributed hugely to the betterment of quality of urban life.

Strangely, there was one very large category of shared space that did not benefit from the waves of laws aimed at improving public health: the interior atmosphere of buildings. Jeffrey Siegel, a University of Toronto professor of civil engineering, describes indoor air quality (IAQ) as the poor cousin of the world of sustainable architecture – an 'incredibly neglected' issue in terms of public health policy, despite the fact that most people spend the lion's share of their time inside, and increasingly in sealed environments (Lorinc 2020).

Stale recycled air in hermetically sealed office buildings contributes to headaches, drowsiness, and colds. Landlords or property managers frequently neglect the maintenance of HVAC equipment. Those physical features are, in turn, exacerbated by the widespread use of synthetic fabrics for carpets or upholstery. These fossil fuel–based materials emit volatile organic compounds and give rise to a condition dubbed 'sick building syndrome.' In residential dwellings, poorly ventilated or damp homes and apartments are susceptible to mould and contribute to respiratory ailments like asthma or allergies. And in the most extreme example, odourless radon gas, which is sequestered in certain types of soil, leaks into basements, causing respiratory illnesses and lung cancer.

However, beyond smoking restrictions and general health and safety standards for industrial workplaces, Canada doesn't really regulate indoor air quality, although other jurisdictions are more activist. 'One reason EPAs (in many countries) did not focus on indoor air was that the indoor environment, especially in the home, was thought of as a private concern with which governments should not interfere,' says Jan Sundell, one of the world's leading IAQ researchers, who notes that serious building science research on IAQ only began in the 1980s (Sundell 2017).

The obscure work of building science researchers was amplified by a surge of media coverage. 'Indoor Air Pollution' was the alarmist headline on an extensive 1986 *Washington Post* feature. The building industry began to respond. In the years prior to the pandemic, HVAC companies were seeing a general increase in private demand for products that claim to improve IAQ, including more robust filters for residential furnaces, air purifiers that use 'germicidal' ultraviolet light to kill airborne microbes, and so-called 'bipolar ionization' air cleaners, which are installed in HVAC equipment, although the efficacy of this latter technology remains controversial.

Yet COVID-19 radically altered the IAQ market. Early in the pandemic, the prevailing scientific consensus was that the virus spread through contact with infected surfaces and the transmission of the disease through droplets that are spread when individuals cough, sneeze, or speak loudly – conclusions that informed public health directives about mask wearing and social distancing. But as the pandemic progressed, a growing number of public health experts began to find evidence that the virus spread with airborne aerosols that were much smaller and lighter than droplets, and circulated in closed environments, from elevators to movie theatres.

The response, in many jurisdictions, involved both low-tech and higher-tech solutions, although there were none that relied specifically on AI, big data, or the other tools in the smart city arsenal. In terms of the former, public health officials directed institutions such as school boards and child care centres to significantly boost existing ventilation rates, so that air in closed environments would be replaced much more frequently than had been the case pre-pandemic. Private building owners were also encouraged to take these measures.

As for the more technologically advanced measures, some jurisdictions began requiring institutions such as school boards to install so-called HEPA (for 'high efficiency particulate air') filters. These devices, which can filter 99.7 per cent of all airborne particles, including extremely small ones, are commonly used in operating rooms or industrial settings such as computer chip manufacturers.

These devices have a curious backstory, because the technology, though sophisticated, is not new. HEPA filters date back to the 1940s, invented as part of the Manhattan Project, the top-secret U.S. government nuclear warhead R&D venture. The filters were intended to protect thousands of employees working in a secret facility from inhaling radioactive particles. Their design centres on a tangled weave of ultra-fine fibres made from fibreglass or other substances that trap some of the most minute particles in the air.

Specialized HVAC equipment until the second year of the pandemic, HEPA filters were suddenly available at hardware stores and through building supply chains. Governments distributed thousands to schools and other congregate settings. Although estimates vary, market researchers estimated that the HEPA filter sector could expand by compound annual growth rates by 7.4 percent by 2026 – a surge few saw coming before COVID-19.

It's worth noting that niche approaches to sustainable/energy-efficient building design, which considerably predate the pandemic, relied heavily on significant investments in ventilation technology as part of an overall philosophy for reducing carbon and providing fresh air in indoor environments. Some of these, in turn, involved ideas that date back to the earliest forms of architecture – designs that allow for windows that open and the virtuous use of cross-drafts for cooling, features that fell to the wayside with so much twentieth-century architecture.

What's more, some smart city tech companies had also identified IAQ as a potential market, developing specialized IoT sensors that were, in turn, integrated into large smart building systems that also controlled lighting, energy consumption, heating and cooling, etc.

Yet it took a global crisis – and not fads from green building architecture or the smart city industry – to change public thinking about indoor air. In that regard, COVID-19's wake-up call evokes another city-transforming public health disaster: the Great Smog of London in December 1952, which killed around 12,000 people. In the aftermath, the British government enacted tough restrictions on the use of coal for home heating and electricity generation, as well as imposing strict air pollution standards on industrial emitters. As the *New York Times* commented, 'The Great Smog is considered a turning point in environmental history' (Nagourney 2003).

2
How Technology is Reshaping the Post-Pandemic City

The global smart city narrative gained tremendous momentum during the 2010s, only to be derailed, as was so much else, by COVID-19.

The crises set in motion by pandemics cast very long shadows. The Black Death – a bacterial infection spread through fleas on rats – ravaged European towns and cities in the mid-fourteenth century, killing tens or even hundreds of millions of people and decimating rural communities. According to Mark Bailey, a professor of medieval history in England, the pandemic of 1347 to 1353 stands 'unchallenged as the greatest catastrophe in human history.'

As Bailey wrote in his 2021 history of the aftermath of the Black Death, 'The tenth to the thirteenth centuries represented a sustained period of efflorescence and expansion, which first slowed, then halted and decisively reversed, during the first half of the fourteenth century due to an exceptional combination of catastrophic events: famine, warfare, bovine disease, human disease, and an unstable climate. Population levels across Europe collapsed in the mid-fourteenth century, and did not recover for two to three centuries' (Bailey 2021, 17).

Over four centuries later, the Spanish flu pandemic of 1918–20 – an H1N1 virus that may have started in the trenches of France at the end of World War I and spread rapidly around the globe – infected an estimated half billion people worldwide and killed at least 50 million over the course of three waves. Young, healthy adults turned out to be especially susceptible ('1918 Pandemic [H1N1 virus]' 2019).

The Spanish flu, compounded by the war's horrific casualties, gutted a generation in its prime, leaving countless families struggling to survive without breadwinners.

Post-pandemic eras, in turn, are often marked by the emergence of far-reaching societal changes. As plague survivors relocated to towns that had been almost wiped out, the generations following the Black Death saw improvements in labour productivity, accelerated urbanization, and a hastened decline of the feudal system of landownership. The waves of infectious disease outbreaks in nineteenth-century industrial cities accelerated and focused scientific research first on the vectors of contagion and then on solutions ranging from handwashing to disinfection technologies and improved infrastructure. The devastation of Spanish flu pushed some countries, including Canada, to establish national health bureaucracies, invest in research that led to early antiviral drugs and antibiotics, and enact sweeping social welfare reforms.

As I write this in early 2022, it is far too soon to draw any meaningful conclusions about the long-term, or even medium-term, impact of the pandemic. But from the earliest days of the outbreak, one fact became abundantly clear: that a range of digital, network, and electronic technologies played a profoundly important role in the ways in which societies responded, both positively and negatively, to the coronavirus that surged out of Wuhan in late 2019.

COVID-19 could, in fact, be described as history's first technology pandemic.

That label deserves parsing. Social media allowed for the rapid dissemination of critical public health information, but it also proved to be a chillingly effective accelerator of lethal misinformation – so much so, in fact, that some epidemiologists regarded the proliferation of anti-vaxxer/anti-masker propaganda as one of the key drivers of infection rates.[16]

---

16. A 2020 paper in *Scientific Reports* analyzed the social media 'infodemic' and concluded, presciently, given the publication date that '[t]he case of the COVID-19 epidemic shows the critical impact of this new information environment. The information spreading can strongly influence people's behavior and alter the effectiveness of the countermeasures deployed by governments' (Cinelli et al. 2020).

Quite apart from the tsunami of digital conspiracy theories, the story of technology's role in the pandemic focused on the ways in which we adapted rapidly by massively scaling up certain digital systems, such as video-conferencing, document-sharing, electronic funds transfer, streaming, e-commerce, automation, 3-D printing, and secure cloud-based computing, among others. All of these technologies existed prior to the pandemic. However, the pandemic restrictions significantly amplified their take-up and importance in a range of sectors, while spurring waves of innovation and billions of dollars in investment in other pandemic-related technologies, such as small-scale battery-powered mobility devices.

The seemingly exponential expansion of information and communications technology applications was transformative. What's more, these emergent digital services were not just crisis work-arounds; rather, they became as integral to modern economies and labour markets as Excel spreadsheets are to accounting, and likely to leave their mark on all sorts of other domains, from culture and education to health services and the media.

But in the context of urban regions, this big family of pandemic-adjacent innovations can be understood as a kind of rebuttal to much of what the smart city industry was promising as it gained momentum during the 2010s. While smart city tech encompasses a diverse array of applications, the common denominator is that these systems are meant to respond to the *concentration* of twenty-first-century city regions. They were created specifically to manage the complex tangle of problems that arise in dense, rapidly evolving city regions. Adapting computing applications designed either for military uses or sprawling multinationals, smart city firms contended that big cities had become so large and so overcrowded that their particular issues – housing, traffic, pollution, the management of public space, goods movement, etc. – could be tamed only by potent new forms of software, hardware, and connectivity.

In other words, if smart city technologies were all about managing the pressures of proximity, then pandemic technologies addressed the opposite, providing pragmatic solutions that enabled part of society and the economy to function in a condition of enforced dispersion.

Obviously, the grind of urban life never came to a halt, even during the strictest lockdowns. Only a portion of the labour force had the luxury of working from home, and there was plenty of anecdotal evidence that traffic worsened as many commuters avoided transit. Yet for just about everyone, the wide sweep of pandemic virtualization touched all aspects of life, from the precipitous rise in e-commerce[17] to the ways in which schools, universities, and colleges, cultural institutions, and health care providers pivoted from in-person to online during the most severe lockdown periods. Mental health care in particular saw a dramatic surge as providers and patients shifted to online sessions, which proved to be more convenient, flexible, and accessible to underserviced communities, as well as less hampered by the stigmas that still cling to in-person counselling (e.g., being seen by an acquaintance entering a psychologist's clinic). Numerous mental health care companies, in fact, raised hundreds of millions of dollars through initial public offerings during the pandemic as remote service delivery took off in response to the demand for counselling and heightened incidence of depression and anxiety.

The earliest video-conferencing systems surfaced in the 1970s but only began to mature in the late 1990s, with improved digital video and connectivity. Even at the beginning of the pandemic, video-conferencing was primarily used in office contexts, typically for virtual gatherings of team members scattered in different cities. The 'consumer' version, Skype, gained some traction as a free alternative to long-distance phone calls, but couldn't shed its reputation as a buggy application.

Some of today's most commonplace technologies – email, cell-phones, smart phones etc. – began as office or business tools and then spread far beyond the world of work. With video-conferencing,

---

17. In Canada, seasonally adjusted e-commerce sales rose 34 per cent between March 2020 and November 2021. A StatsCan survey of online shopping found that 82 per cent of Canadians made online purchases in 2020, up from 73 per cent just two years prior. Among twenty-five- to forty-four-year-olds, the proportion is 95 per cent. Almost one in eight ordered groceries online for the first time in 2020 ('Online Shopping by Canadians in 2020' 2021).

the pandemic dramatically telescoped this process: *Zoom* became a verb, as the use of video-conferencing exploded into almost all spheres of life via every major digital platform and device.

Complaints about virtual meetings and online classes were one of the most common subjects of discussion during the pandemic, and their use in contexts like K–12 classrooms ebbed with the end of lockdowns. Yet the take-up of this technology isn't going to snap back to pre-pandemic levels: during the pandemic, many people, professionals, and organizations also found novel and productive ways to adapt video-conferencing for use in entirely unanticipated contexts, and none of that will go away.[18] What's more, major tech firms continually invest in the development of such applications, making them more user friendly and less painful to use.

The near ubiquity of video-conferencing, streaming, and other lifeline connectivity tools turbocharged the ways in which digital technology is uncoupling experience and place – a trend that has both negative and positive implications. Virtual anything lacks intimacy, atmosphere, the opportunity to collectively participate in a live event, and any sense of occasion. However, the potent combination of necessity, technology, and entrepreneurialism enabled people to take cooking or fitness classes virtually, attend lectures in distant cities or partake in previously overpriced or physically inaccessible live theatre performances. Some of these are extensions of the pre-pandemic online world, but others represent entirely new ways of leaping over the constraints of geography and cost to reach new audiences.

One example: film festivals, which went online during the first year of the pandemic and then sought to navigate in-person versions during later waves. In many ways, film festivals, their brands so heavily associated with specific cities, were emblematic of the type of cosmopolitan experience that characterized global cities: a major elite draw that generates media attention, spinoff economic activity, tourism,

---

18. An example I heard from some professors – most of whom detested online courses – involved virtual office hours, which turned out to be a highly constructive and efficient virtual form of instructor/student interaction.

business network, etc. But the rise of the major streaming services, with their giant production and acquisition budgets, had begun to erode the importance of film festivals to the industry's professionals in the mid-2010s.

The post-pandemic version, predicted pop culture journalist Angela Watercutter in *Wired*, would be hybrid festivals that take place both in person and virtually. '[F]ilm festivals have always struggled with accessibility issues that can be mitigated by allowing people to attend from home,' she observed. 'So perhaps hybrid festivals are the future even in the best of times. Cinema culture exists on multiple planes; it's time film festivals did too' (Watercutter 2022).

Not too many people go to film festivals, although many stream movies. The noteworthy point here is the projected future of these events as 'hybrids' – a term that may come to define the way in-person and virtual/live-streamed experiences or events coexist in the future. These may include trade shows, professional conferences and other smaller events – e.g., board meetings – that migrated online during the pandemic and may return in a more circumscribed form that involves less travel and permanent options for virtual attendance.

The largest post-pandemic hybrid environment seems destined to be the realm of the office, and the ways in which these white-collar workplaces begin to reassemble themselves, both physically and socially. The emergency shift to telework, or 'WFH, in March 2020 represented a dizzyingly swift response to a crisis, enabled by a set of fairly mature technologies, including, but not limited to, video-conferencing. By mid-2020, 42 per cent of the U.S. labour force was working from home, while in Canada the numbers were slightly lower.

For many years, urban planners have talked about the future of telework in big cities, in part as a means of easing rush-hour traffic. 'The phenomenon of working at home rather than in an office – often called "telework" or "telecommuting" – is expected to increase greatly in the years ahead,' a columnist for the *Dallas Morning News* predicted in 1985. 'Working at home has become more practical in recent years because new electronic technologies make it possible for people to perform most office tasks effectively, easily and cheaply over electronic networks between their home and remote offices.'

According to a 2015 Gallup survey, the proportion of U.S. employees who had worked remotely rose from 9 to 37 per cent between 1995 and 2015; most were college educated, higher-income, and white-collar. But 'telecommuting remains much more the exception than the rule,' the pollster concluded, with people working from home a few days a month, typically. Though Gallup's survey found teleworkers were highly productive, the study also noted that some tech firms were moving in the opposite direction, requiring all employees to be on-site (Jones 2015).

The pandemic revealed just how large a proportion of the workforce could, in theory, work from home, and that happened initially because of public health edicts. The adjustment for many was very difficult, carving out a workspace in small apartments shared with partners or children, figuring out how not to be on call all the time, and learning to live without the social environment and habits of the workaday world, from staff meetings to office gossip.

Yet the WFH transition offered as many positives as negatives: no grinding commutes and the associated costs (including environmental), additional time for chores or exercise, and new forms of engagement with colleagues, such as the people who would call in to morning meetings while out walking. And, as Stanford University economist Nicholas Bloom observed, 'The stigma associated with working from home prior to COVID-19 has disappeared' (Wong 2020).

Employers, meanwhile, invested heavily in technology to enable WFH, from remote security systems to monitors, as well as all sorts of home office equipment. They also began scrutinizing their real estate expenses and the amount of space they were renting to house employees who were working as productively if not more from home. As of 2022, it seems increasingly likely that many large organizations will move to hybrid work arrangements and 'hotelling,' i.e., desks that are booked instead of permanently assigned to an individual. The emergence of the hybrid workplace has also attracted a rush of entrepreneurial activity and investment, in everything from hybrid office design to scheduling software and management advice on how to optimize these arrangements.

The transition to hybrid work is very much in its infancy, and what the eventual equilibrium, or at least common practice, looks like remains to be seen. Yet some early indicators offer clues to the ways in which the geography of work has changed. While some employers will insist on a return to the office, others will make it optional, or offer flexibility as a perk. The latter have already begun to cast their recruitment nets wider, hiring from beyond their own commuter sheds. In national and multinational firms, this practice wasn't uncommon pre-pandemic, but it is now available to many more organizations, including some in the public sector. Even for large companies, the separation of office from employee opens up new vistas for hiring people content to work remotely as a permanent condition of employment.

During COVID-19's first year, some pundits and urbanists engaged in a largely speculative and mostly fatuous debate over whether the pandemic would kill cities – a discussion fuelled by empty subway cars, abandoned downtown streets, and darkened office towers. In previous eras, from the Cold War to the out-migration of back offices in the 1980s, the demise of cities has been forecast, incorrectly. The pandemic, similarly, didn't kill the city, although census data reported in 2021 indicated that larger-census metropolitan areas saw a net decline in population and population growth, while rural areas were picking up new residents. In Toronto and Montreal, for example, the populations dropped in the year ending July 2021 by 16,600 and 46,700 residents respectively (Lundy 2022). In the U.S., population growth in major metros fell from a decade-high of 1 per cent in 2013–14 to .39 per cent in the first year of the pandemic, although other factors also contributed, such as slower immigration and higher death rates (Frey 2021).

The shifting patterns of work may have farther-reaching consequences for cities, urban economies, and labour markets, although how these look is not yet clear. For example, transit ridership in some cities may take many years to return to pre-pandemic levels. Indeed, if hybrid work arrangements remain commonplace, then some of the core business assumptions of transit agency planners – like peak period volumes, the take-up of monthly passes, etc. – may fall away, prompting difficult decisions about schedules, fares, and new routes. In the private sector, the business-travel-dependent hospitality sector, already smarting from a decade of Airbnb, seems likely to contract permanently, as will bricks-and-mortar retail of all scales.

Tech-enabled hybrid work could also shift the customers of service businesses – restaurants, after-work bars, gyms, etc. – away from office districts and into neighbourhoods with larger numbers of remote employees. Some office tower owners may seek to convert their assets to residential condo towers as a means of recouping lost revenues due to stubbornly high vacancy rates. And there may even be a boom in new forms of office/commercial development – e.g., smaller-footprint office complexes designed specifically for company gatherings, or shared workspaces in neighbourhood or suburban locales that have been selected by calculating the most convenient location for a gig or hybrid workforce that increasingly chooses to live away from core areas. Such changes, if they happen, won't kill cities so much as loosen them up, decanting some people away from centralized business districts that were once dense and lively, but also congested and overpriced.

It's also clear that some non-smart city technologies played a significant role in shaking up metropolitan labour markets during the pandemic. While automation and robotics have been a presence in manufacturing for many years, the pandemic, combined with the rapid diffusion of AI-driven technologies (e.g., advanced 3-D printing or automated customer service chatbots), significantly accelerated automation, according to several analyses.

Business investment in automation was accelerated by pandemic restrictions, labour shortages, absences due to illness, and a host of other factors. A January 2021 economic assessment by the International Monetary Fund confirmed that Covid factors triggered the surge of investment in automation, and went on to warn that the resulting displacement of low-skill workers will exacerbate income inequality in extended urbanized regions where businesses are investing heavily in robots. 'Our results suggest that the concerns about the rise of the robots amid the COVID-19 pandemic seem justified,' the IMF study concluded (Sedik & Yoo 2021).

Those concerns layer on top of another facet of the interplay between technology, cities, and the pandemic, which involves the issue of access to digital connectivity. As in pandemics past, Covid ruthlessly exposed festering social divisions, which, in this case, manifested themselves in the form of high infection rates in low-income or racialized neighbourhoods, high-rise apartments with poor ventilation and crowded elevators, and industrial/agricultural workplaces managed by companies that were indifferent to workplace safety standards.

While only a portion of the workforce had the option of working from home, every school-age child had to learn from home for extended periods, regardless of the profession or socio-economic status of their parents or caregivers. The reliance by educators on virtual classrooms shone a spotlight on the extent to which critical technologies – laptops or tablets, smart phones, and high-bandwidth internet/wifi – were available in low-income households.

In Canada, the market penetration rate for smart phones is almost 93 per cent, but the availability of high-speed internet is considerably lower. According to Statistics Canada, only three-quarters of households in census metropolitan areas had access to broadband (the proportion is far lower in rural or northern areas), while almost half a million Canadians had a mobile data plan but no home internet ('Access to the Internet in Canada' 2021). In the U.S., meanwhile, broadband access is significantly correlated with income, race, and education levels ('Internet/Broadband Fact Sheet' 2021).

The fact that basic and universal education, government, and health services were suddenly being provided virtually – and were therefore either unavailable or difficult to access for some segment of the urban population – raised critical questions about the technological infrastructure of cities and the so-called digital divide. Many school boards, for example, distributed devices to children in low-income families that didn't have laptops. Some cities sought to provide free wifi to apartment buildings that were home to marginalized tenants. These measures, however, simply underscored the reality that digital access has become a basic, essential form of infrastructure. Despite its central role, broadband is still a commodity distributed by the market and subject to market forces, which means the most vulnerable members of society, i.e., those with the least ability to pay, become that much more isolated from core services and vital information.

Many types of urban infrastructure trace their roots to the market, and to entrepreneurial responses to problems people will pay to fix. With piped access to fresh water in eighteenth-century London, the service was initially targeted at affluent homeowners – a far cry from the way municipal water is now distributed. Firefighting services traced back to the early markets for fire insurance. Waste management is still a service that straddles the public and private sectors. And in many places, electrical grids were never publicly owned, although, as monopolies, they are almost always regulated, if not operated, by the state.

Proponents of smart city tech frequently advocate for faster and more ubiquitous connectivity. Yet the goals for continuing to build out all that digital infrastructure don't necessarily include closing the digital divide or confronting social justice issues.

In a typical op-ed in *Smart Cities World*, a B2B publication, one British Telecom manager expounded on the range of benefits of expanding 5G coverage, yet stopped well short of suggesting it should be a public service. 'By using technology to optimise the city or town, authorities will see benefits across a range of different aspects – from better transport and eased congestion to smart refuse and recycling points and saving electricity. Therefore consistent connectivity is absolutely vital to the functioning of smart cities' (Hayes 2020).

Others have expressed skepticism about the promise of smart city tech in the post-pandemic world. 'In many cities the sky-rocketing expectations about smart city effects have not materialised,' Columbia University urban sociologist Saskia Sassen and Karima Kourtit, a Dutch professor of management, commented in a 2021 essay entitled 'A Post-Corona Perspective for Smart Cities: *"Should I Stay or Should I*

Go?'' 'Chicago calls itself a smart city, but does it excel in urban safety or income inequality? Athens is another smart city, but is it able to solve its congestion and air pollution problems? How is it possible that a city such as Beijing, which is able to control the movements of its citizens, is paralysed when it comes to coping effectively with the smog during the summer? Apparently, there is a significant gap between the myth of the smart city and its actual performance as a healthy or happy city' (Sassen & Kourtit 2021).

Indeed, in other discussions about the post-Covid incarnation of smart cities, the deep divisions exposed by the pandemic may have shifted thinking about the point of these ambitious and costly tech investments. 'How can you become a smart city when thousands of your residents can't connect to the Internet to participate in online learning, to participate in remote work, to do online job training in order to even qualify for unemployment benefits, or to participate in interviews remotely?' wondered Jordan Davis, director of Smart Columbus, in a 2020 interview with *Government Technology* magazine, a U.S. trade publication (Descant 2020).

Davis's question points at something much more fundamental, which has to do with what twenty-first-century cities should aspire to become. In the aftermath of a once-in-a-century health calamity, and with another even more drastic climate crisis looming in the middle distance, the notion of 'smartness' seems not just limiting but blinkered – a utopian brand fuelled by the profit motive and engineered solutions that don't properly address the human challenges of city life while downplaying the crucial role of urban governance in the adoption of transformative systems (Joss et al. 2019). Perhaps we need a better label – one that accounts for inclusiveness and social justice, as well as the most enduring qualities of cities: resilience, adaptability, ingenuity, diversity, serendipity, endurance, and, critically, a sense of place. One size doesn't fit all, and indeed never has.

City-building has always leaned heavily on the problem-solving skills of engineers and inventors. But urban life, with its complicated energy and potential, is about so much more than technical innovation. 'Smart' may be necessary, but it will never be sufficient.

Acknowledgements

Dream States exists because the Atkinson Fellowship's awards jury in 2018 selected my proposal to spend a year reporting on the fascinating and complex issues that had sprung up in response to the development of the multi-billion-dollar smart city technology. That jury included Irene Gentle, Janice Lewis Stein, Armine Yalnizyan, and the late John Honderich, who passed away, to my great regret, the day after I finished the first draft of this manuscript. They were assisted in their evaluation of the many fine proposals by the staff of the Atkinson Foundation: Colette Murphy, Jenn Miller, and Phillip Roh. I cannot thank them enough for a fantastic once-in-a-career opportunity to take a deep dive into a topic that fascinates me.

I must extend my gratitude and heartfelt thanks to all the editors who provide me with work, and the opportunity to write about cities. This, happily, is a long list, and currently (as of 2022) includes Matt Blackett, Dylan Reid, Shawn Micallef, Adria Vasil, D'Arcy McGovern, Scott Colby, Neil Orford, Dawn Calleja, James Cowan, and Steph Chambers. I'd like to also thank the editors who handled some of the first articles I wrote about smart cities – Christina Vardanis and Carmine Starnino – as well as Enid Slack, of the Munk School of Global Affairs, who asked me to prepare a report on smart cities that became the jumping-off point for the original Atkinson Fellowship proposal. Alex Bozikovic, who is a friend and colleague and collaborator, kindly and attentively read the manuscript, and provided insightful feedback.

Sidewalk Labs' short but highly eventful sojourn in Toronto, 2017–20, provided an incredible amount of grist for my mill, and I am grateful to Waterfront Toronto's staff and many other sources, including those at Sidewalk Toronto, for answering all my questions. In particular, I'd like to acknowledge the extraordinary work and dedication of the late Marisa Piatelli, a true city builder and public servant who passed away far too soon.

The University of Toronto has an incredible amount of bench strength when it comes to cities, and I've had the good fortune of drawing on its deep reserve of knowledge. Among the urban scholars who have indulged my interview requests, I'd like to single out Eric Miller, Paul Hess, Andre Sorensen, Susannah Bunce, Richard Florida, Ted Kesik, Robert Wright, and David Wolfe. Pamela Robinson, at Toronto Metropolitan University's school of planning, was a fantastic sounding board early on in my Atkinson research. Finally, Shauna Brail, currently at U of T Mississauga, has been an exemplary collaborator and colleague. She provided me with invaluable access to U of T's bottomless storehouse of scholarship, which helped shape and refine this text.

Book projects, though incredibly rewarding, are time-consuming and stressful. I am extremely fortunate to be supported by many amazing friends and my family – my mother, Eva; my sister Julie; my in-laws in upstate New York (Ron; Trevor, Robin and Corrie; Andy, Lori, Eric, Abby, and Adam); my uncle Adam and his partner, Ellie; my cousins Adam and Mark and their respective families; and Victoria, Jacob, and Sammy, who are my oxygen and so much more.

A bit weirdly (for these kinds of lists), I want to acknowledge my dog, Nora the Lab. Last I checked, she doesn't read and probably doesn't even know what 'acknowledge' means, but I want to give her a shout-out anyway. During the pandemic, she and I walked literally thousands of kilometres around the city. As I said many times, I kept her healthy and she kept me healthy (and sane). Those walks proved to be enormously beneficial, and not just for the workout, the stress-busting, and the quiet time. Early on in the lockdown, I decided to stop walking 'the usual route'; instead, we began exploring, doing a different walk or neighbourhood each day, mainly to counter the Groundhog Day problem. I got to be a tourist in my own city at a time when there wasn't much travel going on. What's more, dog owners also tend to talk to one another, so our meandering urban excursions provided much-needed human interaction at a time when there wasn't a whole lot of human interaction on offer that didn't involve a screen.

Finally, I would like to recognize the amazing staff of Coach House Books, including Crystal Sikma, Tali Voron, James Lindsay, Sasha

Tate-Howarth, Lindsay Yates, Phil Bardach, Rick/Simon, John De Jesus, and Stuart Ross. To Stan Bevington and Alana Wilcox: thank you again for the opportunity to make books together.

Bibliography

'1918 Pandemic (H1N1 virus).' Centers for Disease Control and Prevention. https://www.cdc.gov/flu/pandemic-resources/1918-pandemic-h1n1.html

'About Us.' Crossness Engines Trust. n.d. https://www.crossness.org.uk

'Access to the Internet in Canada, 2020.' Statistics Canada. May 31, 2021. https://www150.statcan.gc.ca/n1/daily-quotidien/210531/dq210531d-eng.htm

Affidavit of Ellen P. Goodman, April 30, 2020, Ontario Superior Court of Justice (Divisional Court), Court File No. 211/19. https://ccla.org/wp-content/uploads/2021/06/Affidavit-of-Ellen-Goodman-Sworn_April-20-2020.pdf

Allegheny Conference on Community Development. *The History of the Allegheny Conference on Community Development: Making the Pittsburgh Region Attractive to Smart People and Smart Investment.* https://www.alleghenyconference.org/wp-content/uploads/2016/08/AlleghenyConferenceHistory.pdf

American Water Works Association. *Water Chlorination/Chloramination Practices and Principles: AWWA Manual M20, 2nd Edition.* Denver: American Water Works Association, 2006. https://www.awwa.org/Portals/0/files/publications/documents/M20LookInside.pdf

Armstrong, Christopher. 'Austin, James.' *Dictionary of Canadian Biography*, Vol. 12. Toronto/Quebec City: University of Toronto/Université Laval, 2003. http://www.biographi.ca/en/bio/austin_james_12E.html

Artyushina, Anna. 'Is Civic Data Governance the Key to Democratic Smart Cities? The Role of the Urban Data Trust in Sidewalk Toronto.' *Telematics and Informatics*, Vol. 55 (December 2020). https://www.sciencedirect.com/science/article/abs/pii/S0736585320301155

Audirac, Ivonne. 'Information Technology and Urban Form.' *Journal of Planning Literature*, Vol. 17, No. 2. Nov. 1, 2002. DOI: 10.1177/088541202762475955

Bai, Shunhua, and Junfeng Jiao. 'Understanding the Shared E-scooter Travels in Austin, TX.' *International Journal of Geo-Information*, Vol. 9, Issue 2. 2020. https://doi.org/10.3390/ijgi9020135

Bailey, Mark. *After the Black Death: Economy, Society, and the Law in Fourteenth-Century England.* Oxford: Oxford University Press, 2021.

Beck, Julie. 'Roman Plumbing: Overrated.' *The Atlantic.* Jan. 8, 2016. https://www.theatlantic.com/health/archive/2016/01/ancient-roman-toilets-gross/423072/

Berman, Marshall. *All That Is Solid Melts into Air: The Experience of Modernity.* New York: Penguin, 1988.

Blau, Eve. *The Architecture of Red Vienna, 1919–1934.* Cambridge: MIT Press, 1999.

Bousquet, Chris. 'How Cities Are Using the Internet of Things to Map Air Quality.' Data-Smart City Solutions, April 19, 2017. https://datasmart.ash.

harvard.edu/ news/article/how-cities-are-using-the-internet-of-things-to-map-air-quality-1025

Bradshaw, Robert, and Rob Kitchin. 'Charting the Design and Implementation of the Smart City: The Case of Citizen-centric Bikeshare in Hamilton, Ontario.' *Urban Geography*. Jan. 15, 2021. https://doi.org/10.1080/02723638.2021.1878439

Brayne, Sarah. *Predict and Surveil: Data, Discretion, and the Future of Policing.* Oxford: Oxford University Press, 2020.

Brustein, Joshua. 'The Diapers.com Guy Wants to Build a Utopian Megalopolis.' *Bloomberg Businessweek*. Sept. 1, 2021. https://www.bloomberg.com/news/features/2021-09-01/how-diapers-com-founder-marc-lore-plans-to-build-utopian-city-telosa

Busbea, Larry. *Topologies: The Urban Utopia in France, 1960–1970.* Cambridge: MIT Press, 2012.

Castells, Manuel. *The Rise of the Network Society.* New York: Wiley-Blackwell, 1996.

Cinelli, Matteo, Walter Quattrociocchi, Alessandro Galeazzi, Carlo Michele Valensise, Emanuele Brugnoli, Ana Lucia Schmidt, Paola Zola, Fabiana Zollo, and Antonio Scala. 'The COVID-19 Social Media Infodemic.' *Scientific Reports*, 10. Oct. 6, 2020. https://www.nature.com/articles/s41598-020-73510-5

City of Toronto. 'Automated Vehicles Tactical Plan.' Toronto: City of Toronto, 2020. https://www.toronto.ca/wp-content/uploads/2020/02/7ec4-TS_AV-Tactical-Plan_Technical-Report.pdf

———. 'Data Governance and Digital Infrastructure: Analysis and Key Considerations for the City of Toronto, Final Report, June 2020.' Steven Coutts and Sarah Gagnon-Turcotte. Toronto: City of Toronto, 2020. https://www.toronto.ca/wp-content/uploads/2020/08/95fb-2020-07-10-Open-North-Data-Governance-Report-Main-report-WEB.pdf

———. 'Non-Competitive Contract with Esri Canada Limited for Proprietary Geographic Information System Software Licenses.' Deanna Hotoyan and Sabrina DiPietro. Toronto: City of Toronto, 2021. https://www.toronto.ca/legdocs/mmis/2021/gl/bgrd/backgroundfile-171693.pdf

Clark, John and Cathy Ross. *London: The Illustrated Story.* London: Penguin UK, 2011.

Clark, Ralph A. 'Viewpoints: ShotSpotter Delivers for 120 Cities and Can Keep Buffalo Safer.' *Buffalo News*. Sept. 18, 2021. https://buffalonews.com/opinion/viewpoints-shotspotter-delivers-for-120-cities-and-can-keep-buffalo-safer/article_d857d12a-1571-11ec-a166-dba2ad5e0d29.html

'Controlling Coronavirus Transmission Using a Mobile App to Trace Close Proximity Contacts.' *Big Data Institute*. March 31, 2020. https://www.bdi.ox.ac.uk/news/controlling-coronavirus-transmission-using-a-mobile-app-to-trace-close-proximity-contacts

Cook, G. C. 'Construction of London's Victorian Sewers: The Vital Role of Joseph Bazalgette.' *Postgrad* Med J, 77, 802–04. Dec. 1, 2001. https://pmj.bmj.com/content/postgradmedj/77/914/802.full.pdf

'Corporate History.' Lloyd's. https://www.lloyds.com/about-lloyds/history/corporate-history

Crook, Lizzie. '15-Minute City concept by Carlos Moreno wins Obel Award 2021.' *dezeen*, October 26, 2021. https://www.dezeen.com/2021/10/26/15-minute-city-carlos-moreno-obel-award

Currier, Russell W., and John A. Widness. 'A Brief History of Milk Hygiene and Its Impact on Infant Mortality from 1875 to 1925 and Implications for Today: A Review.' *Journal of Food Protection*, Vol. 81, Issue 10. Sept. 20, 2018. https://doi.org/10.4315/0362-028X.JFP-18-186

Das, Diganta. 'In Pursuit of Being Smart? A Critical Analysis of India's Smart Cities Endeavor.' *Urban Geography*, Vol. 41, Issue 1, 55–78. 2020. https://doi.org/10.1080/02723638.2019.1646049

Datta, Ayona. 'A 100 Smart Cities, a 100 Utopias.' *Dialogues in Human Geography*, Vol. 5, Issue 1. 2015. https://doi.org/10.1177/2043820614565750

Descant, Skip. 'Social Justice, Broadband Top Priorities for Smart Cities.' *Government Technology*. June 25, 2020. https://www.govtech.com/smart-cities/social-justice-broadband-top-priorities-for-smart-cities.html

'Detailed Biography.' Thomas A. Edison Papers. Rutgers School of the Arts and Sciences. https://edison.rutgers.edu/bio-long.htm

Doucette, Michelle L., Christa Green, Jennifer Necci Dineen, David Shapiro, and Kerri M. Raissian. 'Impact of ShotSpotter Technology on Firearm Homicides and Arrests Among Large Metropolitan Counties: a Longitudinal Analysis, 1999–2016.' *Journal of Urban Health*, 98, 609–21. April 30, 2021. https://doi.org/10.1007/s11524-021-00515-4

Douet, James. 'The Steam Pumping Stations of the London Main Drainage, 1858–75,' *Industrial Archaeology Review*, 43:2, 135–46. Sept. 13, 2021. https://doi.org/10.1080/03090728.2021.1973226

Drapalova, Eliska, and Kai Weigrich. 'Who Governs 4.0? Varieties of Smart Cities.' *Public Management Review*, 22:5, 668–686. Feb. 3, 2020. https://doi.org/10.1080/14719037.2020.1718191

Dyton, Joe. 'Cisco Ends its Smart City Push.' *Connected*, January 7, 2021. https://connectedremag.com/smart-buildings/cisco-ends-its-smart-city-push/

Dugger, Celia W. 'Religious Riots Loom Over Indian Politics.' *New York Times*. July 27, 2002. https://www.nytimes.com/2002/07/27/world/religious-riots-loom-over-indian-politics.html

Eaton, Ruth. *Ideal Cities: Utopianism and the (un)built Environment*. London: Thames & Hudson, 2002.

Eaves, Dave, and Ben McGuire. 'Lessons from Estonia on Digital Government.' *Policy Options.* Feb. 7, 2019. https://policyoptions.irpp.org/magazines/february-2019/lessons-estonia-digital-government

Editorial Board. 'ShotSpotter as an Effective Crime-Fighting Tool? Jury's Still Out.' *Chicago Tribune.* Aug. 30, 2021.

Erhardt, Gregory D., Sneha Roy, Drew Cooper, Bhargava Sana, Mei Chen, and Joe Castiglione. 'Do transportation network companies decrease or increase congestion?' *ScienceAdvances,* Vol. 5, Issue 5. May 2019. https://www.science.org/doi/10.1126/sciadv.aau2670

Eschner, Kat. 'How a Controversial European Architect Shaped New York.' *Smithsonian Magazine.* Oct. 2, 2017. https://www.smithsonianmag.com/smart-news/how-controversial-european-architect-shaped-new-york-180965073/

Freemark, Yonah, Anne Hudson, and Jinhua Zhao. 'Are Cities Prepared for Autonomous Vehicles?' *Journal of the American Planning Association,* Vol. 85, Issue 2. 2019. https://doi.org/10.1080/01944363.2019.1603760

Feathers, Todd. 'Police Are Telling ShotSpotter to Alter Evidence from Gunshot-Detecting AI.' *Vice.* July 26, 2021. https://www.vice.com/en/article/qj8xbq/police-are-telling-shotspotter-to-alter-evidence-from-gunshot-detecting-ai

Ferguson, Andrew Guthrie. *The Rise of Big Data Policing: Surveillance, Race, and the Future of Law Enforcement.* New York: NYU Press, 2017.

Ferguson, Niall. *The House of Rothschild: Money's Prophets 1798–1848.* New York: Penguin, 1999.

Ferretti, Luca, Chris Wymant, Michelle Kendall, Lele Zhao, Anel Nurtay, Lucie Abeler-Dörner, Michael Parker, David Bonsall, and Christophe Fraser. 'Quantifying SARS-CoV-2 Transmission Suggests Epidemic Control with Digital Contact Tracing.' *Science.* Vol. 368, Issue 6491. March 31, 2020. https://doi.org/10.1126/science.abb6936

Fiederer, Luke. 'AD Classics: Master Plan for Chandigarh/Le Corbusier.' *ArchDaily.* Oct. 6, 2018. https://www.archdaily.com/806115/ad-classics-master-plan-for-chandigarh-le-corbusier

Fishman, Robert. *Bourgeois Utopias: The Rise and Fall of Suburbia.* New York: Basic Books, 1987.

Flynn, Meagan. 'The Man Who Discovered That Unwashed Hands Could Kill – and Was Ridiculed for It.' *Washington Post.* March 23, 2020. https://www.washingtonpost.com/nation/2020/03/23/ignaz-semmelweis-handwashing-coronavirus/

Foody, Kathleen. 'Chicago Police End Effort to Predict Gun Offenders, Victims.' *Associated Press.* Jan. 23, 2020. https://apnews.com/article/41f75b783d796b80815609e737211cc6

'Forest City Overview.' Forest City. n.d. https://www.forestcitygpv.com/about-forest-city/overview

Frey, William H. 'Pandemic Population Change Across Metro America: Accelerated Migration, Less Immigration, Fewer Births and More Deaths.' Brookings. May 20, 2021. https://www.brookings.edu/research/pandemic-population-change-across-metro-america-accelerated-migration-less-immigration-fewer-births-and-more-deaths

Geels, Frank. 'The Dynamics of Transitions in Socio-Technical Systems: A Multi-Level Analysis of the Transition Pathway from Horse-Drawn Carriages to Automobiles (1860–1930).' *Technology Analysis & Strategic Management*, Vol. 17, Issue 4, 445–76. 2005. https://doi.org/10.1080/09537320500357319.

Glanz, James, Mike Baker, and Anjali Singhvi. 'Condo Wreckage Hints at First Signs of Possible Construction Flaw.' *New York Times*. July 5, 2021. https://www.nytimes.com/2021/07/03/us/florida-condo-collapse-steel-rebar.html

Goldberg, Michael. 'Berry Gordy: Motown's Founder Tells the Story of Hitsville, U.S.A.' *Rolling Stone*. Aug. 23, 1990. https://www.rollingstone.com/feature/berry-gordy-motown-hitsville-interview-888729/

Goldsmith, Stephen, Betsy Gardener, and Jill Jamieson. 'Toward a Smarter Future: Building Back Better with Intelligent Civil Infrastructure.' Policy Briefs Series, Ash Center for Democratic Governance and Innovation. Sept. 2021. https://ash.harvard.edu/files/ash/files/311026_hks_policy_brief_infrastructure_v2.pdf

Gray, Jeff. 'Toronto Police End ShotSpotter Project Over Legal Concerns.' *Globe and Mail*. Feb. 13, 2019. https://www.theglobeandmail.com/canada/toronto/article-toronto-police-end-shotspotter-project-over-legal-concerns/

Gutiérrez, Gerardo. 'Mexico-Tenochtitlan: Origin and Transformations of the Last Mesoamerican Imperial City.' In *Volume 3: Early Cities in Comparative Perspective, 4000 BCE–1200 CE*, ed. Norman Yoffee, 491–512. Cambridge: Cambridge University Press, 2015.

Hall, Peter Geoffrey. *Cities in Civilization*. New York: Pantheon, 1998.

Halpern, Orit, Jesse LeCavalier, Nerea Calvillo, and Wolfgang Pietsch. 'Test-Bed Urbanism.' *Public Culture*, Vol. 25, Issue 2 70. March 1, 2013. https://doi.org/10.1215/08992363-2020602

Harford, Tim. 'How the Humble S-Bend Made Modern Toilets Possible.' *BBC News*. Oct. 16, 2017. https://www.bbc.com/news/business-41188465

Harris, Mark. 'China's Sponge Cities: Soaking Up Water to Reduce Flood Risks.' *Guardian*. Oct. 1, 2015. https://www.theguardian.com/sustainable-business/2015/oct/01/china-sponge-cities-los-angeles-water-urban-design-drought-floods-urbanisation-rooftop-gardens

Haarstad, Håvard, and Marikken W. Wathne. 'Are Smart City Projects Catalyzing Urban Energy Sustainability?' *Energy Policy*, Vol. 129, 918–25. June 2019. https://doi.org/10.1016/j.enpol.2019.03.001

Hayes, Jamie. 'Smart Cities Are Only as Good as Their Connectivity.' *SmartCities-World.* Aug, 10, 2020. https://www.smartcitiesworld.net/opinions/opinions/smart-cities-are-only-as-good-as-their-connectivity

Heineke, Kersten, Benedikt Kloss, and Darius Scurtu. 'The Future of Micromobility: Ridership and Revenue after a Crisis.' *McKinsey & Company.* July 16, 2020. https://www.mckinsey.com/industries/automotive-and-assembly/our-insights/the-future-of-micromobility-ridership-and-revenue-after-a-crisis

Helft, Miguel. 'You Can't Kill Jack Dangermond's Company. Try, And It Will Only Get Stronger.' *Forbes,* March 31, 2015. https://www.forbes.com/sites/miguel-helft/2015/03/31/you-cant-kill-jack-dangermonds-company-try-and-it-will-only-get-stronger

Highes, Thomas P. 'The Electrification of America: The System Builders.' *Technology and Culture,* Vol. 20, No. 1, 124–61. Jan. 1979. https://www.jstor.org/stable/3103115

'Historical Vaccine Safety Concerns.' Centers for Disease Control and Prevention. https://www.cdc.gov/vaccinesafety/concerns/concerns-history.html

'History of Drinking Water Treatment.' Centers for Disease Control and Prevention. https://www.cdc.gov/healthywater/drinking/history.html

Holder, Sarah. 'In San Diego, "Smart" Streetlights Spark Surveillance Reform.' *Bloomberg CityLab.* Aug. 6, 2020. https://www.bloomberg.com/news/articles/2020-08-06/a-surveillance-standoff-over-smart-streetlights

Information and Privacy Commissioner of Ontario. *Sidewalk Labs' Proposal.* Brian Beamish. 2019. https://www.ipc.on.ca/wp-content/uploads/2019/09/2019-09-24-ltr-stephen-diamond-waterfront_toronto-residewalk-proposal.pdf

'Internet/Broadband Fact Sheet.' Pew Research Center. April 7, 2021. https://www.pewresearch.org/internet/fact-sheet/internet-broadband

Jones, Jeffrey M. 'In U.S., Telecommuting for Work Climbs to 37%.' GALLUP. Aug. 19, 2015. https://news.gallup.com/poll/184649/telecommuting-work-climbs.aspx

Joss, Simon, Frans Sengers, Daan Schraven, Federico Caprotti, and Youri Dayot. 'The Smart City as Global Discourse: Storylines and Critical Junctures across 27 Cities.' *Journal of Urban Technology,* Vol. 26, Issue 1. Feb. 13, 2019. https://doi.org/full/10.1080/10630732.2018.1558387

Kargon, Robert, and Arthur Molella. 'The City as Communications Net: Norbert Wiener, the Atomic Bomb, and Urban Dispersal.' *Technology and Culture,* Vol. 45, No. 4. Oct. 2004. https://www.jstor.org/stable/40060685

Katz, Dana E. *The Jewish Ghetto and the Visual Imagination of Early Modern Venice.* Cambridge: Cambridge University Press, 2017.

Keshaviah, Aparna, Xindi C. Hu, and Marisa Henry. 'Developing a Flexible National Wastewater Surveillance System for COVID-19 and Beyond.' *Environmental Health Perspectives,* Vol. 129, No. 4. April 20, 2021. https://ehp.niehs.nih.gov/doi/10.1289/EHP8572

Khan, Falaah Arif, and Julia Stoyanovich. 'Mirror, Mirror.' Data, Responsibly Comics, Vol, 1. 2020. https://dataresponsibly.github.io/comics/vol1/mirror_en.pdf

Kimmelman, Michael. 'Hudson Yards Is Manhattan's Biggest, Newest, Slickest Gated Community.' New York Times. March 14, 2019. https://www.nytimes.com/interactive/2019/03/14/arts/design/hudson-yards-nyc.html

Kirkbride, T. W., rev. Mike Chrimes. 'Aspdin, Joseph.' Oxford Dictionary of National Biography. Sept. 23, 2004. https://doi.org/10.1093/ref:odnb/37129

Kitchin, Rob. 'Urban Big Data.' Planner. Nov. 3, 2016. https://mural.maynoothuniversity.ie/7327/1/Urban

Koh, Sin Yee, Yimin Zhao, and Hyun Bang Shin. 'Moving the Mountain and Greening the Sea: The Micropolitics of Speculative Green Urbanism at Forest City, Iskandar Malaysia.' Urban Geography. Nov. 15, 2021. https://doi.org/10.1080/02723638.2021.1999725

Kontokosta, Constantine E. 'The Quantified Community and Neighborhood Labs: A Framework for Computational Urban Science and Civic Technology Innovation.' Journal of Urban Technology, 23:4. Oct. 26, 2016. https://doi.org/10.1080/10630732.2016.1177260

Kontokosta, Constantine E., and Boyeong Hong. 'Who Calls for Help? Statistical Evidence of Disparities in Citizen-Government Interactions Using Geo-spatial Survey and 311 Data from Kansas City.' Bloomberg Data for Good Exchange Conference. Sept. 16, 2018. https://data.bloomberglp.com/company/sites/2/2018/09/Who-Calls-for-Help.pdf

Koops, Bert-Jaap. 'The Concept of Function Creep.' Law, Innovation and Technology, Vol. 13, Issue 1. 2021. https://doi.org/10.1080/17579961.2021.1898299

Kostof, Spiro. The City Shaped: Urban Patterns and Meanings Through History. Boston: Little Brown, 1991.

Kovacs, Eduard. 'Tesla Car Hacked Remotely from Drone via Zero-Click Exploit.' SecurityWeek. May 3, 2021. https://www.securityweek.com/tesla-car-hacked-remotely-drone-zero-click-exploit

Kreier, Freda. 'The Myriad Ways Sewage Surveillance Is Helping Fight COVID Around the World.' Nature. May 10, 2021. https://www.nature.com/articles/d41586-021-01234-1

Kresin, Frank. 'Smart Cities Value Their Smart Citizens.' In Urban Europe: Fifty Tales of the City, ed. by Virginie Mamadouh and Anne van Wageningen, 181–86. Amsterdam: Amsterdam University Press, 2015.

Lang, Michael H. 'Town Planning and Radicalism in the Progressive Era: The legacy of F. L. Ackerman.' Planning Perspectives, Vol. 16, Issue 2. Dec. 2, 2010.

Laviv, Ran, Maya Azaria, and Vandana Menon. 'Which Trends Are Driving the Autonomous Vehicles Industry?' World Economic Forum. Nov. 8, 2021. https://www.weforum.org/agenda/2021/11/trends-driving-the-autonomous-vehicles-industry

Le Corbusier. *When the Cathedrals Were White.* New York: McGraw-Hill Book Company, 1964.

LeGates, Richard T., and Frederic Stout, eds. *The City Reader.* Oxfordshire: Routledge, 1996.

Lepore, Jill. *If Then: How the Simulmatics Corporation Invented the Future.* New York: Liveright, 2020.

Lewis, Dyani. 'Contact-Tracing Apps Help Reduce COVID Infections, Data Suggest.' *Nature.* Feb. 26, 2021. https://www.nature.com/articles/d41586-021-00451-y

Li, Hua, Alana Glecia, Arlene Kent-Wilkinson, Donald Leidl, Manal Kleib, and Tracie Risling. 'Transition of Mental Health Service Delivery to Telepsychiatry in Response to COVID-19: A Literature Review.' *Psychiatric Quarterly,* 1–17. June 8, 2021. https://doi.org/10.1007/s11126-021-09926-7

Light, Jennifer S. *From Warfare to Welfare: Defense Intellectuals and Urban Problems in Cold War America.* Baltimore: Johns Hopkins University Press, 2005.

Liu, Pearl. 'Country Garden Shrinks Its Malaysia Staff as Sales of Forest City's Property Trickle to a Stop Amid Covid-19 Travel Bans.' *South China Morning Post.* Sept. 1, 2021. https://www.scmp.com/business/companies/article/3147020/country-garden-shrinks-its-malaysia-staff-forest-citys

———. 'How Cities Are Searching for Solutions Among Massive Mounds of Data.' *Globe and Mail.* Feb. 20, 2015. https://www.theglobeandmail.com/news/world/how-cities-are-searching-for-solutions-among-massive-mounds-of-data/article23131733/

Lorinc, John. 'The Push to Pump Fresh Air into Schools.' *Corporate Knights.* Oct. 27, 2020. https://www.corporateknights.com/built-environment/the-push-to-pump-fresh-air-into-schools/

Lundy, Matt. 'Toronto, Montreal Populations Decline as Urban Exodus Accelerates.' *Globe and Mail.* Jan. 13, 2022. https://www.theglobeandmail.com/business/article-toronto-montreal-populations-decline-as-urban-exodus-accelerates/

MacDougall, Heather. 'Hastings, Charles John Colwell Orr.' *Dictionary of Canadian Biography,* Vol. 16. Toronto/Quebec City: University of Toronto/Université Laval, 2018. http://www.biographi.ca/en/bio/hastings_charles_john_colwell_orr_16E.html

Martin, Reinhold. 'The Organizational Complex: Cybernetics, Space Discourse.' *Assemblage* by the MIT Press, No. 37, 102–27. Dec. 1998. https://doi.org/10.2307/3171358

Mattern, Shannon. 'Instrumental City: The View from Hudson Yards, circa 2019.' *Places Journal.* April 2016. https://placesjournal.org/article/instrumental-city-new-york-hudson-yards

McFadden, Christopher. 'John Loudon McAdam: The Father of the Modern Road.' *Interesting Engineering.* April 5, 2021. https://interestingengineering.com/john-loudon-mcadam-the-father-of-the-modern-road

Meadows, Paul. 'Giovanni Botero and the Process of Urbanization.' *The Midwest Sociologist*, Vol. 21, No. 2 (May 1958): 90–95. Taylor & Francis Ltd. https://www.jstor.org/stable/i25515013

Mikesell, Stephen. 'Ernest Leslie Ransome: A Vital California Engineer and Builder.' *California History*, Vol. 96, Issue 3, 77–96. Aug. 1, 2019. https://online.ucpress.edu/ch/article-abstract/96/3/77/109713/Ernest-Leslie-RansomeA-Vital-California-Engineer

'Milestones: Pearl Street Station, 1882.' ETHW. Engineering and Technology History Wiki, n.d. https://ethw.org/Milestones:Pearl_Street_Station,_1882

'Minutes of the 1st Meeting of the Digital Strategy Advisory Panel of the Toronto Waterfront Revitalization Corporation.' June 7, 2018. https://waterfrontoronto.ca/nbe/wcm/connect/waterfront/15c75e47-67e6-4db4-9601-3052a9368f12/FINAL+Minutes+Meeting+01+DSAP+-+June+7+2018.pdf

Muggah, Robert, and Greg Walton. '"Smart" Cities Are Surveilled Cities.' *Foreign Policy*. April 17, 2021. https://foreignpolicy.com/2021/04/17/smart-cities-surveillance-privacy-digital-threats-internet-of-things-5g/

Mulligan, Kate. *Meet Me at the Narrows [microform]: the Historic Mnjikaning Fish Fence and the Transformative Power of Place*. M.A. Thesis, University of Toronto, 2003.

Mumford, Lewis. *The City in History: Its Origins, Its Transformations, and Its Prospects*. New York: Harcourt, Brace and World, 1961.

Murdoch, William. 'An Account of the Application of the Gas from Coal to Economical Purposes.' *Philosophical Transactions*, Royal Society. 1808. https://catalogues.royalsociety.org/CalmView/Record.aspx?src=CalmView.Catalog&id=PT%2f2%2f10&pos=3

Nagourney, Eric. 'Why the Great Smog of London Was Anything but Great.' *New York Times*. Aug. 12, 2003.

Nonko, Emily. 'Hudson Yards Promised a High Tech Neighborhood – It Was a Greater Challenge Than Expected.' *Metropolis Mag*. Feb. 5, 2019. https://metropolismag.com/viewpoints/hudson-yards-technology-urbanism

Nye, David E. *American Illuminations : Urban Lighting, 1800–1920*. Cambridge: MIT Press, 2018.

'Online Shopping by Canadians in 2020: Results from the Canadian Internet Use Survey.' Statistics Canada. June 22, 2021. https://www150.statcan.gc.ca/n1/pub/11-627-m/11-627-m2021048-eng.htm

Pacey, Arnold. 'Five Chinese Cities before 1840.' In *Pre-Industrial Cities and Technology, 1st Edition*, edited by Colin Chant and David Goodman. London: Routledge, 1998.

Paiva, Sara, Mohd Adbdul Ahad, Sherin Zafar, Gautami Tripathi, Aqeel Khalique, and Imran Hussain. 'Privacy and Security Challenges in Smart and Sustainable Mobility.' *SN Applied Sciences*, 2:1175. June 6, 2020. https://doi.org/10.1007/s42452-020-2984-9

Patrick, Brooks. 'Honolulu Planners Visualize Housing Patterns with an Eye on Affordability.' *Esri Blog*, June 25, 2019. https://www.esri.com/about/newsroom/blog/honolulu-planners-visualize-urban-development-patterns

Penn State. 'Maya Plumbing: First Pressurized Water Feature Found in New World.' *ScienceDaily*. May 5, 2010. https://www.sciencedaily.com/releases/2010/05/100504155421.htm

Pinder, David. *Visions of the City: Utopianism, Power and Politics in Twentieth-Century Urbanism*. Edinburgh: Edinburgh University Press, 2005.

Prevost, Lisa. 'Building a Connected City From the Ground Up.' *New York Times*. April 3, 2018. https://www.nytimes.com/2018/04/03/business/smart-city.html

Rebentisch, Hannah, Caroline Thompson, Laurence Côté-Roy, and Sarah Moser. 'Unicorn Planning: Lessons from the Rise and Fall of an American "Smart" Mega-Development.' *Cities*, Vol. 101. June 2020. https://doi.org/10.1016/j.cities.2020.102686

Riding, Alan. 'Britain Confronts Legacy of Slave Trade.' *New York Times*. March 20, 2007. https://www.nytimes.com/2007/03/20/arts/design/20slav.html

'Rio de Janeiro's centre of operations: COR.' Centre for Public Impact. March 25, 2016. https://www.centreforpublicimpact.org/case-study/ioe-based-rio-operations-center

Roberts, Gerrylynn K., and Philip Steadman. *American Cities and Technology: Wilderness to Wired City*. London: Routledge, 1999.

Rocher, Luc, Julien M. Hendrickx, and Yves-Alexandre de Montjoye. 'Estimating the Success of Re-identifications in Incomplete Datasets Using Generative Models.' *Nature Communications*, 10, 3069. 2019. https://doi.org/10.1038/s41467-019-10933-3

Rose, Mark H. 'Machine Politics: The Historiography of Technology and Public Policy.' *Public Historian*, Vol. 10, No. 2 (Spring). 1988. https://www.jstor.org/stable/3378667

Rulf, Kristen. 'A Warning Shot for AV Policy Action.' *Harvard Kennedy School Autonomous Vehicles Policy Initiative*, August 7, 2018. https://medium.com/harvard-kennedy-school-autonomous-vehicle-policy/a-warning-shot-for-av-policy-action-45699d129320

Ryan-Mosley, Tate, and Jennifer Strong. 'The Activist Dismantling Racist Police Algorithms.' *MIT Technology Review*. June 5, 2020. https://www.technologyreview.com/2020/06/05/1002709/the-activist-dismantling-racist-police-algorithms

Sadowski, Jathan. '"Anyway the Dashboard Is Dead": On Trying to Build Urban Informatics.' *New Media & Society*. Nov. 27, 2021. https://doi.org/10.1177/14614448211058455

San Diego Union-Tribune Editorial Board. 'Editorial: Mayor Was Right to Shut Off Smart Streetlights.' *San Diego Union-Tribune*. Sept. 10, 2020. https://www.

sandiegouniontribune.com/opinion/editorials/story/2020-09-10/smart-streetlights-san-diego-surveillance-faulconer-activists

Sassen, Saskia, and Karima Kourtit. 'A Post-Corona Perspective for Smart Cities: "Should I Stay or Should I Go?"' *Sustainability*, Vol. 13, Issue 17. Sept. 6, 2021. https://www.mdpi.com/2071-1050/13/17/9988/htm

Scassa, Teresa, Pamela Robinson, and Ryan Mosoff. 'The Datafication of Wastewater: Legal, Ethical and Civic Considerations.' *Technology and Regulation*, Vol. 2022. Feb. 11, 2022. https://techreg.org/article/view/11192

Schladweiler, Jon C., Jan McDonald, Richard Cunningham, and Charles King. 'Home.' History of Sanitary Sewers. http://www.sewerhistory.org

Sedik, Tahsin Saadi, and Jiae Yoo. 'Pandemics and Automation: Will the Lost Jobs Come Back?' *International Monetary Fund.* Jan. 15, 2021. https://www.imf.org/en/Publications/WP/Issues/2021/01/15/Pandemics-and-Automation-Will-the-Lost-Jobs-Come-Back-50000

'See How Your Community Is Moving around Differently Due to COVID-19.' COVID-19 Community Mobility Reports. Google, reports created on Feb. 23, 2022. https://www.google.com/covid19/mobility/

'Sensing Platform.' Senseable Stockholm Lab. Last changed April 19, 2022. https://www.senseablestockholm.org/projects/sensing-platform-1.1153679

Sharara, Nour, Noriko Endo, Claire Duvallet, Newsha Ghaeli, Mariana Matus, Jennings Heussner, Scott W. Olesen, Eric J. Alm, Peter R. Chai, and Timothy B. Erickson. 'Wastewater Network Infrastructure in Public Health: Applications and Learnings from the COVID-19 Pandemic.' *PLOS Global Public Health.* Dec. 2, 2021. https://journals.plos.org/globalpublichealth/article? id=10.1371/journal.pgph.0000061

Sinclair, Ryan G., Christopher Y. Choi, Mark R. Riley, and Charles P. Gerba. 'Pathogen Surveillance through Monitoring of Sewer Systems.' *Adv Appl Microbiol.*, 65: 249–69. Nov. 20, 2008. https://www.ncbi.nlm.nih.gov/pmc/articles/PMC7112011

Singer, Natasha. 'Mission Control, Built for Cities.' *New York Times*, March 3, 2012. https://www.nytimes.com/2012/03/04/business/ibm-takes-smarter-cities-concept-to-rio-de-janeiro.html

'Sir Edwin Chadwick.' UCL Department of Civil, Environmental and Geomatic Engineering. https://www.ucl.ac.uk/civil-environmental-geomatic-engineering/about/sir-edwin-chadwick

'Smart City Observatory.' IMD. International Institute for Management Development. https://www.imd.org/smart-city-observatory/home/#_smartCity

Spiro Jr., Robert H. 'John Loudon McAdam and the Metropolitan Turnpike Trust.' *Journal of Transportation History.* Nov. 1, 1956. https://journals.sagepub.com/doi/abs/10.1177/002252665600200402

Sponholtz, Shirley. 'A Brief History of Road Building.' Triple Nine Society. n.d. http://www.triplenine.org/V dya/OtherArticles/ABriefHistoryofRoadBuilding.aspx

Stanley, Jay. 'Four Problems with the ShotSpotter Gunshot Detection System.' American Civil Liberties Union. Aug. 24, 2021. https://www.aclu.org/news/privacy-technology/four-problems-with-the-shotspotter-gunshot-detection-system

Sundell J. 'Reflections on the History of Indoor Air Science, Focusing on the Last 50 Years.' *Indoor Air*, 27(4), 708–24. Feb. 27, 2017. https://doi.org/10 1111/ina.12368

Tarr, Joel. 'The Changing Face of Pittsburgh: A Historical Perspective.' In *Ensuring Environmental Health in Postindustrial Cities: Workshop Summary*, ed. B. D. Goldstein, B. Fischoff, S. J. Marcus et al. Washington: National Academies Press, 2003. https://www.ncbi.nlm nih.gov/books/NBK222035/

Tiku, Nitasha. 'Creator of GhettoTracker.com Surprised by All the "Negative Baggage."' *Gawker*. Sept. 4, 2013. https://www.gawker.com/creator-of-ghettotracker-com-surprised-by-all-the-nega-1249859432

Tham, Irene. 'Coronavirus: Google Launches New Tool to Help Public Health Officials Plan Social Distancing Measures.' *Straits Times*. April 6, 2020. https://www.straitstimes.com/tech/google-launches-new-tool-to-help-public-health-officials-plan-social-distancing-measures

Thomasen, Kristen, Suzie Dunn, Kate Robertson, Pam Hrick, Cynthia Khoo, Rosel Kim, Ngozi Okidegbe, Christopher A. Parsons. 'Submission to the Toronto Police Services Board's Use of New Artificial Intelligence Technologies Policy – LEAF and the Citizen Lab.' Available at SSRN. Dec. 15, 2021. https://ssrn.com/abstract=3989271

Tomor, Zsuzsanna, Albert Meijer, Ank Michels, and Stan Geertman. 'Smart Governance For Sustainable Cities: Findings from a Systematic Literature Review.' *Journal of Urban Technology*, Vol. 26, Issue 4. 2019. https://doi.org/10.1080/10630732.2019 1651178

Tomory, Leslie. 'London's Water Supply before 1800 and the Roots of the Networked City.' *Technology and Culture*, Vol. 56, No. 3, 704–37. July 2015. https://doi.org/10.1353/tech.2015.0082

Toronto Police Services Board. *Toronto Police Services Board – Enforcement Investments to Combat Gun Violence*. Andy Pringle. Toronto: Toronto.ca, 2018. https://www.toronto.ca/legdocs/mmis/2018/cc/bgrd/backgroundfile-119232.pdf

'Turning on Toronto: A History of Toronto Hydro.' Toronto. n.d. https://www.toronto.ca/explore-enjoy/history-art-culture/online-exhibits/web-exhibits/web-exhibits-local-government/turning-on-toronto-a-history-of-toronto-hydro

van Lieshout, Carry. '"The Most Valuable Means of Extinguishing the Destroying Fires": Fire-fighting and the London Water Companies in the Long Eighteenth

Century.' *London Journal*, 42:1, 53–69. Feb. 13, 2017. https://doi.org/10.1080/03058034.2017.1279869

Wainwright, Olivier. 'Story of Cities #4: Beijing and the Earliest Planning Document in History.' *Guardian*. March 17, 2016. https://www.theguardian.com/cities/2016/mar/17/story-cities-beijing-earliest-planning-document-history

Walton, Robert. 'Global EV Sales Rise 80% in 2021 as Automakers Including Ford, GM Commit to Zero Emissions: BNEF.' *Utility Dive*. Nov. 12, 2021. https://www.utilitydive.com/news/global-ev-sales-rise-80-in-2021-as-automakers-including-ford-gm-commit-t/609949

Wattercutter, Angela. 'Film Festivals Are Evolving for the Better.' *Wired*. Jan. 21, 2022. https://www.wired.com/story/film-festivals-hybrid

Wayman, Erin. 'The Secrets of Ancient Rome's Buildings.' *Smithsonian Magazine*. Nov. 16, 2011. https://www.smithsonianmag.com/history/the-secrets-of-ancient-romes-buildings-234992/#H8i51lguDAYVKbRH.99

West, Geoffrey. *Scale: The Universal Laws of Growth, Innovation, Sustainability, and the Pace of Life in Organisms, Cities, Economies, and Companies*. New York: Penguin, 2017.

'What is a Civic Digital Trust?' MaRS. Last modified in 2019. https://marsdd.gitbook.io/datatrust/trusts/what-is-a-civic-digital-trust

White, Chris. 'South Korea's "Smart City" Songdo: Not Quite Smart Enough?' *South China Morning Post*. March 25, 2018. https://www.scmp.com/week-asia/business/article/2137838/south-koreas-smart-city-songdo-not-quite-smart-enough

Williams, Rebecca. *Whose Streets? Our Streets! (Tech Edition): 2020–21 'Smart City' Cautionary Trends & 10 Calls to Action to Protect and Promote Democracy*. Cambridge: Belfer Center for Science and International Affairs, 2021.

Wong, May. 'Stanford Research Provides a Snapshot of a New Working-from-Home Economy.' *Stanford News*. June 29, 2020. https://news.stanford.edu/2020/06/29/snapshot-new-working-home-economy/

'Zero Emission Vehicle and Infrastructure Statistics.' California Energy Commission. https://www.energy.ca.gov/data-reports/energy-insights/zero-emission-vehicle-and-charger-statistics

Zuboff, Shoshana. *The Age of Surveillance Capitalism: The Fight for a Human Future at the New Frontier of Power*. London: Profile Books, 2019.

———. 'You Are the Object of a Secret Extraction Operation.' *New York Times*. Nov. 12, 2021. https://www.nytimes.com/2021/11/12/opinion/facebook-privacy.html

Index

John Lorinc is a Toronto freelance journalist and editor. He writes about cities, politics, business, climate change, and local history for various media, including *Spacing* magazine, the *Globe and Mail*, the *Toronto Star*, *The Walrus*, *Corporate Knights*, and, previously, the *New York Times*, the *Washington Post*, and *Readers' Digest*. John has won numerous National Magazine Awards for his journalism and was the 2019–20 Atkinson Fellow in Public Policy, which produced a series of ten articles on smart cities that were the basis of *Dream States*. He is the author of three previous books, including *The New City* (Penguin, 2006), and has co-edited several Coach House uTOpia anthologies including *The Ward: The Life and Loss of Toronto's First Immigrant Neighbourhood* (2015) and *Any Other Way: How Toronto Got Queer* (2017).

Typeset in Albertina and Circular Standard.

Printed at the Coach House on bpNichol Lane in Toronto, Ontario, on Rolland Natural paper. This book was printed with vegetable-based ink on a 1973 Heidelberg KORD offset litho press. Its pages were folded on a Baumfolder, gathered by hand, bound on a Sulby Auto-Minabinda, and trimmed on a Polar single-knife cutter.

Coach House is on the traditional territory of many nations, including the Mississaugas of the Credit, the Anishnabeg, the Chippewa, the Haudenosaunee, and the Wendat peoples, and is now home to many diverse First Nations, Inuit, and Métis peoples. We acknowledge that Toronto is covered by Treaty 13 with the Mississaugas of the Credit. We are grateful to live and work on this land.

Edited by Alana Wilcox
Cover design by David Gee
Interior design by Crystal Sikma
Author photo by Samuel Lorinc

Coach House Books
80 bpNichol Lane
Toronto ON M5S 3J4
Canada

416 979 2217
800 367 6360

mail@chbooks.com
www.chbooks.com